Galatians

REFORMED EXPOSITORY COMMENTARY

A Series

Series Editors

Richard D. Phillips
Philip Graham Ryken

Testament Editors

Iain M. Duguid, Old Testament
Daniel M. Doriani, New Testament

Galatians

Philip Graham Ryken

P&R
PUBLISHING
P.O. BOX 817 • PHILLIPSBURG • NEW JERSEY 08865-0817

Page design and typesetting by Lakeside Design Plus

Printed in the United States of America

Library of Congress Cataloging-in-Publication Data

Ryken, Philip Graham, 1966–
    Galatians / Philip Graham Ryken.
      p. cm. — (Reformed expository commentary)
    Includes bibliographical references and index.
    ISBN-13: 978-0-87552-782-6 (cloth)
    ISBN-10: 0-87552-782-5 (cloth)
    1. Bible. N.T. Galatians—Commentaries. I. Title. II. Series.

BS2685.53.R95 2005
227'04077—dc22

2005047401

To

William S. Barker, Sinclair B. Ferguson,
and my other mentors on the faculty of
Westminster Theological Seminary in Philadelphia,
whose superior scholarship, brotherly friendship,
and godly leadership
brought reformation to my life and ministry.

We know that a person is not justified by works of the law
but through faith in Jesus Christ,
so we also have believed in Christ Jesus,
in order to be justified by faith in Christ
and not by works of the law,
because by works of the law no one will be justified.

Galatians 2:16

CONTENTS

Contents

SERIES INTRODUCTION

In every generation there is a fresh need for the faithful exposition of God's Word in the church, for the world. At the same time, the church must constantly do the work of theology: reflecting on the teaching of Scripture, confessing its doctrines of the Christian faith, and applying them to contemporary culture. We believe that these two tasks—the expositional and the theological—are interdependent. Our doctrine must derive from the biblical text, and our understanding of any particular passage of Scripture must arise from the doctrine taught in Scripture as a whole.

We further believe that these interdependent tasks of biblical exposition and theological reflection are best undertaken in the church, and most specifically in the pulpits of the church. This is all the more true since the study of Scripture properly results in doxology and praxis—that is, in praise to God and practical application in the lives of believers. In pursuit of these ends, we are pleased to present the Reformed Expository Commentary as a fresh exposition of Scripture for our generation in the church. We hope and pray that pastors, teachers, Bible study leaders, and many others will find this series to be a faithful, inspiring, and useful resource for the study of God's infallible, inerrant Word.

The Reformed Expository Commentary has four fundamental commitments. First, these commentaries aim to be *biblical*, presenting a comprehensive exposition characterized by careful attention to the details of the text. They are not exegetical commentaries—commenting word by word or even verse by verse—but integrated expositions of whole passages of Scripture. Each commentary will thus present a sequential, systematic treatment of an entire book of the Bible, passage by passage. Second, these commentaries are unashamedly *doctrinal*. We are committed to the Westminster Confession of Faith and Catechisms as containing the system of doctrine taught in the Scriptures of the Old and New Testaments. Each volume will teach, promote, and defend the doctrines of the Reformed faith as they are found in the Bible. Third, these commentaries are *redemptive-historical* in their orientation. We believe in the unity of the Bible and its central message of salvation in Christ. We are thus committed to a Christ-centered view of the Old Testament, in which its characters, events, regulations, and institutions are properly understood as pointing us to Christ and his gospel, as well as giving us examples to follow in living by faith. Fourth, these commentaries are *practical*, applying the text of Scripture to contemporary challenges of life—both public and private—with appropriate illustrations.

The contributors to the Reformed Expository Commentary are all pastor-scholars. As pastors, each author will first present his expositions in the pulpit ministry of his church. This means that these commentaries are rooted in the teaching of Scripture to real people in the church. While aiming to be scholarly, these expositions are not academic. Our intent is to be faithful, clear, and helpful to Christians who possess various levels of biblical and theological training—as should be true in any effective pulpit ministry. Inevitably this means that some issues of academic interest will not be covered. Nevertheless, we aim to achieve a responsible level of scholarship, seeking to promote and model this for pastors and other teachers in the church. Significant exegetical and theological difficulties, along with such historical and cultural background as is relevant to the text, will be treated with care.

We strive for a high standard of enduring excellence. This begins with the selection of the authors, all of whom have proven to be outstanding communicators of God's Word. But this pursuit of excellence is also reflected in a disciplined editorial process. Each volume is edited by both a series editor and a testament editor. The testament editors, Dr. Iain Duguid for the Old Testament and Dr. Daniel Doriani for the New Testament, are accomplished pastors and respected scholars who have taught at the seminary level. Their job is to ensure that each volume is sufficiently conversant with up-to-date scholarship and is faithful and accurate in its exposition of the text. As series editors, we oversee each volume to ensure its overall quality—including excellence of writing, soundness of teaching, and usefulness in application. Working together as an editorial team, along with the publisher, we are devoted to ensuring that these are the best commentaries our gifted authors can provide, so that the church will be served with trustworthy and exemplary expositions of God's Word.

It is our goal and prayer that the Reformed Expository Commentary will serve the church by renewing confidence in the clarity and power of Scripture and by upholding the great doctrinal heritage of the Reformed faith. We hope that pastors who read these commentaries will be encouraged in their own expository preaching ministry, which we believe to be the best and most biblical pattern for teaching God's Word in the church. We hope that lay teachers will find these commentaries among the most useful resources they rely upon for understanding and presenting the text of the Bible. And we hope that the devotional quality of these studies of Scripture will instruct and inspire each Christian who reads them in joyful, obedient discipleship to Jesus Christ.

May the Lord bless all who read the Reformed Expository Commentary. We commit these volumes to the Lord Jesus Christ, praying that the Holy Spirit will use them for the instruction and edification of the church, with thanksgiving to God the Father for his unceasing faithfulness in building his church through the ministry of his Word.

Richard D. Phillips
Philip Graham Ryken
Series Editors

PREFACE

This commentary originated with a series of sermons preached in the Sunday evening service at Tenth Presbyterian Church in Philadelphia. Its overall interpretation is in line with classic Reformation teaching on Galatians, especially with regard to the doctrine of justification by faith alone. By trying to base their justification on their sanctification, the Galatians were in danger of exchanging God's grace in the gospel for performance-based Christianity. But the apostle Paul rightly warned them that any form of works-righteousness is inimical to the good news of salvation, arguing "that a person is not justified by works of the law but through faith in Jesus Christ" (Gal. 2:16).

Properly understood, the gracious gospel of Galatians liberates us from legalism. Since we are legalists by nature, the book challenges many of our preconceptions about what it means to have a right relationship with God. F. F. Bruce wrote in his commentary on the epistle:

> When, from time to time, someone appeared who understood and proclaimed the genuine message of Galatians, he was liable to be denounced as a subversive character—as, indeed, Paul was in his own day. But the letter to the Galatians, with its trumpet-call to Christian freedom, has time and again released the true gospel from the bonds in which well-meaning but misguided people have confined it so that it can once more exert its emancipating power in the life of mankind, empowering those who receive it to stand fast in the freedom with which Christ has set them free.[1]

1. F. F. Bruce, *The Epistle to the Galatians: A Commentary on the Greek Text*, New International Greek Testament Commentary (Grand Rapids: Eerdmans, 1982), 278.

Like every other aspect of my ministry, this commentary was written within the context of Christian community. I praise God for everyone who helped to bring this book into print:

- Josh, Kirsten, Jack, Kathryn, Karoline, and especially Lisa, who remind me to live the gospel I preach;
- the members of Tenth Presbyterian Church, who sustain me by their prayers for God's work in my life and ministry;
- the elders at Tenth, whose blessing enables writing to be an important part of my work as a pastor;
- the Tenth staff, who share with me in the blessings and burdens of ministry;
- Dan Doriani, Iain Duguid, and Rick Phillips—my colleagues and teachers—who improved my work immensely by making many exegetical, theological, and practical suggestions;
- Jonathan Rockey, who read and commented on my original manuscript (as he does for nearly all my books);
- Robert and Katherine Arthur, who generously allowed our family to stay at Weston Farms on the Chesapeake while I worked on the final revision;
- Al Fisher and the fine staff at P&R, who have the vision and skill to attempt a full new series of commentaries;
- and James Montgomery Boice, who set the standard for expositional commentaries.

My prayer is that God will use this commentary on Galatians—the first volume in the Reformed Expository Commentary series—to help people understand and teach the gospel of grace in all its liberating power.

Galatians

THE GOSPEL OF FREE GRACE

1

DEAR RECOVERING PHARISEE

Galatians 1:1—5

*Paul, an apostle—not from men nor through man, but through
Jesus Christ and God the Father, who raised him from the dead—
and all the brothers who are with me, To the churches of Galatia.*
(Gal. 1:1–2)

alatians is a letter for recovering Pharisees. The Pharisees who
lived during and after the time of Christ were very religious.
They were regular in their worship, orthodox in their theology,
and moral in their conduct. Yet something was missing. Although God was
in their minds and in their actions, he was not in their hearts. Therefore,
their religion was little more than hypocrisy.

The Pharisees were hypocrites because they thought that what God would
do for them depended on what they did for God. So they read their Bibles,
prayed, tithed, and kept the Sabbath as if their salvation depended on it.
What they failed to understand is that God's grace cannot be earned; it only
comes free.[1]

---

1. I am well aware of the efforts of E. P. Sanders and others to rehabilitate first-century Judaism as
a religion of grace. However, our best and most reliable resource for understanding Pharisaism is still
the New Testament, which plainly shows that the religion of the Pharisees was infected by a reliance on
human effort for salvation. For a full and accurate assessment of the prevailing legalism of first-century
Judaism, see D. A. Carson, Peter T. O'Brien, and Mark A. Seifrid, eds., *Justification and Variegated
Nomism*, 2 vols. (Tübingen: Mohr Siebeck, 2001, 2004).

There is a way out of Pharisaism. The way out is called the gospel. It is the good news that Jesus Christ has already done everything necessary for our salvation. If we trust in him, he will make us right with God by giving us the free gift of his grace. When we reject our own righteousness to receive the righteousness of Jesus Christ, we become former Pharisees.

Most former Pharisees have a problem, however. It is hard for them to leave their legalism behind. Although initially they received God's grace for free, they keep trying to put a surcharge on it. They believe that God loves them, but secretly they suspect that his love is conditional, that it depends on how they are doing in the Christian life. They end up with a performance-based Christianity that denies the grace of God. To put this in theological terms, they want to base their justification on their sanctification.

This means that most former Pharisees—indeed, most Christians—are still in recovery. There is still something of the old legalist in us. Although we have been saved by grace, we do not always know how to live by grace. The gospel is something we received some time in the past, but not something we live and breathe. Galatians was written for people like us.

Freedom Letter

Paul's epistle to the Galatians has been called the Magna Carta of Christian liberty. Its theme verse is a declaration of independence: "We know that a person is not justified by works of the law but through faith in Jesus Christ" (Gal. 2:16). Whenever the church has understood this gospel message, Galatians has brought life and freedom to recovering Pharisees.

This was true in the life of Martin Luther (1483–1546), the father of the Reformation. Luther had tried everything he knew to be a good Christian. He wrote, "I was a good monk and kept my order so strictly that I could claim that if ever a monk were able to reach heaven by monkish discipline I should have found my way there. All my fellows in the house, who knew me, would bear me out in this. For if it had continued much longer I would, what with vigils, prayers, readings and other such works, have done myself to death."[2] Yet as hard as Luther worked, his conscience was still troubled by

2. Martin Luther, quoted in Bernard M. G. Reardon, *Religious Thought in the Reformation* (London: Longman, 1981), 51.

4

the thought that he was not good enough for God. He didn't understand the gospel of grace. His breakthrough came when he discovered that Christianity was not about what he had to do for God; it was about what God had done for him in Jesus Christ.

The free grace of God in Christ, received by faith, was the great theme of Luther's famous lectures on Galatians, which he began by saying: "I do not seek [my own] active righteousness. I ought to have and perform it; but I declare that even if I did have it and perform it, I cannot trust in it or stand up before the judgment of God on the basis of it. Thus I . . . embrace only . . . the righteousness of Christ . . . which we do not perform but receive, which we do not have but accept, when God the Father grants it to us through Jesus Christ."[3]

Through Martin Luther, the book of Galatians taught the same lesson to the great Puritan preacher John Bunyan (1628–1688). In his spiritual autobiography, *Grace Abounding to the Chief of Sinners*, Bunyan describes how a battered old copy of Luther's commentary came into his possession. He was surprised how old the book was, but he was even more surprised when he read it. He wrote, "I found my condition in his experience, so largely and profoundly handled, as if his book had been written out of my heart . . . I do prefer this book of Mr. Luther upon the Galatians, (excepting the Holy Bible) before all the books that ever I have seen."[4]

Why does this epistle have such a liberating influence? Because the church is always full of recovering Pharisees who need to receive the gospel again, as if for the very first time.

Who Was Paul?

The letter opens with more argumentation than salutation: "Paul, an apostle—not from men nor through man, but through Jesus Christ and God the Father, who raised him from the dead" (Gal. 1:1). The author's name comes first, as was customary in ancient letters, and then his name is followed immediately by his credentials. Paul identifies himself as an apostle sent by God

---

3. Martin Luther, *Lectures on Galatians, 1535*, trans. and ed. Jaroslav Pelikan, in *Luther's Works* (St. Louis: Concordia, 1963), 26:6.
4. John Bunyan, *Grace Abounding to the Chief of Sinners*, ed. W. R. Owens (1666; repr. New York: Penguin, 1987), 35.

rather than men. Two things are obvious from this return address. One is that Paul was upset. In the Greek original, his words are terse: "Paul, apostle, *not*." It is equally obvious that the reason Paul was upset was that enemies were trying to undermine his authority.

In the ancient world, an apostle was an official messenger, like an emissary or ambassador. The messenger had the authority to represent his superior, something like an agent who holds the power of attorney. In the New Testament, the term "apostle" has a more specific meaning. It denotes the official spokesmen for Jesus Christ, especially his original twelve disciples. These men were chosen, called, and commissioned by Christ himself to teach on his behalf (Luke 6:13–16; Mark 3:14–19).

Apparently, some critics were quick to point out that Paul was not one of the original twelve disciples. He was a latecomer, they claimed, who had not been commissioned directly by Christ himself. Therefore, he was only a second-rate apostle—his gospel was just hearsay.

If this is what people were saying about Paul, it is easy to see why he dispensed with the customary pleasantries and started his letter by defending his credentials. He was not merely being defensive. He understood that his opponents were making a personal attack in order to advance a theological error. They were devaluing Paul to disparage his gospel. If they could show that he was an impostor rather than an apostle, they could discredit his message of grace.

What was at stake, therefore, was not simply Paul's reputation, but our salvation. The great New Testament scholar J. B. Lightfoot (1828–1889) began his commentary on Galatians by saying, "The two threads which run through this epistle—the defence of the Apostle's own authority, and the maintenance of the doctrine of grace—are knotted together in the opening salutation."[5] Paul was not defending himself as much as he was defending the independence of his apostleship in order to defend the gospel. When it came to the good news about salvation by grace through faith, he refused to budge so much as a single micron.

The truth is that Paul was not sent from men. His apostolic commission did not come, for example, from the church at Antioch. Nor was he sent by a man, as if his call had come through someone like Barnabas or Peter. No,

5. J. B. Lightfoot, *St. Paul's Epistle to the Galatians* (1865; repr. Lynn, MA: Hendrickson, 1981), 71.

Paul was an apostle by the will of God. God had set him apart from birth, called him by grace, and revealed his Son to him (see Gal. 1:15–16). Thus his commission was neither originated nor mediated by mere human beings.

Paul's opponents said that his gospel was not God's word to man, but a man's word about God. Skeptics make the same argument today. They accuse Paul of Tarsus of inventing Christianity. They say that Jesus of Nazareth was a teacher of love and a model of sacrifice, but then Paul came along with all his complicated Greek concepts and turned Christ into Christianity.

At the beginning of his letter to the Galatians, which was one of his earliest letters, Paul explains where his Christianity came from. It came straight from the mouth of Christ. Paul was "an apostle—not from men nor through man, but through Jesus Christ" (Gal. 1:1). His authority was not human, but divine. Therefore, Paul's message is God's own message about salvation from sin. Anyone who sets aside his apostolic teaching sets aside the gospel truth of Jesus Christ.

WHO WERE THE GALATIANS?

Paul addressed his pastoral letter "to the churches of Galatia" (Gal. 1:2). This apparently simple phrase has generated a good deal of scholarly discussion. Who were the Galatians?

The old theory was that the Galatians were the Celts and the Gauls (literally, the "Gaulatians") who lived in northern Asia Minor. Luke reports that Paul and his companions "went through the region of Phrygia and Galatia, having been forbidden by the Holy Spirit to speak the word in Asia" (Acts 16:6; cf. 18:23). Perhaps both Luke and Paul (see Gal. 3:1) were referring to the ethnic Galatians who lived in the north.

The main problem with this view is that none of the churches in northern Asia Minor are mentioned anywhere else in the New Testament. This would be surprising if those churches were the scene of a major theological conflict and the recipients of one of Paul's most important letters.

The newer theory is that Paul was writing to churches in southern Asia Minor. Ethnically speaking, the people who lived there were not Galatian. However, the Romans had turned Asia Minor into one large province, and they had been calling it "Galatia" since before the time of Christ. Paul, who was a Roman citizen, may well have been using a proper provincial title to refer to Christians who were not necessarily Galatian by birth. Indeed, "Galatians" may have been the only suitable term that included all the people in all these churches.

To give a modern example, consider the way the Russians incorporated Georgians, Lithuanians, Ukrainians, and other ethnic groups into the former Soviet Union. Although these groups retained their ethnic identities, they were sometimes referred to as "Russians."

One good reason for thinking that Paul was writing this circular letter to churches in the south is that he had planted churches there himself. The main cities in the southern part of the province of Galatia were Pisidian Antioch, Iconium, Lystra, and Derbe—the very cities Paul visited on his first missionary journey.

Furthermore, Paul's recollection of the way the Galatians responded to the gospel (Gal. 4:12–15) corresponds to Luke's description of those cities in his history of the early church (Acts 13:1–14:28). The way Luke summarizes Paul's preaching to these churches is especially striking: "Therefore, my brothers, I want you to know that through Jesus the forgiveness of sins is proclaimed to you. Through him everyone who believes is justified from everything you could not be justified from by the law of Moses" (Acts 13:38–39 NIV). As we shall see, justification by faith in Jesus Christ, apart from the law, is exactly the message Paul wanted to urge the Galatians not to forget.

Whether the Galatians who received this correspondence lived in the north or the south, which is more likely, there is little doubt as to why Paul was writing to them. One of the best summaries of his message comes from the first Latin commentary written on the letter, by the theologian Marius Victorinus (d. c. 303): "the Galatians are going astray because they are adding Judaism to the gospel of faith in Christ. . . . Disturbed by these tendencies Paul writes this letter . . . in order that they may preserve faith in Christ alone."[6]

Religious traditionalists, probably from Jerusalem, were trying to teach the Galatians a new gospel. These men dogged Paul's footsteps all over Asia

---

6. C. Marius Victorinus, *Ad Galatas*, quoted in F. F. Bruce, *The Epistle to the Galatians: A Commentary on the Greek Text*, New International Greek Testament Commentary (Grand Rapids: Eerdmans, 1982), 21.

Minor. Often they are called the "Judaizers" because they wanted to require Gentiles to follow Jewish customs. They taught that a Gentile had to become a Jew before he could become a Christian. In short, their gospel was Jesus Christ plus the law of Moses.

To be specific, the Judaizers wanted Gentile believers to be circumcised. Their theology is summarized in Acts 15, where we read that "some men"—possibly the very men who caused trouble in Galatia—went down from Judea to Antioch and were teaching: "Unless you are circumcised according to the custom of Moses, you cannot be saved" (Acts 15:1). Not surprisingly, this teaching was especially popular among believers who were former Pharisees (Acts 15:5). The church has always been full of recovering Pharisees who want to add human effort to God's grace.

THE RISEN CHRIST

To help Christians—especially recovering Pharisees—rediscover the gospel of grace, where should one start? Well, before receiving the gospel again for the first time, people have to know what the gospel is. So the obvious place to start is with the gospel itself. This is precisely where Paul begins his letter to the Galatians. He starts with the good news about the cross and the empty tomb. The gospel is made up of these two great saving events—the crucifixion and the resurrection of Jesus Christ.

Whenever Paul preached the good news, he started with the facts. He simply recounted what Jesus Christ had done in human history to save his people from their sins. This is the strategy he adopted when he wrote to the Corinthians: "Now I would remind you, brothers, of the gospel I preached to you, which you received, in which you stand, and by which you are being saved. . . . that Christ died for our sins in accordance with the Scriptures, that he was buried, that he was raised on the third day in accordance with the Scriptures" (1 Cor. 15:1–4). The gospel is the atoning death and the bodily resurrection of Jesus Christ.

Paul adopted a similar strategy when he wrote to the Galatians, only this time he started with the fact of the resurrection: "Jesus Christ and God the Father, who raised him from the dead" (Gal. 1:1). This Jesus was no ordinary man. Although it is not the apostle's main point, there is a hint here of the doctrine of the incarnation. Paul mentions Jesus in the same breath with

God the Father. The calling of God and the calling of Christ are one and the same. Thus Paul distinguishes Jesus from mortal men ("not from men nor through man") and uses a preposition to pair him with Almighty God ("but through Jesus Christ and God the Father").

Jesus is a man, of course. Later Paul will say that he was "born of woman" (Gal. 4:4). But the man Jesus of Nazareth is divine as well as human. He shares an essential and eternal unity with God the Father. Between them there is "no distinction of essence."[7] "There is no other God," wrote Luther, "than this Man Jesus Christ. . . . We must look at no other God than this incarnate and human God."[8] Although he was a man among men, Jesus is very God of very God.

This Jesus is the God-man whom God the Father raised from the dead. But why would Paul start with the resurrection? He does not mention the crucifixion until verse 4, so he seems to be taking things out of their chronological order.

The reason Paul does this may have to do with his autobiography. Remember how he first came to Christ. He did not meet him at the cross. Rather, his calling as a Christian and his commission as an apostle began with his encounter with the risen Christ. Paul's conversion happened while he was on his way to Damascus, breathing murderous threats against the Christian church: "Now as he went on his way, he approached Damascus, and suddenly a light from heaven flashed around him. And falling to the ground he heard a voice saying to him, 'Saul, Saul, why are you persecuting me?' And he said, 'Who are you, Lord?' And he said, 'I am Jesus, whom you are persecuting' " (Acts 9:3–5). So in Galatians, where Paul has to defend both his own apostolic authority and the truth of his gospel message, he quite naturally begins with Christ and his resurrection.

The resurrection of Jesus Christ was a stupendous divine miracle. The body of Jesus of Nazareth was taken down from a Roman gibbet and placed in a Jewish tomb, where it remained until the third day. Then, by his infinite power, God raised Jesus from the dead. Not only did he bring him back to

---

7. John Chrysostom, *Homilies on the Epistles of St. Paul the Apostle to the Galatians and Ephesians,* trans. Gross Alexander, ed. Philip Schaff, in *Nicene and Post-Nicene Fathers,* First Series (1889; repr. Peabody, MA: Hendrickson, 1994), 13:3.

8. Luther, *Galatians,* 26:29.

life, but he also gave him a glorious and immortal body with supernatural powers.

Paul never would have believed this unless he had seen it with his own eyes. But we do not have to take just Paul's word for it. The resurrection of Jesus of Nazareth, also called Christ, is recorded in reliable documents as a fact of human history. There are multiple eyewitness accounts of the risen Christ. Over the course of many weeks, Jesus was seen in his resurrection body by women as well as men, by skeptics as well as believers. These men and women had the opportunity to see Jesus with their own eyes. They walked with him and talked with him. Their unanimous testimony is that they had been in the presence of the risen Christ.

CHRIST CRUCIFIED

The resurrection of Jesus Christ is gospel truth, but by itself, the resurrection is not the gospel. Although it proved God's victory over death, it did not take away our sins. This is where the crucifixion comes in. In his letter to the Galatians, Paul describes that saving event by saying that the Lord Jesus Christ "gave himself for our sins to deliver us from the present evil age, according to the will of our God and Father" (Gal. 1:4). This verse teaches four important things about the cross of Christ.

First, it shows the *willingness* of Jesus to go to the cross. The crucifixion was a voluntary self-sacrifice. Jesus gave the most precious gift of all. He "gave himself" (Gal. 1:4). He "gave himself up" (Eph. 5:25), or he "gave himself for us" (Titus 2:14). No one took Christ's life away from him; he freely gave it away: "I lay down my life"—Jesus said—"that I may take it up again. No one takes it from me, but I lay it down of my own accord" (John 10:17–18). This is also emphasized in the gospel of Matthew, where an unusual phrase is used to show that at the moment of his death Jesus "yielded up his spirit" (Matt. 27:50).

Second, this verse shows the *purpose* of the cross. The reason Christ gave himself away was "for our sins" (Gal. 1:4). A transaction took place on the cross. We were the ones who deserved to die because we owe God an infinite debt for our sin. But Christ took our place on the cross. He became our substitute, our sin-offering. He gathered up all our sins, put them on his own shoulders, and paid for them with his death. Thus the crucifixion of Jesus

Christ was not merely an example of supreme sacrifice, but an actual atonement for sin. It enabled God to forgive us by satisfying his pure justice.

We learn from this substitutionary atonement how impossible it is to pay for our own sins. Full atonement requires nothing less than the blood of Jesus Christ, the very God. Our confidence lies in the fact that Jesus gave his lifeblood for our own personal sins. Luther could even imagine having this confidence when facing the devil himself: "When the devil accuses us and says: 'You are a sinner; therefore you are damned,' then we can answer him and say: 'Because you say that I am a sinner, therefore I shall be righteous and be saved.' 'No,' says the devil, 'you will be damned.' 'No,' I say, 'for I take refuge in Christ, who has given Himself for my sins.'"[9]

Third, this verse shows the *effect* of the cross. Christ was crucified "to deliver us from the present evil age" (Gal. 1:4). When we think of the cross, we usually think first of the atonement. As we have seen, Christ died to pay for our sins. But Christ was also crucified to emancipate us from this evil age. The gospel is a rescue, like being released from servitude or freed from prison.

By "the present evil age," Paul means "the course and current of this world's affairs as corrupted by sin."[10] In the words of another commentator, he means "the totality of human life dominated by sin and opposed to God."[11] Ours is an age of corruption, decay, and death. It is dominated by the evils of war, murder, oppression, slavery, incest, and abortion.

Jesus died on the cross to save us from all of it, not just individually, but together, as a new humanity. As Timothy George puts it, "Here Paul described what Jesus' death accomplished not only in terms of our personal salvation but also in regard to God's redemptive purpose in the wider historical and cosmic arenas."[12] Even though we continue to live in this evil realm, we are being rescued from it through the cross. The age to come has burst into the present age. We ourselves no longer have to live the way we used to live when

9. Ibid., 26:36.
10. Marvin R. Vincent, *Word Studies in the New Testament*, 2d ed., 4 vols. (1888; repr. Peabody, MA: Hendrickson, n.d.), 4:84.
11. Ronald Y. K. Fung, *The Epistle to the Galatians*, New International Commentary on the New Testament (Grand Rapids: Eerdmans, 1988), 41.
12. Timothy George, *Galatians*, New American Commentary 30 (Nashville: Broadman & Holman, 1994), 87.

we were under the power of evil. Already we are beginning to live the life of the age to come, when God's will is always done.

When we pray—as we do in the Lord's Prayer—that God would "deliver us from evil" (Matt. 6:13), we are asking God to finish the work Christ began to do on the cross. This is why Galatians is the epistle of the soul set free. It announces that Jesus died on the cross to deliver us from evil. Deliverance is "the keynote of the epistle," wrote J. B. Lightfoot. "The Gospel is a rescue, an emancipation from a state of bondage."[13]

Fourth, this verse shows the *origin* of the cross. Christ died "according to the will of our God and Father" (Gal. 1:4). The execution of Jesus of Nazareth was not an unforeseen tragedy, a mere accident of history; it was part of God's plan for the salvation of sinners. The apostle Peter said as much to the very men who nailed Jesus to the cross. In his famous sermon in Jerusalem, he declared, "This Jesus, delivered up according to the definite plan and fore-knowledge of God, you crucified and killed by the hands of lawless men" (Acts 2:23).

Paul said the same thing to the Galatians. The cross had been in God's mind from all eternity. Thus it demonstrates the love of God as well as the love of Christ. There could be no conflict within the Trinity, as if a loving Son had to rescue us from an angry Father. On the contrary, the willingness of the Son was in response to the Father's will. The Father does not love us because the Son died for us. Rather, the Son died for us because the Father loves us. The cross had its origin in our Father's heart.

To God Be the Glory

The crucifixion and the resurrection, the cross and the empty tomb— these are the simple facts of the gospel. The good news is that Jesus Christ, whom God raised from the dead, gave himself for our sins to rescue us from this present evil age, according to the will of God our Father.

These facts do not contain a single word about anything we do. They simply document what God has done in human history through Jesus Christ. The gospel is not about what we do for God; it is about what God has done for us. God the Father is the one who came up with the gospel plan. God the

13. Lightfoot, *Epistle to the Galatians*, 73.

Son is the one who made the willing sacrifice, in keeping with the Father's will. God the Father is the one who raised Jesus from the dead. Together the Father and the Son accomplished our salvation through the cross; together they announce it to the world through the teaching of the apostles; and together they apply it to our hearts through the Holy Spirit.

Therefore, all the glory goes to God, which is precisely how Paul ends the beginning of his letter: "To whom be the glory forever and ever. Amen" (Gal. 1:5). If salvation is God's work from beginning to end, then all the honor and majesty belong to him forever. Literally, his glory "is into the ages of the ages," which, unlike this present evil age, will never pass away.

If all the glory goes to God, what comes to us is only grace, which is what Paul's letter to the Galatians is all about. It holds out "grace to you and peace from God our Father and the Lord Jesus Christ" (Gal. 1:3). These are not pious clichés; they are God's free gifts for sinners. Grace is the favor God has shown to undeserving sinners through the death and resurrection of Jesus Christ. And grace is exactly what recovering Pharisees need. We are tempted to forget, sometimes, that Jesus is all we need, and when we forget, we need to rediscover the gospel of God's free grace.

2

NO OTHER GOSPEL

Galatians 1:6—10

I am astonished that you are so quickly deserting him who called
you in the grace of Christ and are turning to a different gospel. . . .
As we have said before, so now I say again: If anyone is preaching
to you a gospel contrary to the one you received,
let him be accursed. (Gal. 1:6, 9)

Quintilian probably would not have given Paul an "A" for his letter to the Galatians. Quintilian (c. 35–95) was the master of the classical style. If people wanted to know how to write or speak in a refined manner, they read his *Institutio oratoria*. Quintilian had strong opinions about proper rhetoric, and he despised speakers who began with loud or angry words: "I do not . . . understand why they should open in such a wild and exclamatory manner. When a man is asked to express his opinion on any subject, he does not, if he is sane, begin to shriek, but endeavors as far as possible to win the assent of the man who is considering the question by a courteous and natural opening."[1]

"A courteous and natural opening"—these are hardly the words to describe the way Paul addressed the Galatians: "I am astonished that you are so quickly deserting him who called you" (Gal. 1:6). The apostle was not

---

1. Marcus Fabius Quintilianus, *Institutio oratoria* 3.8.59, quoted in Ben Witherington III, *Grace in Galatia: A Commentary on Paul's Letter to the Galatians* (Edinburgh: T & T Clark, 1998), 32–33.

insane (although perhaps Quintilian would have had his doubts), but he was obviously alarmed. And not just alarmed; he was stunned.

The British have a good expression for Paul's attitude. They would say that he was "gob-smacked." "Gob" is slang for "mouth." To be smacked is to be slapped with an open hand. So someone who is "gob-smacked" opens his mouth, claps his hand over it, and lifts his eyebrows in amazement. Paul was gob-smacked. He was amazed and astonished. He was shocked and out-raged. Thus the body of his letter seethes with righteous indignation.

The apostle did not even pause to say a few kind words to the Galatians. This is in sharp contrast to his other letters, where invariably he thanked God for the good work the church was doing. Even the Corinthians, for all their immorality, received Paul's lavish praise. But he barely gave the Galatians his common courtesy. After the doxology in verse 5, we might have expected a blessing. What Paul gives instead is a curse.

Another Gospel?

There was a good reason for Paul's urgency. He was facing a crisis. What must have happened was something like this: A messenger had brought him a letter or report about the churches in Galatia. The word was that the Galatians were adding the law of Moses to the gospel of Jesus Christ. This was the teaching of the Judaizers, the Jewish-Christian legalists who came from Jerusalem to do follow-up on Paul's evangelism. They wanted to make Gentiles become Jews before they could become Christians. They wanted to add works of the law on top of faith in Jesus Christ as the basis for salvation.

No sooner did Paul hear this than he started composing his response. We can imagine how he did it, grabbing a parchment, slamming an inkwell on his desk, and calling for his secretary. As he paced back and forth in his chamber, he dictated his letter in short, angry outbursts: "Paul . . . apostle . . . I'm surprised at you!"

The reason Paul wrote the Galatians was that he was afraid they were abandoning the Christian faith. They were turning away. "Deserting" is a good translation because the word was first used in a military context for traitors and turncoats. Later it was used to describe anyone who converted from one religion or philosophy to another. The Galatians were betraying their allegiance to Jesus Christ and going over to the other side. The fact that the verb occurs here in the present tense is significant. It describes something the Galatians were in the process of doing at that very moment. But they had not done it yet, so there was still a chance to stop them.

What perplexed Paul was how rapidly the Galatians were leaving the faith. As the New English Bible puts it, they were "turning so quickly away." This may refer to how quickly they accepted the new gospel of the law. More likely, it means that Paul had recently been at the church himself.

Paul's short-term missions trip to Galatia had been a rousing success. Here are some of the press clippings. In Pisidian Antioch "many Jews and devout converts to Judaism followed Paul and Barnabas. . . . When the Gentiles heard this, they began rejoicing and glorifying the word of the Lord; and . . . the word of the Lord was spreading throughout the whole region" (Acts 13:43, 48–49). At Iconium Paul and Barnabas "spoke in such a way that a great number of both Jews and Greeks believed" (14:1). In Lystra they were welcomed like gods (Acts 14:11–13). Then at Derbe "they had preached the gospel to that city and had made many disciples" (Acts 14:21).

It was quite a trip. Sinners were saved. Miracles were performed. Churches were planted. It was one of the most successful missionary journeys in the history of Christianity, which is why Paul could hardly believe that the Galatians were falling away already. As soon as he left, the Judaizers came. In no time at all, the church was giving up the gospel. How fickle! Yet this is a reminder how easy it is to fall away unless we are kept safe by God's grace.

The apostle was going through what Moses went through when he came down from Mount Sinai to find God's people worshiping the golden calf. The great prophet had been up with God having the ultimate mountaintop experience. "And the LORD said to Moses, 'Go down, for your people, whom you brought up out of the land of Egypt, have corrupted themselves. They have turned aside quickly out of the way that I commanded them'" (Ex. 32:7–8).

Paul was as angry as Moses had been. Only instead of throwing down stone tablets, he tried to get in touch with the Galatians before it was too late. His letter shows the urgency of a man who is trying to stop a disaster before any more damage can be done. J. Gresham Machen (1881–1937)

17

offers a helpful paraphrase of these verses: "You are falling away from the gospel and I am writing to stop you."[2]

The gospel—this is what the Galatians were giving up. To use the proper term for it, they were "apostatizing." They were abandoning the good news about the cross and the empty tomb. The good news of God's grace is his unmerited favor for undeserving sinners. The gospel proclaims that Jesus Christ died and rose again to save us from sin. When the Galatians turned away from this gracious gospel, they were not just adopting a new philosophical position. They were not simply trading one set of ideas for another. No, Paul said to them, "you are so quickly deserting him who called you" (Gal. 1:6), meaning God himself. This put their betrayal in personal terms. They could not give up the gospel without giving up God himself.

THE UPSIDE-DOWN GOSPEL

The Galatians were turning away from God and his gospel of free grace. This was the problem, and Paul went on to identify its cause: "Evidently some people are throwing you into confusion and are trying to pervert the gospel of Christ" (Gal. 1:7 NIV).

Who were these people? Maybe Paul didn't know himself, or maybe he knew and didn't want to say. Apparently, they came from somewhere besides Galatia, probably Jerusalem. Throughout this letter Paul addresses the Galatians directly, calling them "you." But when he refers to the teachers of the other gospel, he refers to them as "they."

Whoever they were, they were causing a disturbance in the church. They were creating turmoil. They were "troubling" the Galatians (Gal. 1:7). These people were agitators. Since they were stirring up trouble, the best term for them is "troublemakers."

Many things can disturb the peace of the church, but these troublemakers were doing the most disturbing thing of all. As John Stott says, "The church's greatest troublemakers (now as then) are not those outside who oppose, ridicule and persecute it, but those inside who try to change the

---

2. J. Gresham Machen, *The New Testament: An Introduction to Its Literature and History*, ed. W. John Cook (Carlisle, PA: Banner of Truth, 1976), 127.

gospel."[3] This is what the Judaizers were doing. They wanted "to distort the gospel of Christ" (Gal. 1:7). They were distorting things. They were taking sound theology and twisting it.

The word "pervert" refers to something reversed, something turned upside down. When the good news about Jesus is right side up, we have the gospel. If we take it and stand it on its head, we end up with the law. But it is not always easy to tell the difference. If you had been in the Galatian church, would you have been able to tell which end was up? Would you have been able to identify the one true gospel? Realize how plausible this other gospel sounded, especially to the Galatians, who were relatively new in the faith. It sounded almost good enough to be the good news.

Remember that the people who came to the Galatians with this "other gospel" were baptized members of the Christian church. Their teaching started something like this: "We believe that Jesus Christ is the Son of God and the Savior of the world. He is the Messiah, the chosen one of Israel, who died on the cross for our sins and rose again from the dead. You must repent of your sins and trust in Jesus Christ to be saved."

The teachers who were getting Paul all hot and bothered were using the same terminology that he used. They were preaching salvation in Christ. All they wanted to do was take it a little further. Paul's opponents were "*Christian-Jewish missionaries* who had come to Galatia to improve or correct Paul's gospel and to 'complete' his converts by integrating them fully into the heirs of Abraham through circumcision and by thus bringing them 'under the law.' "[4]

The Judaizers wanted to add something to Paul's gospel of free grace. "Yes, yes, what Paul preaches is fine," they said, "as far as it goes. But we've been worshiping God for a long time, a lot longer than you Gentiles. In fact, we've been keeping the law of Moses for over a thousand years. And you know what Jesus said? He said that he did not come to abolish the law, but to fulfill it. If you want the full gospel, you need to be circumcised in order to get it. This is what Gentiles have *always* had to do to become part of God's people."

3. John R. W. Stott, *The Message of Galatians: Only One Way*, The Bible Speaks Today (Downers Grove, IL: InterVarsity, 1968), 23.
4. James D. G. Dunn, *The Epistle to the Galatians*, Black's New Testament Commentary (Peabody, MA: Hendrickson, 1993), 11.

19

What could be more reasonable? If you had gone to church in Iconium, or Lystra, would you have been able to get the gospel right side up?

MODERN GOSPELS

More importantly, can you distinguish between the true gospel and all the false gospels in the contemporary church? We worship in a church of many gospels. There is the gospel of material prosperity, which teaches that Jesus is the way to financial gain. There is the gospel of family values, which teaches that Jesus is the way to a happy home. There is the gospel of the self, which teaches that Jesus is the way to personal fulfillment. There is the gospel of religious tradition, which teaches that Jesus is the way to respectability. There is the gospel of morality, which teaches that Jesus is the way to be a good person.

What makes these other gospels so dangerous is that the things they offer are all beneficial. It is good to be prosperous, to have a happy home, and to be well behaved. Yet as good as all these things are, they are not the good news. When they become for us a sort of gospel, then we are in danger of turning away from the only gospel there is.

Raymond Ortlund Jr. has tried to imagine the church without the gospel. "What might our evangelicalism, without the evangel, look like?" he asks. "We would have to replace the centrality of the gospel with something else, naturally. So what might take the place of the gospel in our sermons and books and cassette tapes and Sunday school classes and home Bible studies and, above all, in our hearts?"[5] Ortlund lists a number of possibilities:

- "a passionate devotion to the pro-life cause"
- "a confident manipulation of modern managerial techniques"
- "a drive toward church growth"
- "a deep concern for the institution of the family"
- "a clever appeal to consumerism by offering a sort of cost-free Christianity Lite"
- "a sympathetic, empathetic, thickly-honeyed cultivation of interpersonal relationships"

5. Raymond Ortlund Jr., *A Passion for God* (Wheaton, IL: Crossway, 1994), 205.

- "a determination to take America back to its Christian roots through political power"
- "a warm affirmation of self-esteem"

In other words, the church without the gospel would look very much the way the evangelical church looks at this very moment. We cannot simply assume that we have the gospel. Unless we keep the gospel at the center of the church, we are always in danger of shoving it off to one side and letting something else take its place. Martin Luther rightly warned that "there is a clear and present danger that the devil may take away from us the pure doctrine of faith and may substitute for it the doctrines of works and of human traditions. It is very necessary, therefore, that this doctrine of faith be continually read and heard in public."[6] The good news of the cross and the resurrection must be preached, believed, and lived. Otherwise, it will be lost.

The church's greatest danger is not the anti-gospel outside the church; it is the counterfeit gospel inside the church. The Judaizers did not walk around Pisidian Antioch wearing T-shirts that said, "Hug me, I'm a false apostle." What made them so dangerous was that they knew how to talk the way Christians talk. They used all the right terminology. They talked about how they "got saved." They told people to "trust in Christ." They "presented the gospel."

Only they did not have the gospel after all. We should expect, therefore, that the most serious threat to the one true gospel is something that is also called the gospel. The most dangerous teachers are the ones who preach a different Christ but still call him "Jesus."

So, for example, a preacher in a well-established church always talks about the gospel, but never gets around to confronting sin. Or a Mormon invites people to belong to the Church of Jesus Christ (of Latter-day Saints). Or a Roman Catholic signs a statement that says, "We are justified by faith in Christ," but without ever specifying that justification comes by faith in Christ alone. Or a theologian who calls himself an evangelical teaches that there are many ways to God, and that Jesus will save people through other religions. They all seem like such nice people. They all say that they believe in Jesus. But who is the Jesus they believe in? Is he the Christ who is God as

---

6. Martin Luther, *Lectures on Galatians, 1535*, trans. and ed. Jaroslav Pelikan, in *Luther's Works* (St. Louis: Concordia, 1963), 26:3.

well as man? Is he the Christ whose cross is the only atonement for sin? Is he the Christ who is the Judge as well as the Savior? Is he the Christ whose righteousness alone can make us right with God?

Not everyone who calls himself a Christian serves Christ, and not everything called the gospel *is* the gospel. It is not mere words that save; it is the realities of the one true gospel that save—Jesus Christ in his death and resurrection for sinners.

THE ONLY GOSPEL THERE IS

There is one and only one gospel of free grace. In verse 6 Paul described the teaching of his opponents as "a different gospel." But in reality there is no other gospel. So no sooner has he hinted that there might be, than he has to clarify himself by saying, "not that there is another one" (Gal. 1:7). Paul did not want anyone to think, even for a moment, that there is any other true gospel because, in fact, there isn't.

To prove his point, the apostle tried to imagine a situation in which it would be okay to believe another gospel. What if Paul himself came back to Galatia with a different gospel? After all, he had been arguing that he was a genuine apostle, one of God's official spokesmen. Maybe someday God might give him a new gospel. Or what if an angel came from heaven? Paul probably mentions the angels because the Jews thought that the law had been given through the angels (see Gal. 3:19). So imagine a bright angelic being showing up and saying, "Fear not! Behold, I bring you a new gospel. Sincerely, God." What then?

God's Holy Word rejects the very possibility of God's ever giving a new gospel: "But even if we or an angel from heaven should preach to you a gospel contrary to the one we preached to you, let him be accursed" (Gal. 1:8). The good news of justification by grace alone, through faith alone, in Christ alone, is the only gospel there is. Anyone who says anything different—Paul doesn't care who—deserves to go to hell! There is no other gospel, there has never been any other gospel, and there never will be any other gospel.

Martin Luther said, "That which does not teach Christ is not apostolic, even if Peter and Paul be the teachers. On the other hand, that which does teach Christ is apostolic, even if Judas, Annas, Pilate or Herod should propound it."[7] Luther was exaggerating to make a point, as he often did. But the point itself is valid. The true standard for Christianity is not the messenger, but the message: "The gospel preached by Paul is not the true gospel because it is Paul who preaches it; it is the true gospel because the risen Christ gave it to Paul to preach."[8] The gospel is the gospel because it is God's gospel.

Because the gospel is God's gospel, there will never be another. To be sure, the gospel has its rivals. There are religions such as Islam that claim to be based on the revelation of angels. There are cults that claim to have a special message about how to be saved from the coming judgment. There are even Bible scholars who take Galatians and say that the Protestant Reformers were wrong: it is not really about justification by faith alone after all. This is the approach taken by advocates of the New Perspective on Paul and the law, in which Galatians is reinterpreted as focusing on Jewish-Gentile relations and not on the more ultimate question as to how sinners can be righteous before God.

To any and all challengers we give the same answer that Paul gave to the Galatians: "But even if we or an angel from heaven should preach to you a gospel contrary to the one we preached to you, let him be accursed" (Gal. 1:8). To show that this was not a rash exaggeration, fueled by excessive passion, but his mature and settled judgment, Paul virtually repeated himself: "As we have said before, so now I say again: If anyone is preaching to you a gospel contrary to the one you received, let him be accursed" (Gal. 1:9). In this verse the apostle speaks in the indicative rather than in the subjunctive. Verse 8 was hypothetical ("if anyone should preach"). Verse 9 is actual ("if anyone does preach"). Paul is addressing the real situation in Galatia, where false teachers were preaching a false gospel.

The true gospel is not only the one that Paul preached, but also the one that the Galatians accepted. Anyone who preaches any other gospel is, to put it literally, "anathema." This is the Old Testament idea of "a person or thing set apart and devoted to destruction, because hateful to God."[9] To be anathema is to be under the divine curse, like the Canaanite cities that God utterly destroyed. Paul is saying that he would be damned if he ever preached another gospel. Anyone who teaches another gospel is subject to the wrath and curse of God.

---

7. Martin Luther, quoted in F. F. Bruce, *The Epistle to the Galatians: A Commentary on the Greek Text*, New International Greek Testament Commentary (Grand Rapids: Eerdmans, 1982), 83.

8. Bruce, *Epistle to the Galatians*, 83.

9. J. B. Lightfoot, *St. Paul's Epistle to the Galatians* (1865; repr. Lynn, MA: Hendrickson, 1981), 78.

There is no other gospel. Sinners must either receive this one true gospel or be eternally condemned. God offers the free gift of eternal life, through faith in his Son Jesus Christ, who died for our sins and rose again. If we reject this gift, what else can God possibly do to save us?

FOR HIS PLEASURE

Paul's harsh words about eternal condemnation do not sound very tolerant. Martin Luther comments, "This is not preaching that gains favor from men and from the world. For the world finds nothing more irritating and intolerable than hearing its wisdom, righteousness, religion, and power condemned. . . . For if we denounce men and all their efforts, it is inevitable that we quickly encounter bitter hatred, persecution, excommunication, condemnation, and execution."[10]

The apostle Paul faced all these things himself—including execution—because of his life-or-death commitment to the one true gospel. He was willing to face them because he knew whose approval really mattered.

As committed as he was, apparently Paul was accused of being inconsistent. Verse 10 gives a clue what his enemies were saying: "For am I now seeking the approval of man, or of God? Or am I trying to please man? If I were still trying to please man, I would not be a servant of Christ" (Gal. 1:10).

Paul's opponents said that he was a people-pleaser. They claimed that he would say or do anything to be popular. When he was with Jews, he behaved like a Jew; but when he was with Gentiles, he told them they didn't have to keep the law or get circumcised. All he really cared about was his own reputation. For example, Paul had Timothy circumcised right in Galatia, just to keep the Jews happy (Acts 16:3). But Titus wasn't circumcised at all (Gal. 2:3). Not surprisingly, Paul was accused of being inconsistent. After all, he was the man who said, "I have become all things to all people, that by all means I might save some" (1 Cor. 9:22).

The truth is that however inconsistent he seemed, Paul was always consistent with the gospel. Timothy was circumcised so that he could be effective in Jewish evangelism. An uncircumcised man would not have the respect he needed for social access to orthodox Jews. The situation with Titus was dif-

10. Luther, *Galatians*, 26:58.

ferent because Paul rightly perceived that some Jewish Christians were making his circumcision a matter of salvation. For Paul, circumcision was a matter of indifference until people tried to make it essential for salvation, and then it became, for them, a matter of gospel truth. For proof that Paul was not simply out to win people's approval, look at his anathemas (Gal. 1:8–9). These are hardly the words of a man who cared very much what people thought! So the apostle posed the question, "Am I now seeking the approval of man, or of God? Or am I trying to please man?" (Gal. 1:10). Obviously not.

Paul was one of those rare individuals who did not live to please anyone except God. If we ask how he was able to do this, the answer is that he was living by the one true gospel. To be sure, there was a time when the most important thing in his life was what people thought of him. He refers to this at the end of verse 10: "If I were *still* trying to please man, I would not be a servant of Christ" (Gal. 1:10). Before he came to Christ, back when he was still a Pharisee, Paul did everything he could to keep up appearances. He put his confidence in his circumcision, his ethnicity, his family connections, his cultural background, and especially the way he kept the law (Phil. 3:4–6). Back then he was living by a different gospel, which was no gospel at all.

Then Paul left Pharisaism behind and came to Christ. He stopped trying to please anyone else and put all his confidence in Jesus Christ. He no longer cared what other people thought of him. He stopped living for his own publicity and started living for God's pleasure.

This is a question every person has to answer: Whose pleasure do I seek? If we try to please ourselves, or other people, then we are living by a different gospel. Pleasing God and pleasing others are mutually exclusive. We cannot follow our own ambitions and follow Jesus Christ at the same time. For us, the "good news" is a bigger paycheck, a better job, a new romance, or some other personal accomplishment. But once we understand the one true gospel, then we stop living for ourselves, or for others, and start living for God.

Consider what the gospel says. It does not tell us what we have to do to please God. Instead, it announces that God is already pleased with us through the death and resurrection of Jesus Christ. God is as pleased with us as he is with his own Son. This liberates us from seeking the approval of others. At the same time, it frees us from striving for God's favor. We already have the tender affection of his eternal love. What more do we need? Nothing more, which is why the one true gospel is such amazingly good news.

3

THE ORIGIN OF PAUL'S RELIGION

Galatians 1:11—24

For I would have you know, brothers, that the gospel that was preached by me is not man's gospel. For I did not receive it from any man, nor was I taught it, but I received it through a revelation of Jesus Christ. (Gal. 1:11–12)

efore going any further, it will be helpful to have the outline of Galatians clearly in mind. The letter falls neatly into three sections—biography, theology, and ethics—each two chapters in length.

In the first two chapters Paul recounts his spiritual autobiography. His life story shows that he is a true apostle who preaches the true gospel of free grace. The first section of the letter may be summarized like this: "For I would have you know, brothers, that the gospel that was preached by me is not man's gospel. For I did not receive it from any man, nor was I taught it, but I received it through a revelation of Jesus Christ" (Gal. 1:11–12). Paul understood that people had to accept his apostleship before they would accept his gospel.

The theology of the one true gospel is expounded in chapters 3 and 4. Essentially, it is the theology of justification by faith alone in Christ alone. A good theme verse for this section of Paul's letter comes in the middle of the third chapter: "Now it is evident that no one is justified before God by the law, for 'The righteous shall live by faith'" (Gal. 3:11).

Finally, the book concludes with two chapters of ethics. Paul takes his theology—as he does in all his letters—and applies it to daily life, where "neither circumcision nor uncircumcision counts for anything, but only faith working through love" (Gal. 5:6).

This is the logic of Galatians: live by the gospel that you can receive only by faith. What God has done (the biography of chapters 1 and 2) teaches us what we should believe (the theology of chapters 3 and 4) and how we should live (the ethics of chapters 5 and 6).[1]

PAUL: THE EARLY YEARS

We begin with Paul's spiritual autobiography. At the time he wrote to the Galatians, both the apostle and his gospel were under attack. Certain men had come from Jerusalem to correct Paul's teaching. They wanted to add the law of Moses to the gospel of Jesus Christ. They taught that Gentiles had to become Jews in order to become Christians. This was so completely different from what Paul preached that they had to say something to discredit his message. Thus they claimed that he was a second-rate apostle with a secondhand gospel.

This smear on Paul's reputation has persisted through the succeeding centuries. Thomas Jefferson, among others, dismissed the great apostle as "the first corruptor of the doctrines of Jesus."[2] This accusation strikes at the heart of Christianity. The New Testament offers eternal life through the atoning death and bodily resurrection of Jesus Christ. Is this offer human or divine? Is the gospel of the cross and the empty tomb something that the first Christians invented, or does it come from God himself?

By this point in the letter we can already anticipate Paul's answer. The first thing he wrote was that his gospel was "not from men nor through man, but through Jesus Christ" (Gal. 1:1). Now he says the same thing again: "the

1. See Timothy George, *Galatians*, New American Commentary 30 (Nashville: Broadman & Holman, 1994), 66.
2. Thomas Jefferson, letter to W. Short (1820), quoted in S. L. Johnson, *Galatians: Believers' Bible Bulletin* 3 (Dallas: Believers' Chapel, 1978), 1.

gospel that was preached by me is not man's gospel" (Gal. 1:11). Literally, Paul "gospeled" the gospel that comes from God.

In order to prove that what he preached was God's own true gospel, Paul denied that it could have come from anyone or anywhere else. Verse 11 is his denial that what he preached was something he made up (or that anyone else made up, for that matter). The gospel is not man's good news about God; it is God's good news for man.

Verse 12 is Paul's denial that his gospel was something he received from a mere human being. Unlike the Galatians themselves (see Gal. 1:9), he "did not receive it from any man" (Gal. 1:12). Nobody witnessed to Paul. He didn't read a tract or go forward at an evangelistic crusade. No one explained to him the plan of salvation. No one even discipled Paul. He was not, he insists, "taught" the gospel (Gal. 1:12). Nor did he consult with anyone to get it (Gal. 1:16). Why would he need to? Once he had seen the risen Christ for himself, there was nothing he needed to double-check. In particular, Paul did not go running to the apostles in Jerusalem for confirmation: "Nor did I go up to Jerusalem to see those who were apostles before I was, but I went immediately into Arabia and later returned to Damascus" (Gal. 1:17 NIV).

From all this we can guess what Paul's opponents were saying. After all, they were from the mother church in Jerusalem, and as far as they were concerned, Jerusalem was the only place to get the apostolic gospel. In effect, they claimed that Paul did not get his gospel from an authorized dealer, or that if he did, he had departed from it.

Paul's response was that he was an apostle in his own right years before he ever went to Jerusalem. The first thing he did after his conversion was to go to Arabia (Gal. 1:17). Some scholars have thought that this refers to the region around Mount Sinai. Perhaps like the prophets of old, Paul retreated to the wilderness to commune with God and study what the Scriptures taught about the Messiah. However, it is more likely that he was referring to the kingdom of Nabatea, known in those days as "Arabia." The Nabatean kingdom included the city of Damascus, and in one of his other letters, Paul tells how "the governor under King Aretas was guarding the city of Damascus in order to seize me, but I was let down in a basket through a window in the wall and escaped his hands" (2 Cor. 11:32–33).

This raises an interesting question: Why would the Nabateans want to arrest Paul? Probably for the same reason anyone ever wanted to arrest Paul: he was preaching the gospel of free grace. If so, then he started preaching the gospel long before he went back to Jerusalem.

PETER AND PAUL

Eventually Paul did travel to Jerusalem. The book of Acts gives the impression that he went right after he was converted (Acts 9:26). However, Luke does not actually indicate when he made the trip, and Galatians helps provide the real timetable: "Then after three years [meaning the third year since Paul's conversion] I went up to Jerusalem to visit Cephas [meaning Peter] and remained with him fifteen days" (Gal. 1:18).

Fifteen days with Peter—not long enough to be trained in the rabbinic style, but long enough to get to know someone. Undoubtedly the two apostles talked about Jesus and the gospel. The Greek word for "visit" (*historēsai*) is a word for getting a report. Presumably Paul interviewed Peter, taking his personal history to learn more about the life, death, and resurrection of Jesus Christ.

The other person Paul met in those days was James the brother of Jesus (who may or may not have been regarded as an apostle): "But I saw none of the other apostles except James the Lord's brother" (Gal. 1:19). To show how serious he was about all this, Paul took the kind of oath someone would swear in a court of law: "In what I am writing to you, before God, I do not lie!" (Gal. 1:20). If it seems surprising that Paul did not meet any other apostles in Jerusalem, we should remember that they were still afraid of him because of his former persecution of the church (Acts 9:26).

Paul undoubtedly learned many things from Peter and James. He must have asked both of them about their encounters with the risen Christ, because Peter and James are the only two individuals he mentions by name in his list of the people who saw Christ after his resurrection (see 1 Cor. 15:5–7). But one thing Paul definitely did not learn from Peter, James, or any of the other apostles was the gospel. This was something he already knew. He did not receive the good news by instruction because he had already received it by revelation. John Stott summarizes by saying, "Paul's first visit to Jerusalem was only after three years, it lasted only two weeks, and he saw only two apostles. It was, therefore, ludicrous to suggest that he obtained his gospel from the Jerusalem apostles."[3]

The last thing Paul denied was that he had picked up his gospel anywhere else in the church: "Then I went into the regions of Syria and Cilicia" (Gal. 1:21). These areas were well to the north. Paul preached to Gentiles there, apparently with some success (Acts 15:41). But as for the rest of the Christians in Judea, they did not even know Paul by sight: "I was still unknown in person to the churches of Judea that are in Christ" (Gal. 1:22). This completes Paul's airtight alibi. He neither invented nor inherited his gospel. He did not make it up on his own and he did not get it from anyone else—not before his conversion, not during his conversion, and not after.

WHERE THE GOSPEL COMES FROM

If Paul did not get the gospel from his own fertile imagination, or from Peter or the other apostles, or from somewhere else in the church, then where did it come from? The answer is that the gospel came from God himself. Paul received it "through a revelation of Jesus Christ" (Gal. 1:12). The gospel was not an invention, or a tradition, but a revelation.[4] That is to say, it was something previously unknown that was unveiled by God.

There is some question as to whether Jesus was the one who was revealed or the one who did the revealing. Probably Jesus was the one revealed, since Paul later says that God revealed Jesus to him (Gal. 1:16), but it makes little difference. The important thing is that Jesus was revealed to Paul. This refers to Paul's experience on the Damascus road, when he looked up into the heavens and saw Jesus in all his glory. What was unveiled for him in that moment was the essence of the gospel. To see the glorious Christ was to know the reality of his cross and empty tomb.

Presumably Paul had heard some of the facts about Jesus of Nazareth before his conversion, only to reject them because they sounded like blasphemy. But then he saw the same Jesus who had been crucified, now disclosed as Son of God and risen Lord. His eyes were opened, spiritually speak-

---

3. John R. W. Stott, *The Message of Galatians: Only One Way*, The Bible Speaks Today (Downers Grove, IL: InterVarsity, 1968), 35.

4. Ibid., 30.

ing. In an instant he realized that he could never get right with God by keeping the law, but only by coming to Christ. Therefore, Paul received the good news from Jesus himself.

Yet the origins of Paul's gospel go further back. His calling as a Christian and his commission as an apostle were on God's mind long before he was even born. God "was pleased to reveal his Son to me," he writes in verse 16, and to speak of God's pleasure in this way is to speak of his eternal election, the secret purpose of his predestinating love. What God was pleased to do was to set Paul apart before he was born (Gal. 1:15). This was a clever phrase because the Pharisees considered themselves set apart by keeping God's law. Paul had been a Pharisee himself, but God did not set him apart merely to keep the law after all; he set him apart to preach the gospel. Literally, he set him apart "from the womb." Paul was like some great Old Testament prophet (see Jer. 1:5): God claimed his life and ministry while he was still in his mother's womb.

Many years later, when the time was right, God was pleased to call Paul "by his grace" (Gal. 1:15). Calling refers to the life events that lead a person to repentance for sin and faith in Jesus Christ. Such effectual calling is always by grace because the call shows God's undeserved favor. Yet calling also refers to God's special plan for someone's life work. What God had planned for Paul to do was to take the gospel to the Gentiles: God "was pleased to reveal his Son to me, in order that I might preach him among the Gentiles" (Gal. 1:16). This verse summarizes Paul's whole life. He preached Christ to the Gentiles. He preached Christ crucified and Christ risen, and the Christ he preached was the very same Christ that God had revealed to him.

HOW THE GOSPEL COMES TO US

The great New Testament scholar J. Gresham Machen once wrote a book called *The Origin of Paul's Religion.* Through his study of Paul, Machen reached the same conclusion the apostle himself had reached: The origin of Paul's religion was God in Christ. But this is not simply the origin of Paul's religion. God in Christ is the origin of any true religion.

Not surprisingly, the religions that human beings invent always end up glorifying human beings. There is some law to keep, some teaching to follow, some ritual to perform, some penance to endure, or some state of consciousness to achieve that will bring salvation. One way or another, we can climb up to heaven and reach God.

Christianity is different. What distinguishes it from other world religions is that it actually comes from God. The one true gospel is not man-made, which is why it gives all the glory to God. The good news of the cross and the empty tomb could come only from God because it is about what God has done to save us through Jesus Christ. It does not teach that we can reach up to heaven; it teaches that God has come down to earth. In Christ, God has entered human history and the human heart.

We cannot receive this gospel the same way Paul received it. Even if we traveled the Damascus road, we would not find it there. The heavens will not part so we can see Jesus in all his glory. Yet ultimately the good news of our salvation comes from the same place: it comes from God. As Luther put it, "The knowledge of Christ and of faith is not a human work but utterly a divine gift."[5] God is the one who set us apart from birth. He knew us even when we were in our mother's womb. This is part of the doctrine of election, which is "God's gracious choice of certain individuals unto eternal life in consequence of which they are called, justified, sanctified and glorified."[6]

God's gracious choice goes all the way back to eternity past: "he chose us in him [Christ] before the foundation of the world, that we should be holy and blameless before him. In love he predestined us for adoption through Jesus Christ, according to the purpose of his will" (Eph. 1:4–5). God chose us in love long before we were able to choose him.

Then he called us by his grace. It was "by grace" because it was more than we could ever deserve. Nevertheless, and however he did it—whether with the help of a parent, the witness of a babysitter, the message of a radio preacher, or the invitation of someone from work—God called us. And when he called us, he showed us his Son. We read in the Scriptures that Jesus Christ is the Son of God, we heard in a sermon that he is the Savior of the world, and we believed that it is all true. We believed it because God revealed his Son to our hearts by his Holy Spirit.

---

5. Martin Luther, *Lectures on Galatians, 1535*, trans. and ed. Jaroslav Pelikan, in *Luther's Works* (St. Louis: Concordia, 1963), 26:64.

6. "Abstract of Principles," Southern Baptist Theological Seminary (Louisville, Kentucky).

One man was searching for the meaning of his existence. His life was full of emptiness and despair. He knew there had to be something more, but he had no idea what it was. Then one day he found what he was looking for. While he was working as a pathologist in a hospital, he went down to the morgue. Another hospital worker there looked straight at him and asked, "Do you know Jesus Christ?" Something in the man's heart cried out and he said, "That's it! That's the answer. I've been looking for Jesus Christ."

Every Christian's story is different, but the story line is always the same. God chose you and called you to faith. He revealed his Son to your heart. Then he gave you a particular place of service. Do you know what God has called you to do?

A university student in Vietnam decided to become a Christian, a choice that proved to be very costly. He fell out of favor with the communist leaders, and as a result he was turned down for a job as a lecturer and forced to perform menial labor. At first the young man was very angry, not only with God, but also with his parents, who had raised him in the church. "You work only for the church," he complained. "Why don't you help me?" His father had a simple answer. He said, "You are for God." In other words, "You do not live for yourself any more, my son; you belong to God. You cannot go and seek some great position for yourself; you must receive your place in life as a gift from him."

Are you for God? Have you been set apart for his service? God is calling you by his grace. At this very moment, he is inviting you to turn away from sin and trust in him. He is showing you his Son, Jesus Christ, who died on the cross for sins and was raised again to conquer death. If you believe this gospel, you will live for him forever.

WHAT THE GOSPEL DOES

The gospel comes from God, but what does it do when it arrives? The answer is that it changes a person's whole life.

Consider what the gospel did for Paul. The details of his story were well known to the Galatians: "For you have heard of my former life in Judaism, how I persecuted the church of God violently and tried to destroy it" (Gal. 1:13). Before Paul came to Christ, he was one of God's most violent enemies. The historical records show that he went from house to house, dragging Christians away by brute force, attacking women as well as men. When they were brought up on charges, he cast his vote for the death sentence (Acts 26:10). In one famous incident—the execution of Stephen—he even ran the coat-check for the firing squad (Acts 7:58).

Paul was obsessed with destroying the church. The word he uses for this (*eporthoun*) is the word that the Greeks used for sacking a city. John Chrysostom (c. 350–407) said it signified "an attempt to extinguish, to pull down, to destroy, to annihilate, the Church."[7] Paul's goal was nothing less than the total extermination of Christianity. He was such a fanatic that no one would have even attempted to change his mind.

All this time, Paul was making great strides in the Jewish religion. He was at the head of his class: "And I was advancing in Judaism beyond many of my own age among my people, so extremely zealous was I for the traditions of my fathers" (Gal. 1:14). His parents had reared him well. They could have displayed a proud bumper sticker: "Our Son Is an Honor Student with Gamaliel" (see Acts 22:3). Paul knew the Torah, the Old Testament law, with all its interpretations and applications. He drew the hardest possible line between Christianity and Judaism.

That was the "before." The "after" came by word of mouth, as people heard it said: "He who used to persecute us is now preaching the faith he once tried to destroy" (Gal. 1:23).

What happened to Paul was such a radical transformation that it made people nervous. He had earned his reputation by terrorizing the church, as his opponents were quick to point out. Wherever he first went after he was converted, such as Damascus and Jerusalem, he received a chilly reception. But the change in Paul's life proved to be genuine, and it proved to be total. Not only did he stop persecuting Christians, but he also started to promote Christianity. He began to preach the very gospel he had once tried to destroy.

What could account for the transformation in Paul's life? Certainly nothing in his religious background. The only thing that could explain it is the supernatural work of God. Notice that when Paul described his life before Christ, he used the first person as the subject of his sentences: I persecuted the church, I advanced in Judaism, and so forth. His life afterwards was totally

---

7. John Chrysostom, *Homilies on the Epistles of St. Paul the Apostle to the Galatians and Ephesians*, trans. Gross Alexander, ed. Philip Schaff, in *Nicene and Post-Nicene Fathers*, First Series (1889; repr. Peabody, MA: Hendrickson, 1994), 13:10.

different, and when he described it (Gal. 1:15–16), he had to use "God" as the subject: God chose him, God called him, and God revealed his Son to him.

More literally, Paul said that God's Son was revealed "in him" (Gal. 1:16). Grammatically it is possible for this phrase to mean that Jesus was revealed "to" him or "through" him. But more likely it refers to the fact that Jesus Christ actually entered Paul's heart. As he went on to write in the next chapter, "Christ . . . lives in me" (Gal. 2:20). When Paul met Christ on the Damascus road, he was changed from the inside out. His knowledge of Christ was not just historical and factual; it was also spiritual and personal.

When people heard about the total change that had taken place in Paul's life, all they could do was give God the glory: "And they glorified God because of me" (Gal. 1:24). They knew that only the direct intervention of God can change a sinner's heart, and when God does intervene, to him alone goes all the glory.

GOD'S LIFE-CHANGING GOSPEL

The gospel will do the same thing in our lives that it did in Paul's life. Not exactly the same thing, of course, because there was only one Paul. But it is the same gospel. Perhaps we have never persecuted anyone, or kidnapped people, or voted for their execution. But we are still sinners who need the gospel. We are evil by nature, and thus we need the gospel to take us from where we are to where we ought to be.

One man whose life was changed by the gospel is Tom Papania, who actually went from the Mafia to the ministry. Papania's grandfather was a criminal who helped bring organized crime from Sicily to America. Papania himself was a hard man. When he was only ten years old, during one of the many beatings he received from his father, he vowed that he would never shed another tear as long as he lived. He became a thief, an extortionist, and a murderer. Eventually he became the number-two man in the New York Mafia. His heart was so cold that when hardened criminals looked into his eyes, they saw nothing but death.

Eventually God began to speak to Papania's heart, but he refused to listen. He did not want God to have any power over him. So he decided to outsmart God. He figured he was probably about to die for his sins, but before

God had the chance to kill him, he was going to kill himself. As Papania put the gun to his head, the telephone rang. It was a man who had been inviting him to church. Just to prove that God did not have any power over him, Papania decided to go to church after all. When the service was finished, he met the minister at the back door of the church. The minister said to him, "I have something I want to say to you, but I don't want to offend you. The eyes are the windows of the soul. When you first came in here, I looked into your eyes, and all I could see was a little boy crying, wanting to be loved."

By saying this, the pastor exposed Papania's most painful secret. But Papania did not want anyone to know that he had a weakness, so he went back to the church later that night to murder the minister. When he got to the church, he found to his amazement that he couldn't go through with it. As the two men began to talk, the minister asked him if he knew Jesus and told him that he needed to be born again. Papania just laughed. He said, "Pastor, if these people in this church found out who I was, they'd throw both of us out of here. I'm probably the biggest sinner you'll ever see if you live to be a million years old. These people here don't want me. I'm a sinner."

Then Papania began to recount all his crimes. He was trying to get the minister off his back about being born again. He wanted to convince him that he was so bad that God was about to kill him; he was just one step ahead of God. But what he was really doing was confessing his sins. Before he knew it, Papania found himself kneeling on the ground, with thirty years of tears freely flowing down his cheeks, opening the door of his heart to let Jesus in. He said, "I've found Jesus, and I've been searching for him all my life, and now that I have him, I'm not letting him go." Papania went on to become a prison evangelist. His life was changed by God's gospel.[8]

I also see lives changed by the gospel in my own church. I think about the lives we would still be leading if we had never come to Christ. Or I think about the way we used to live. Some of us were thieves. Some of us were felons. Some of us were violent and abusive. Some of us were in bondage to sexual sin. Some of us were liars and cheats. The rest of us seemed like relatively nice people, but we lived only for ourselves.

Then God changed us. First, he called us by his grace. Someone told us that there was a way to have a friendship with God. Next, God revealed to

---

8. As recounted in a radio broadcast from Focus on the Family in Colorado Springs.

us his Son. He showed us the gospel of the cross and the empty tomb. We saw that our sins could be forgiven through the death and resurrection of Jesus Christ. Then he set us apart for his service. We began to love others and to live for God. This is what the gospel does. It changes a person's whole life. God can bring the same change to your life. It is very simple: all you need to do is trust in Jesus Christ.

4

GOSPEL FREEDOM FIGHTER

Galatians 2:1–10

*But even Titus, who was with me, was not forced to be circum-
cised, though he was a Greek. Yet because of false brothers secretly
brought in—who slipped in to spy out our freedom that we have
in Christ Jesus, so that they might bring us into slavery—to them
we did not yield in submission even for a moment, so that the
truth of the gospel might be preserved for you. (Gal. 2:3–5)*

"Free at last! Free at last! Thank God Almighty, we're free at last!"
These famous words express the joyful release of freedom.
They were spoken by Dr. Martin Luther King Jr. at the close
of his address at the 1963 March on Washington for Civil Rights. Dr. King's
words conveyed something besides freedom's joy; they also hinted at its
long, hard struggle. They were spoken a full century after liberty was first
proclaimed for African-Americans. Free at last! At last, after centuries of
bondage and enslavement. At last, after another long century of prejudice
and injustice.

Our experience with slavery in America teaches that proclaiming emancipation and possessing liberty are two very different things. Freedom is not
easily gained, and once gained, it is easily lost.

THE ENEMIES OF FREEDOM

Freedom has as many joys and struggles in the spiritual realm as it does in human society. Dr. King knew this, for he borrowed his famous words from an old Negro spiritual: "Free at last! Free at last! Thank God Almighty, we're free at last!" The song's first and primary meaning was about freedom from sin through Jesus Christ.

Freedom in Christ was the apostle Paul's concern as he wrote Galatians, a letter sometimes known as the Magna Carta of Christian liberty. Paul knew how precious spiritual freedom is. He knew the price that Jesus paid on the cross to gain it. He also knew how easy it is to squander that freedom and return to spiritual bondage.

This is why Paul wrote to the Galatians with such urgency. They believed the gospel of the cross and the empty tomb. They had gained true spiritual freedom by putting their faith in Christ crucified and Christ risen. But now they were under the spell of teachers who wanted to add the law of Moses to the gospel of Christ (see Gal. 3:1). As a result, they were in danger of becoming enslaved all over again (see Gal. 5:1).

What was happening in Galatia reminded Paul of an almost identical situation he had faced some years before, probably in Antioch, where Judaizers secretly entered the church—false brothers "who slipped in to spy out our freedom that we have in Christ Jesus, so that they might bring us into slavery" (Gal. 2:4). Here Paul borrows his vocabulary from the world of espionage. His opponents were conducting covert operations in the church. Like undercover agents, they had sneaked into the church to see what the Gentile Christians were up to. But they were more than informants; they were slave-traders. They were conspiring to hold the church hostage to the law.

These men are sometimes called "the Judaizers" because they confused Judaism with Christianity. They taught that Gentiles had to become Jews in order to become Christians. Their slogan was, "Unless you are circumcised according to the custom of Moses, you cannot be saved" (Acts 15:1). Since they opposed Paul's law-free gospel, one might call them "the Torah police." But Paul knew them for what they really were: "false brothers" (Gal. 2:4)— "brothers" because they claimed to be Christians, but "false" because they did not follow Christ after all.

39

Whatever we call these men, they were enemies of freedom, which is why Paul took such a strong stand against them: "to them we did not yield in submission even for a moment, so that the truth of the gospel might be preserved for you" (Gal. 2:5). Paul was a freedom fighter. He knew that people who want to keep their freedom in Christ have to fight for it.

Notice that the gospel he was fighting for is not *a* truth; it is *the* truth. It is the truth that Jesus had in mind when he said, "You will know the truth, and the truth will set you free" (John 8:32). It is the same truth that Jesus was talking about when he said that he was the truth (John 14:6). There is only one Christ, one truth, and one gospel. Therefore, there is only one ultimate freedom worth fighting to preserve. From Paul's example we learn that the price of spiritual freedom is constant vigilance. It is not enough to share the gospel or even to preach it. The gospel has to be defended.

It is not easy to defend the truth in an age of lies. These days people want to make up their own good news. They do not want to be told that there is one and only one way of salvation. They will put up with Christianity only as long as it minds its own business. Therefore, the church is under great pressure to compromise its message. But there is one thing we will not give up, and that is the freedom we have in Christ. Salvation comes only by his death and resurrection. We will not let anyone add to or subtract anything from his cross and empty tomb. With Martin Luther, we say that "we can stand the loss of our possessions, our name, our life, and everything else; but we will not let ourselves be deprived of the Gospel, our faith, and Jesus Christ. And that is that."[1]

WHEN DID PAUL GO TO JERUSALEM?

Paul would not let himself be deprived of faith in Jesus Christ either, which is why he went up to Jerusalem to fight for the freedom of the gospel. The apostle's account of his visit raises an important question: How do the details of his spiritual autobiography in Galatians match up with the historical account Luke gives in the book of Acts? The outstanding New Testament scholar C. K. Barrett calls this "the most celebrated and complicated

---

1. Martin Luther, *Lectures on Galatians, 1535*, trans. and ed. Jaroslav Pelikan, in *Luther's Works* (St. Louis: Concordia, 1963), 26:99.

historical problem in the whole epistle—perhaps in the whole of the New Testament."[2]

The book of Acts mentions at least four visits Paul made to Jerusalem. He made the first not long after his conversion (Acts 9:26–30). It was on this occasion that he got acquainted with Peter (Gal. 1:18–19). His second trip was to take a gift to the poor who had suffered during a severe famine (Acts 11:27–30). Paul's third visit to Jerusalem was perhaps the most famous. He went up with Barnabas and others for what is known as the Jerusalem Council (Acts 15). It was at this council that the apostles officially declared that Gentiles were welcome in the church. The apostle's fourth visit to Jerusalem was his last, for he was arrested and sent to Rome (Acts 21–28).

So which visit did Paul have in mind when he wrote: "Then after fourteen years I went up again to Jerusalem with Barnabas, taking Titus along with me. I went up because of a revelation and set before them (though privately before those who seemed influential) the gospel that I proclaim among the Gentiles, in order to make sure I was not running or had not run in vain" (Gal. 2:1–2)? Here Paul indicates that he went to Jerusalem "after fourteen years." This probably means fourteen years after his conversion, or eleven years after his first visit to Peter. His companions were Titus and Barnabas— a Greek and a Jew. They went in response to divine revelation, not in response to an apostolic summons. But while they were there, they had a private interview with the other apostles to talk about the gospel for the Gentiles.

Some of those details match Luke's description of the Jerusalem Council in Acts 15. The same parties were present: Paul and Barnabas presented their gospel to the other apostles, opposed by the false brothers. They were discussing a similar issue: whether or not Gentiles had to be circumcised to be accepted in the church. And the meeting had the same basic result: Paul's message of grace for the Gentiles was affirmed.

There do seem to be some differences, however. Galatians says the meeting took place in private, but Acts gives the impression it was more public (15:4, 22). Galatians says Paul went in response to a revelation, but Acts says he was part of an official delegation from the church in Antioch (15:2). But the real problem is that if Galatians 2 describes the same events as Acts 15, then Paul has left out the visit he made to Jerusalem in Acts 11. This would

---

2. C. K. Barrett, *Freedom and Obligation* (Philadelphia: Westminster, 1985), 10.

be misleading, to say the least. What he is trying to show in Galatians is that he did not get his gospel from the other apostles. That being the case, it would not be right for him to cover up his visit to Jerusalem in Acts 11.

Perhaps these discrepancies can be reconciled in some way, but the other possibility is that Galatians 2 describes the visit Paul made to Jerusalem in Acts 11 rather than the one he made in Acts 15. Most of the details seem to fit. Paul made the earlier trip with Barnabas (Acts 11:30). He did so in response to a revelation (Acts 11:28). He made the trip to help the poor, which would fit in with what he says in Galatians 2:10: "Only, they asked us to remember the poor, the very thing I was eager to do."

So where does Galatians fit in the chronology of Acts? At first glance, Galatians 2 seems to describe the events surrounding Paul's third visit to Jerusalem—his attendance at the Jerusalem Council in Acts 15. However, not all the facts seem to match. Furthermore, there are some important similarities between Galatians 2 and Acts 11, Paul's second visit to Jerusalem.

There is one more thing to consider. Remember that the Jerusalem Council settled the Gentile question once and for all. At the end of the council, an official decree was issued about the status of Gentiles in the Christian church (Acts 15:23–29), a decree that was distributed to all the churches (Acts 16:4). If Galatians 2 refers to Acts 15, then Paul wrote to the Galatians *after* the Jerusalem Council. But if that is so, why did he not mention the decision that was made there? This would have ended the argument and stopped the Judaizers from claiming that Jerusalem was on their side.

All things considered, it seems likely that Galatians 2 refers to Paul's second visit to Jerusalem, and not to the Jerusalem Council. If so, we can offer a rough chronology for Paul's life to this point. He was converted not long after the death and resurrection of Jesus Christ, possibly in A.D. 32. He then spent up to three years in the region near Damascus. Sometime around A.D. 34 he made a short trip to Jerusalem to get acquainted with the apostle Peter. This is the visit described in Galatians 1:18–19. Paul did not return to Jerusalem until A.D. 45. His main purpose for going was famine relief. While he was there, however, he consulted privately with the other apostles about his gospel for the Gentiles, as we read in Galatians 2:1–2.

Not long afterwards, the apostle embarked on his first missionary journey, during which he planted the major churches of Galatia. But the Judaizers continued to oppose his mission, especially in Antioch (Acts 15:1; Gal.

2:11–14). The conflict grew so fierce that eventually the church held an official council to resolve it, the minutes of which are recorded in Acts 15. And sometime before that council was held in Jerusalem, Paul wrote his famous pastoral letter to the Galatians.

TITUS: A TEST CASE

Some of the questions we have about Paul's chronology cannot be settled with absolute certainty. Yet the answers do not greatly affect our understanding of Galatians 2. Whenever Paul made this visit to Jerusalem, we know that he won his fight for freedom. The trip had two positive results: Paul's convert (namely, Titus) was accepted, and his commission was acknowledged.

First, Paul's convert was accepted. In verse 1 Paul mentions that he brought Titus with him to Jerusalem. Titus was a Gentile convert whom Paul considered one of his co-workers. In fact, Titus was practically like a son to him (Titus 1:4). Eventually he became a prominent leader in the early church, serving as pastor of the church in Crete.

Taking Titus to Jerusalem was a daring move. Because he was a Greek rather than a Jew, Titus was uncircumcised. And if anything was bound to enrage the Judaizers, it was bringing an uncircumcised man into their holy city! Circumcision meant everything to the Jews. It was the sacred mark of Jewish identity, the symbol of salvation. Since the days of Abraham, the removal of the male foreskin had been the visible sign of belonging to God's people. According to the command of God (Gen. 17:9–14), circumcision determined whether someone was inside or outside the covenant.

In the past, if a Gentile decided to become a Jew, he had to be circumcised. This was what the law required. Then Paul came along with his law-free gospel, preaching the good news of the cross and the empty tomb. He said that Jesus Christ had already met the requirements of the law, so that circumcision didn't even matter. All it took to belong to God was faith in Jesus Christ. Titus served as the perfect test case for the freedom of Paul's gospel. Here was a man who had received Jesus Christ as his Lord and Savior. Did he or did he not also have to meet the requirements of the law, epitomized by circumcision?

The answer the apostles gave was that Titus did not have to be circumcised to be saved. As Paul put it: "But even Titus, who was with me, was not forced to be circumcised, though he was a Greek" (Gal. 2:3). The good news

43

is not salvation by faith in Christ plus circumcision; the good news is salvation by faith in Christ alone.

Circumcision is no longer a hot topic for the church, but the deeper issue here is still relevant. Paul regarded circumcision as a synecdoche for the entire law (see Phil. 3:2–9); it represented law-keeping in general. Thus the apostle was fighting for something fundamental to Christianity at all times and in all places: What does it take to become a first-class member of God's family? Is it simply a matter of faith in Christ, or is there something else, too?

The answer is that there are no second-class Christians. How could there be? Every Christian is saved exactly the same way: by grace alone through faith alone in Christ alone. Therefore, there can be no discrimination in the church. The church cannot exclude people from salvation on the basis of race, gender, class, age, or anything else. The church cannot even discriminate on the basis of relative righteousness. Christians have a way of ranking sins. If someone is struggling with pride and lust, that's okay. Who isn't? But someone who is battling with depression, or whose marriage is falling apart, or who is tempted to commit homosexual sin, or who is addicted to drugs had better keep it quiet. Otherwise, people will know that he or she does not really belong in the church.

This seems to be the way that some Christians think, but it is not the way God thinks. Christians have different gifts, of course. We have different backgrounds. We have different cultures, in some cases. We have different ministries and callings, so there is order in the church. We have different trials and temptations. But there is no difference in our standing before God. And if there is no difference in our standing before God, there should be no differences in our standing with one another.

Titus was the perfect example. He could hardly have been more different from the apostles than he was, standing before them as an uncircumcised Gentile. But he also stood before them as a man saved by the cross and the empty tomb. God had accepted him solely on the basis of what Jesus had done for him. And on this same basis the apostles even in Jerusalem accepted him as a first-rate brother in Christ, thereby proving that justification comes by grace through faith in Christ alone.[3]

3. The New Perspective on Paul and the law would emphasize the ecclesiological dimension of Paul's example: the gospel provides the basis for a Gentile like Titus to be accepted by Jews. N. T. Wright, among others, claims that "the question at issue in the church at Antioch, to which Paul refers in chap-

MISSION TO THE GENTILES

One result of Paul's trip to Jerusalem was that his convert was accepted. Titus was not required to be circumcised. The second result of this apostolic summit meeting was that Paul's commission was acknowledged.

Notice Paul's attitude toward the other apostles. He describes them as men "who seemed to be influential" (Gal. 2:2, 6), or "who seemed to be pillars" (Gal. 2:9). Paul's comments about the other apostles may seem a bit standoffish, or even derogatory. But remember that his opponents were making a big deal about them, as if the Jerusalem apostles were the only ones that counted. Paul responded by saying, "What they were makes no difference to me" (Gal. 2:6). What God had done in Paul's life was different from what he had done in Peter's life, and Paul knew it. He was not one of the original twelve disciples (Gal. 1:17). But "what they were"—namely, companions of Christ during his earthly ministry—did not make them a higher authority. Paul had respect for the other apostles, but he was not intimidated by them. He did not make a fuss over their credentials because he knew that "God shows no partiality" (Gal. 2:6). John Stott explains that "although he [Paul] accepts their *office* as apostles, he is not overawed by their *person* as it was being inflated by the Judaizers."[4]

The important thing is not what Paul thought about the other apostles, however, but what they thought about him and his gospel of free grace. Paul puts it plainly: the men "who seemed influential added nothing to me" (Gal. 2:6). The other apostles did not have to give official approval to Paul; they simply acknowledged that he already had God's approval because he was an apostle in his own right. Nor did the other apostles add anything to Paul's message. They did not try to amend, edit, change, or otherwise alter his gospel. They added nothing to it. They removed nothing from it. They changed nothing about it. They simply accepted it as it was.

Contrast the attitude of the apostles with that of Paul's opponents—the enemies of freedom. The members of the Torah police taught that Paul's

---

ter 2, is not how people came to a relationship with God, but who one is allowed to eat with" (*What Saint Paul Really Said* [Grand Rapids: Eerdmans, 1997], 121). But Paul is using the example of Titus to make a more fundamental point pertaining to soteriology: the apostolic embrace of Titus proved that the basis for a man's acceptance by God (and not merely by other people) is not works, but grace.

4. John R. W. Stott, *The Message of Galatians: Only One Way*, The Bible Speaks Today (Downers Grove, IL: InterVarsity, 1968), 45.

gospel was all right as far as it went; it just didn't go far enough. They wanted to add law to faith as the basis for salvation. But the apostles understood that nothing should or even could be added to Paul's gospel. They knew that it is impossible to refinish the finished work of Christ. The gospel says that through his death and resurrection, Jesus Christ has done everything that needs to be done for our salvation. If we were to try to add anything to that free and gracious gospel, it would be like taking an Olympic gold medal and having it bronzed! The good news of the cross and the empty tomb cannot be improved; it can only be destroyed.

This is a perennial danger for the church. Christians are always trying to add something to the gospel. They elevate some aspect of Christianity to a place of supreme importance, so that the good news becomes faith in Christ plus something else. Usually what gets added to the gospel is something good in itself. Some particular experience of the Holy Spirit, perhaps. Some special ministry (usually the ministry we are involved with). Some methodology for having devotions, growing a church, or raising a family. Some distinctive doctrine or style of worship. Some political or social cause. Some way of doing, or of not doing, what the world does. But for the gospel to be the gospel, it has to stand alone. The gospel is Christ plus nothing. The old hymn by Edward Mote (1797–1874) claims that our "hope is built on nothing less than Jesus' blood and righteousness." But our hope is also built on nothing *more* than Jesus' blood and righteousness. Back in chapter 1, Paul told the Galatians to accept no alternatives. Here in chapter 2, he tells them to accept no additives.

What more do we need to save us from sin than the death and resurrection of Jesus Christ? Nothing more. The apostles knew this, which is why they acknowledged Paul's commission to preach the gospel: "when James and Cephas and John, who seemed to be pillars, perceived the grace that was given to me, they gave the right hand of fellowship to Barnabas and me" (Gal. 2:9). The right hand of fellowship was more than a handshake. It was a symbolic gesture of partnership in the gospel. It showed that in the division of their labor, the other apostles endorsed Paul's mission to the Gentiles.

PARTNERS IN THE GOSPEL

The way the first apostles treated one another is a model for ministry. An older commentary on Galatians states:

46

The true way to avoid strife, is just that which is here proposed. Let there be on both sides perfect frankness—let there be a willingness to explain and state things just as they are—and let there be a disposition to rejoice in the talents, and zeal, and success of others, though it should far outstrip our own,—and contention in the church would cease; and every devoted and successful minister of the gospel would receive the right hand of fellowship from all . . . who love the cause of true religion.[5]

The apostles did everything they could to avoid strife. For starters, they were perfectly frank with one another. When Paul met with the apostles, he "set before them" his gospel for the Gentiles (Gal. 2:2). This is a term for making a full disclosure. Paul did not hide anything. He told the others exactly what he preached so there could be an honest discussion of the issues.

At the same time, the apostles all rejoiced in the talents and success of others. They were not interested in building their own little kingdoms. The Jerusalem apostles did not envy Paul's global success as a missionary. "On the contrary, . . . they saw that I had been entrusted with the gospel to the uncircumcised, just as Peter had been entrusted with the gospel to the circumcised (for he who worked through Peter for his apostolic ministry to the circumcised worked also through me for mine to the Gentiles)" (Gal. 2:7–8). The apostles knew the work of God when they saw it. They also understood that the gospel is a partnership. They were unwilling to rob Paul to pay Peter, but recognized that each man had his own legitimate sphere of ministry. Peter was to take the gospel primarily to the Jews in Judea. Paul mainly was to take the gospel to the Gentiles of the world. Although Peter sometimes evangelized Gentiles (Cornelius, for example), and Paul got thrown out of his share of synagogues, each man had his own unique calling.

The evangelization of the world depends on this kind of cooperation in the church. Rather than taking pride in our own ministry, we should celebrate what God is doing through others. We can participate in different campus groups, for example, or belong to various church denominations. We can engage in various means of outreach. We can take diverse approaches to evangelism. We can allow space for different styles of music, according to the cultural context. We not only allow for these differences, but rejoice in

5. Barnes, in John Brown, *An Exposition of the Epistle of Paul the Apostle to the Galatians* (Edinburgh, 1853; repr. Evansville, IN: Sovereign Grace, 1957), 80–81.

them, *provided that we are all preaching the same gospel.* This qualification needs to be emphasized. Partnership in the gospel goes only as far as the gospel itself goes, and no further, which is precisely why the apostles took the time to discuss exactly what they were preaching.

Bible scholars often call attention to the differences among the New Testament apostles. They speak of the gospel according to Paul, for example, and contrast it with the gospel according to Peter. It is true that each of the apostles had his own way of preaching the gospel. But whatever differences there may have been in terms of experience, emphasis, or style, there was no difference in content. Paul's gospel was independent, but not different. Any variations had more to do with where he was preaching than what he was preaching. Thus the gospel according to Paul and the gospel according to Peter, or John, or even James, was always the same gospel of free grace.

The principle here is that the church can allow diversity of mission only where there is unity of message. The gospel itself sets the limits on our cooperation with others who call themselves Christians. We are willing to compromise on many things, but we are completely obstinate when it comes to the gospel. We refuse to recognize as Christian any church or any other organization that does not teach the one true gospel. Where there is no fellowship in the gospel, there can be no partnership in mission.

Paul had a genuine partnership with the Jerusalem apostles. They demanded only one thing from him: "Only, they asked us to remember the poor, the very thing I was eager to do" (Gal. 2:10). "The poor" refers specifically to the church in Jerusalem. Whereas most Gentile churches had some wealthy members, the Christians back in Jerusalem were destitute, especially in times of famine.

Helping the poor is not the gospel, but it is one necessary result of the gospel. Martin Luther wrote, "Next to the proclamation of the Gospel it is the task of a good pastor to be mindful of the poor."[6] A gospel-preaching church does not forget the poor—especially suffering Christians around the world—but remembers to care for them. And when it came to the poor, the apostle Paul set a good example. He never forgot what the apostles asked him to do. Several of his later epistles refer to the collections he took to relieve the suffering church (e.g., 1 Cor. 16:1–4; 2 Cor. 8:1–9:15). Paul sent the money

---

6. Luther, *Galatians*, 26:105.

back to Jerusalem to demonstrate the unity of the church. He and the other apostles all shared in the partnership of the gospel.

WHAT IF PAUL HAD LOST?

By the time Paul's visit to Jerusalem was over, he had won his fight for spiritual freedom. His convert was accepted and his commission was acknowledged. He had successfully defended the gospel truth that salvation comes by grace alone through faith alone in Christ alone. Yet we may well ask what difference this makes. To be sure, it made a difference to Paul. He met with the others "to make sure," he wrote, "I was not running or had not run in vain" (Gal. 2:2). This did not mean that there was any doubt in Paul's mind that he had the right gospel. He knew he had the right gospel because he had received it from Christ himself and had been preaching it for more than a decade. He hardly needed the Jerusalem apostles to reassure him that he had the right gospel!

Paul's fear did not have to do with his own commission, but with the church's commission. Unless he and the other apostles were all preaching the same gospel, the church would never fulfill its mission to the world. In particular, Paul was worried about a permanent division in the church between Jews and Gentiles. Here is how F. F. Bruce describes his concern: "His commission was not derived from Jerusalem, but it could not be executed effectively except in fellowship with Jerusalem. A cleavage between his Gentile mission and the mother-church would be disastrous: Christ would be divided, and all the energy which Paul had devoted, and hoped to devote, to the evangelizing of the Gentile world would be frustrated."[7]

To describe his fears, Paul used the illustration of a footrace, such as a relay race. Paul knew that he would complete his leg of the race, but he needed to be sure that the other apostles were also carrying the gospel baton. Otherwise, his efforts would be wasted and the church would never make it to the finish line. So imagine for a moment what would have happened if Paul had lost his fight for freedom. What would the church look like today

---

7. F. F. Bruce, *The Epistle to the Galatians: A Commentary on the Greek Text*, New International Greek Testament Commentary (Grand Rapids: Eerdmans, 1982), 111.

if the first apostles had required Gentiles to become Jews in order to become Christians?

If Paul had failed to defend his gospel for the Gentiles, then Christians would still have to follow the law of Moses down to the last detail. Our salvation would depend on such things as being circumcised, keeping the Old Testament dietary laws, and following the more obscure regulations in Leviticus. The church would be imprisoned within the Jewish culture. Not that there is anything wrong with Judaism as a culture. God never asked the Jews to leave their ethnic identity behind. It was fine for them to be circumcised. It was even appropriate for them to follow the law of Moses, *provided they understood that they were not saved by it.*

It would be wrong, however, for Christianity to be held prisoner by Jewish culture. Christianity is multicultural as a matter of principle, which is one reason it has changed the world. Part of the secret of the gospel's success is that it can be translated into any cultural context. Paul rightly understood that the Gentile question would affect the entire future of Christianity. He was afraid that if the Judaizers had their way, Christianity would become another Jewish sect rather than good news for the whole world.

Free at Last!

Galatians is partly about ethnocentrism, about turning a cultural distinctive into a theological necessity. But the deeper issue is the perpetual danger of adding our own requirements to the only thing God requires for salvation, which is faith in Jesus Christ. One of the fundamental errors of the New Perspective on Paul and the law is that it focuses on the horizontal relationship between Jews and Gentiles to the neglect of the vertical relationship between God and sinners, which for Paul was the more crucial concern. Indeed, the conflict between Jews and Gentiles had significance for him only insofar as it threatened to corrupt the true gospel of grace. Here is how John Stott defines the terms of Paul's engagement of this issue: "The Christian has been set free from the law in the sense that his acceptance before God depends entirely upon God's grace in the death of Jesus Christ received by faith. To introduce the works of the law and make our acceptance depend on our obedience to rules and regulations was to bring a free man into bondage again."[8]

This spiritual bondage is what Paul was fighting against when he went up to Jerusalem, which is why the whole future of Christianity was at stake. When Paul contended for the theology of justification through faith in Christ alone (especially in Galatians 3 and 4), it was not because his overarching concern was for better relations between Jews and Gentiles. On the contrary, for Paul the relationship between the two issues (the horizontal issue of Jewish-Gentile relations and the vertical issue of a sinner's standing before a righteous God) was exactly the opposite: he fought for spiritual freedom from Jewish regulations in order to preserve the justifying grace of God in the gospel.

By the grace of God, Paul won his fight for gospel freedom. Gentiles were accepted in the church on the basis of the gospel alone. In fact, according to a work known as *The Epistle of Barnabas*, circumcision had been abolished everywhere in the church by the second century.[9] Yet the fight for freedom in Christ will not end until Christ returns to make us free forever. For this reason, the gospel still needs freedom fighters today. One of the great freedom fighters in the history of the church was Martin Luther, who wrote:

> The issue before us is grave and vital; it involves the death of the Son of God, who, by the will and command of the Father, became flesh, was crucified, and died for the sins of the world. If faith yields on this point, the death of the Son of God will be in vain. Then it is only a fable that Christ is the Savior of the world. Then God is a liar, for he has not lived up to his promises. Therefore our stubbornness on this issue is pious and holy; for by it we are striving to preserve the freedom we have in Christ Jesus and to keep the truth of the gospel. If we lose this, we lose God, Christ, all the promises, faith, righteousness, and eternal life.[10]

These things are worth as much of a fight today as they were for Luther. Fight for them we must!

---

8. Stott, *Message of Galatians*, 43.
9. *Epistle of Barnabas* 9.4, in *The Apostolic Fathers*, trans. Kirsopp Lake (Cambridge, MA: Harvard University Press, 1912), 370–71.
10. Luther, *Galatians*, 26:90–91.

5

THE BATTLE FOR THE GOSPEL

Galatians 2:11—16

But when Cephas came to Antioch, I opposed him to his face,
because he stood condemned. . . . We ourselves are Jews by birth
and not Gentile sinners; yet we know that a person is not justified
by works of the law but through faith in Jesus Christ, so we also
have believed in Christ Jesus, in order to be justified by faith in
Christ and not by works of the law, because by works of the law
no one will be justified. (Gal. 2:11, 15–16)

*I*t was an awkward moment, to say the least. It's always embar-
rassing when a fight breaks out at church, but this one was a
real doozy. For one thing, it took place during a church potluck,
where everyone was supposed to be having a good time. For another thing,
the combatants were the pillars of the church. It was Peter against Paul, two
apostles in a face-to-face, knock-down, drag-out showdown.

The battle was completely unexpected. The two men had been friends
ever since they got acquainted in Jerusalem. The last time they were together,
Peter had given Paul the right hand of fellowship. But this time Paul was
opposing Peter right to his face.

The idea of an open conflict between two apostles has made many commentators extremely uncomfortable. Some of the early church fathers said the
two men didn't really disagree: it must have been some other Peter. More recent

scholars have argued that the breach was permanent—that Peter and Paul were never reconciled. Perhaps this was what the Judaizers had been saying to the Galatians. Everyone knew there had been some kind of argument at Antioch, and it would have been easy to use the incident to discredit Paul's gospel.

Yet according to Paul, the altercation was the final proof that he was a genuine apostle of the one true gospel of free grace. Here it may help to review his argument to this point. First Paul argued that he had been an apostle long before he met any other apostles (1:13–24). Next he showed how the other apostles recognized him as an apostle in his own right (2:1–10). In case any further proof was needed, he now shows that he even had the authority to rebuke another apostle who stepped out of line (2:11–14).

A PLACE AT THE TABLE

To understand why Paul was so upset with Peter, it helps to understand a few things about dining habits. Eating is a cultural event. What we eat (and with whom) says something about who we are. Sometimes certain people refuse to eat with certain other people. This is something the black Hall of Fame pitcher Bob Gibson discovered when he made it to the big leagues. He walked onto the team bus and saw a white ballplayer drinking an orange soda. "That looks really good," he said. "Can I have a swig?" Gibson's teammate looked down at his drink, looked back at Gibson, and said, "I'll save you some." What he meant was that his white lips would not share a drink with a black man.[1]

One of the reasons the incident at Antioch was so ugly was its racial overtones. Here is how the Cotton Patch Bible renders Galatians 2:11–13: "But in spite of all of this, when Rock [Peter] came to Albany, I had to rebuke him to his face, because he was clearly in error. For, before the committee appointed by Jim [James] arrived, he was eating with Negroes. But when they came, he shrank back and segregated himself because he was afraid of the whites. He even got the rest of the white liberals to play the hypocrite with him, so that even Barney [Barnabas] was carried away by their hypocrisy."

This paraphrase helps capture the ethnic tension in Antioch. However, what was going on in the church involved something more than racism.

1. David Halberstam, *October 1964* (New York: Villard, 1994), 220–21.

Keeping the Old Testament food laws was one way for the Jews to show that they belonged to God: "In Judaism table-fellowship means fellowship before God, for the eating of a piece of broken bread by everyone who shares in the meal brings out the fact that they all have a share in the blessing which the master of the house has spoken over the unbroken bread."[2] Mealtimes were sacred to the Jews. Remember the way people reacted when Jesus ate with sinners and tax collectors?

Jewish dining habits created a crucial problem for the church in the cosmopolitan city of Antioch. Of a population of nearly half a million, at least 10 percent were Jews. So the Antiochene church became a multicultural melting pot. It was the place where the diverse followers of Christ were first called "Christians." People could tell that whatever this strange religion was, it was not exclusively Jewish, so it needed a special name.

Antioch thus became the first place where the early church had to wrestle with the issue of table fellowship. At their former meeting in Jerusalem (Gal. 2:1–10), the apostles had already agreed that the Gentiles belonged in the church. They didn't have to keep the Old Testament law to be saved. At the same time, it was still appropriate for Jewish Christians to maintain their heritage by keeping the ceremonial law. Just as the Gentiles could behave like Gentiles, so the Jews could behave like Jews. But how was a Jew supposed to relate to a Gentile when they both worshiped in the same church? Did they have to *eat* together? Table fellowship with Gentiles had always been forbidden! In the words of one old tradition, "Eat not with them ... for their works are unclean."[3] How could Jewish Christians keep kosher if they had to eat with Gentiles who ate the wrong foods, prepared the wrong way, and in some cases offered to the wrong gods?

Although the apostles had already settled the theological question of salvation for the Gentiles, they had not settled the practical question of fellowship with the Gentiles. J. Gresham Machen summarized the problem like this:

> The Gentile Christians, it will be remembered, had been released from the obligation of being circumcised and of undertaking to keep the Mosaic Law.

2. Joachim Jeremias, *New Testament Theology: The Proclamation of Jesus* (London: SCM, 1971), 115.
3. *The Book of Jubilees* 22.16, quoted in James D. G. Dunn, *The Epistle to the Galatians*, Black's New Testament Commentary (Peabody, MA: Hendrickson, 1993), 119.

The Jewish Christians, on the other hand, had not been required to give up their ancestral mode of life. But how could the Jewish Christians continue to live under the Law if they held companionship with Gentiles in a way which would render the strict observance of the Law impossible?[4]

God revealed the radical solution to this problem in a vision. As Peter was praying before lunch one day, he "saw the heavens opened and something like a great sheet descending, being let down by its four corners upon the earth. In it were all kinds of animals and reptiles and birds of the air" (Acts 10:11–12). In other words, the sheet was full of animals that the Jews were absolutely forbidden to eat. Then a voice from heaven said something remarkable: "Rise, Peter; kill and eat" (Acts 10:13). God had to be kidding! So Peter said, "By no means, Lord; for I have never eaten anything that is common or unclean" (Acts 10:14). But the voice told him, "What God has made clean, do not call common" (Acts 10:15).

Through this vision God was preparing Peter to take the gospel to a Gentile. Immediately afterwards he was called to Caesarea, where he baptized a Roman named Cornelius (Acts 10:48). Peter learned a vital lesson from all of this. He said, "Truly I understand that God shows no partiality, but in every nation anyone who fears him and does what is right is acceptable to him" (Acts 10:34–35). Later, when he faced public criticism for his actions, he said, "If then God gave the same gift to them as he gave to us when we believed in the Lord Jesus Christ, who was I that I could stand in God's way?" (Acts 11:17).

Eventually Peter came to understand that his vision was not just about evangelism; it was also about fellowship. "He was eating with the Gentiles" (Gal. 2:12), Paul wrote, meaning that it was his usual custom to sit down with them at the table. Peter did not have any scruples about sharing a meal with his uncircumcised brothers in Christ. His radical solution to the problem of table fellowship was to consider them not separate, but equal.

PETER'S PRETENSE

To an orthodox Jew, sitting down to eat with pagans was an act of defiant rebellion. So imagine what these men who "came from James" (Gal. 2:12)

---

4. J. Gresham Machen, *The Origin of Paul's Religion* (New York: Macmillan, 1921), 100.

thought when they went to Antioch! James the brother of Jesus had given Paul the right hand of fellowship. But apparently James also had his groupies in Jerusalem—what we might call "the James gang"—and sometimes they lacked the balance of their hero. In fact, the Jerusalem Council's letter to the churches makes a telling comment about such men: "We have heard that some persons have gone out from us and troubled you with words, unsettling your minds, although we gave them no instructions" (Acts 15:24).

This was exactly what happened in Antioch, where members of the "James gang" went to check up on Peter. These extremists were Christians, of course, but as former Pharisees (in all likelihood) they were very traditional in their faith (Acts 15:5). They still followed the rituals of Moses, especially circumcision. The first thing they noticed was how lax Peter was when it came to the old traditions. He was behaving practically like a pagan! As Paul would later put it, he lived "like a Gentile and not like a Jew" (Gal. 2:14). There he was, sitting down to have table fellowship with unwashed, uncircumcised heathens. He might as well have gone the whole hog and hosted a pig roast for the singles fellowship!

The pressure group from Jerusalem put Peter in an awkward situation. Frankly, he found himself "fearing the circumcision party" (Gal. 2:12). He knew how traditional they were, and he did not want to offend them. After all, he was called to take the gospel to the Jews, not the Gentiles, so why worry about the Gentiles?[5] So Peter did an about-face: "He drew back and separated himself" (Gal. 2:12). He stopped inviting Gentiles to sit at his table. He started eating on the other side of the church basement. Or perhaps, since the first Christians met in private homes, he stopped eating with them altogether, even for the Lord's Supper.

What Peter did was not a matter of principle; it was a case of cowardice. This was not the first time Peter had given in to peer pressure, but at least the fourth (see Matt. 26:69–75). From this we learn that even great Christians can fall into sin, sometimes more than once. We also learn how necessary it is for Christian ministers to have the courage to defend the gospel against all opposition, including opposition that comes from within the church.

---

5. Ben Witherington III, *Grace in Galatia: A Commentary on Paul's Letter to the Galatians* (Edinburgh: T & T Clark, 1998), 132.

Peter's poor example also teaches us to stick up for the gospel. It was his firm conviction that salvation came by grace through faith, not by the law. He not only believed that Gentiles could be first-class Christians; he also lived in a way that demonstrated that they were. Nevertheless, Peter retreated from his former position. He "pulled back" from his brothers and sisters. The Greek term (*hypestellen*) is sometimes used to describe a military withdrawal. In effect, Peter was ashamed of the gospel. When push came to shove, he did not stand his ground for the truth that all Christians are saved by the same grace.

It takes courage to stand for the gospel. A former archbishop of Canterbury was once asked by a reporter if he believed in God. Unfortunately, the question caught him off guard. He said, "Well, sort of. It depends on what you mean by God." The man was ashamed of the gospel, afraid to take a stand for God. Or take another example. A rather nervous woman on the airplane turned to me and asked, "Are you religious?" I think she hoped I was praying we wouldn't crash into the mountains. My answer was so noncommittal that she was surprised when I later had to admit that I was in seminary. "Well, you don't need to be afraid," she said. I was so ashamed that the next day I started sharing the gospel with strangers on the ski lift. When the fear of people overcomes the fear of God, we are likely to deny the gospel. Unless we are willing to stand up for God at work on Monday, we are just pretending at church on Sunday.

PAUL'S PROTEST

Some people are like Peter. They hate confrontation. They do not want to cause any trouble or make a scene, so they avoid conflict. However, Paul was not one of those people. He really didn't care what anybody else thought. Even when it came to another apostle, Paul cared enough to confront. For him, it was not peace at any price, but the gospel at all costs.

Here was Paul's protest to Peter's pretense: "But when I saw that their conduct was not in step with the truth of the gospel, I said to Cephas before them all, 'If you, though a Jew, live like a Gentile and not like a Jew, how can you force the Gentiles to live like Jews?'" (Gal. 2:14).

There were many situations in which Paul was willing to keep things private, or to work out some kind of compromise. But not this time. He opposed

Peter right to his face, and he did it out in the open, right in front of the whole church. Paul did not do this to be argumentative, or because he considered Peter a rival. He did it because the gospel was at stake, and because Peter's sin was so obvious: "He stood condemned" (Gal. 2:11), meaning condemned before God by his own actions.

Not only was Peter in the wrong, but he was also setting a bad example. This is why Paul had to confront him in public. A private offense deserves a private rebuke, but a public scandal demands public exposure (see 1 Tim. 5:20). Peter was the leader. His example influenced what everyone else did. Suddenly, observing Old Testament dietary laws was all the rage: "The rest of the Jews acted hypocritically along with him, so that even Barnabas was led astray by their hypocrisy" (Gal. 2:13). We can sense Paul's shock and disbelief. Even Barnabas! Even Barnabas, his close friend, who had introduced him to the church and defended him before the other apostles. Even Barnabas, who had helped him in his mission to the Gentiles. Paul could hardly believe it.

What Paul objected to was the hypocrisy of Peter, Barnabas, and the others. The word "hypocrite" comes from the Greek theater, where actors wore masks to play their parts. Eventually the word came to have a religious significance. A good example comes from the Stoic philosopher Epictetus (c. 55–135): "When we see a man trimming between two faiths we are wont to say, 'He is no Jew, but is acting a part.' "[6] Paul saw that Peter, Barnabas, and the others were putting on a charade. They did not *really* believe that Gentiles were second-class Christians, but they were acting as if they did. Their actions were not consistent with their theology.

The real effect of this hypocrisy was to deny the gospel. John Stott explains the situation well: "He [Peter] knew perfectly well that faith in Jesus was the only condition on which God will have fellowship with sinners; but *he* added circumcision as an extra condition on which *he* was prepared to have fellowship with them, thus contradicting the gospel."[7]

It was almost as if Peter and the others had gone back on the agreement they had reached in Jerusalem (2:1–10). They were not acting in line with the truth of the gospel. They were talking the talk, but not walking the walk.

6. Epictetus, "The Discourses," in *The Stoic and Epicurean Philosophers*, ed. Whitney J. Oates (New York: Random House, 1940), 2:9.
7. John R. W. Stott, *The Message of Galatians: Only One Way*, The Bible Speaks Today (Downers Grove, IL: InterVarsity, 1968), 56.

Their lifestyle was no longer in line with the gospel. Even worse, they were knocking the Gentiles out of line too. Paul accused Peter of forcing the Gentiles to "Judaize," or adopt Jewish customs and practices, in order to be accepted in the church. Peter did not really believe that salvation came from being Jewish, but in this case his actions spoke louder than his words. By refusing to eat with Gentiles, he was communicating that he thought they were unclean. Gentiles were getting the picture that if they wanted to become Christians, they had no choice but to live like Jews.

This is another warning for the contemporary church. Our behavior can undermine our belief. It is possible for Christians to believe the gospel in their hearts and even confess it with their mouths, yet deny it with their lives.

A tragic example comes from the history of the Southern Presbyterian Church prior to the Civil War.[8] In those days it was customary for Presbyterian elders to give their parishioners tokens signifying that they were eligible to participate in the Lord's Supper. Sadly, in some churches African slaves were not given the customary silver token, but one made of base metal. Nor were they allowed to receive the sacrament until all the white church members had been served. This was a divisive and prejudicial way of handling a sacrament that God intends to signify our union together in Christ. Whether the elders believed the gospel or not, their actions clearly denied it.

What do our actions say? Do our friendships, our dinner invitations, and our ministry partnerships demonstrate our commitment to the unity and community we have in Christ? Or are our actions out of step with the gospel?

JUSTIFIED BY FAITH, NOT BY LAW

When Paul squared off against Peter in Antioch, he was dealing with something more than a social problem. He was not concerned simply about cliques that were forming in the church, or about who was washing his hands before dinner. He was not even concerned about the ugly sin of racism exclusively, although the Judaizers were using their theology to justify their prejudice.

Paul understood that his skirmish with Peter was nothing less than a battle for the gospel of free grace. On the surface, the issue was unity between

8. Andrew E. Murray, *Presbyterians and the Negro: A History* (Philadelphia: Presbyterian Historical Society, 1966), 62.

Jews and Gentiles at the table. But beneath the surface lurked the deeper issue of what God requires for salvation. This is one of the places where the New Perspective on Paul and the law falls short in its understanding of New Testament theology. The New Perspective views the Jewish-Gentile conflict primarily in terms of cultural boundaries. But for Paul the main issue was soteriological, not cultural. Thus the letter to the Galatians brings us back, yet again, to the good news about Jesus Christ.

The gospel proclaims that through his death on the cross and his resurrection from the grave, Jesus has done everything God requires for our salvation. There is nothing else we need to do to gain forgiveness for sins, enjoy fellowship with God, or have the hope of eternal life except trust in Christ alone. This is the gospel of free grace, and anyone who believes it is a Christian.

After the gospel tells us how to get right with God—or rather, after it tells us what God has done to make us right with him through the cross and the empty tomb—it proceeds to tell us how to live with one another. We must have fellowship with anyone and everyone who is in fellowship with God through faith in Jesus Christ. If we refuse to have fellowship with them, then our actions deny the gospel. We are making a distinction that God himself does not make. We are adding some qualification to the only thing God requires, which is faith in Jesus Christ.

The problem with the "James gang" is that they were recovering Pharisees. They were concerned about outward appearances. They kept a list of things people had to do to be good Christians. When Gentile converts didn't do some of these things—get circumcised, for example—they were treated as second-class Christians. Such Pharisaism runs deep in human nature. People always want to add something they do to what God has done, and they want to look down on people who haven't done it, whatever "it" is.

When Paul stood up to confront Peter, he spoke as one recovering Pharisee to another. First he appealed to what they shared in common: "We ourselves are Jews by birth and not Gentile sinners" (Gal. 2:15). Peter and Paul had the same birthright. They were natural-born Jews rather than pagans. They had always been on the inside with God's people, not outside in the world.

Then Paul appealed to the gospel that he and Peter had both discovered to be true. This point is worth emphasizing. The apostles had come to complete agreement about the good news of Jesus Christ. Their only difference of opinion was over what the good news meant for table fellowship. The battle for the gospel, then, was not a contest between two different gospels. Rather, Paul was fighting to make sure that the church would continue to live by the gospel it had always preached.

The gospel that Peter and Paul both preached was the gracious gospel of faith, not works: "We know that a person is not justified by works of the law but through faith in Jesus Christ, so we also have believed in Christ Jesus, in order to be justified by faith in Christ and not by works of the law, because by works of the law no one will be justified" (Gal. 2:16). This is the famous doctrine of justification by grace alone through faith in Christ alone. "Justification" is a legal term, a word used in a court of law. It means to be proclaimed innocent, to be acquitted, to be cleared of all charges. In its biblical sense, to be justified means to be declared righteous before the bar of God's justice.[9]

Justification must be an important doctrine, because Paul mentions it three different times in three different ways, all in a single verse. First, he states the doctrine in *general* terms: "A person is not justified by works of the law but through faith in Jesus Christ" (Gal. 2:16). This explains God's general method for salvation. How does a person get right with God? Not by keeping God's law, but by trusting in Jesus Christ.

The phrase "faith in Christ" may also be taken as a subjective genitive, meaning "the faith[fulness] of Christ." This option is generally preferred by advocates of the New Perspective on Paul and the law, who tend to downplay the classic Reformation doctrine of justification by faith alone. However, linguistically the case for the objective genitive ("faith in Christ") is much stronger. Mark Seifrid concludes, "When Paul speaks of 'the faith of Christ' he is speaking of faith which has Christ as its object, particularly since he nowhere speaks of Christ's faithfulness in clear terms."[10]

9. Contrary to N. T. Wright and other advocates of the New Perspective on Paul and the law, justification is *not* a declaration that someone belongs to the covenant community. This is another clear example of the way that the New Perspective confuses ecclesiology with soteriology. See Donald A. Hagner, "The Law in Paul's Letter to the Galatians," *Modern Reformation* 12.5 (Sept./Oct. 2003): 38.

10. Mark A. Seifrid, *Christ, Our Righteousness: Paul's Theology of Justification*, New Studies in Biblical Theology (Downers Grove, IL: InterVarsity, 2000), 142. See also Moises Silva, "Faith Versus the Works of the Law in Galatians," in *Justification and Variegated Nomism, Vol. 2, The Paradoxes of Paul*, ed. D. A. Carson, Mark A. Seifrid, and Peter T. O'Brien (Tübingen: Mohr Siebeck, 2004).

Paul's reference to the "works of the law" includes but is not limited to the ceremonial law of the Old Testament.[11] Recently, some scholars have sought to restrict Paul's idea of law-keeping to ceremonial matters such as circumcision and food laws—the so-called ethnic boundary markers that distinguished Jews from Gentiles. Their position is, in part, that Paul's argument against Peter had to do with ritual obedience rather than moral righteousness. But in the course of Paul's long polemic against legalism, it is clear that he views the problem of works-righteousness to include *both* ritual ceremonies and supposed moral attainments (see Rom. 2:6–29 and Phil. 3:2–9). The "works of the law," then, "always refers primarily to what the law requires *in general and in its entirety*."[12] And Paul "opposes the false opinion which supposes that such works contribute to a right standing before God, whether personally or nationally."[13]

A striking example of the typical Jewish attitude toward the law as a means of justification comes from the epitaph on a first-century tomb:

> Here lies Regina . . . She will live again, return to the light again, for she can hope that she will rise to the life promised, as a real assurance, to the worthy and the pious in that she has deserved to possess an abode in the hallowed land. This your piety has assured you, this your chaste life, this your love for your people, this your observance of the Law, your devotion to your wedlock, the glory of which was dear to you. For all these deeds your hope for the future is assured.[14]

As this inscription indicates—and contrary to what advocates of the New Perspective on Paul and the law are saying—first-century Judaism generally was a religion of law, not grace. And when Judaizing theology began to infect the New Testament church, Paul responded by saying (as Martin Luther was later to say in the context of the Protestant Reformation) that anyone who thinks he can win acceptance from God by keeping the law, or any part of it, has fallen into a soul-destroying form of legalism. He (or she) is trying to

---

11. See Seifrid, *Christ, Our Righteousness*, 99–105, and also A. Andrew Das, *Paul, the Law, and the Covenant* (Peabody, MA: Hendrickson, 2001), 155–60.

12. Das, *Paul, the Law, and the Covenant*, 158 (emphasis in original).

13. Seifrid, *Christ, Our Righteousness*, 99.

14. Pieter W. Van Der Horst, "Jewish Funerary Inscriptions," *Biblical Archaeology Review* 18.5 (Sept./Oct. 1992): 55.

be justified by doing what the law commands. Yet when it comes to being accepted by God, observing the law is completely ruled out. Here Paul makes an absolute distinction between salvation by works of the law and salvation by faith in Christ. Law-keeping cannot justify anyone.

Not that there is anything wrong with the law itself, which comes from the righteous character of God. As Paul said to the Romans, "the law is holy, and the commandment is holy and righteous and good" (Rom. 7:12). The problem with the law is our lawlessness! The reason we cannot be justified by the law is that we cannot keep it. Even if we could keep God's commandments outwardly, we break them inwardly: "No human deeds, however well motivated and sincerely performed, can ever achieve the kind of standing before God that results in the verdict of justification."[15]

Happily, there is another way for us to be justified, which is by faith. Here Paul is not talking about faith in general. President Eisenhower once said that America "is founded in a deeply felt religious faith—and I don't care what it is."[16] Ike may not have cared, but Paul certainly did! For him, the important thing is what we believe in, not the mere fact that we believe.

We must believe in Jesus Christ. Paul says it three times in this verse. We must put our faith "in Jesus Christ," "in Christ Jesus," "in Christ" (Gal. 2:16). Faith is a total surrender to Jesus Christ, a complete acceptance of all that he is and all that he has done for our salvation. The reason faith justifies is that it takes hold of Christ, and Christ is the one who makes us right with God. We are acceptable to God—not by keeping the law ourselves, but by trusting in the only man who ever did keep it, Jesus Christ. The doctrine of justification can be stated in these general terms: we get right with God not by observing the law, but only by trusting in his Son.

Second, Paul states the doctrine of justification in *personal* terms: "So we also have believed in Christ Jesus, in order to be justified by faith in Christ and not by works of the law" (Gal. 2:16). Here Paul is reminding Peter that he himself had become a Christian by putting his faith in Jesus Christ (see Matt. 16:16). He knew from experience that when it came to dealing with his sinful nature, keeping the law would not help. It certainly did not stop

---

15. Timothy George, *Galatians*, New American Commentary 30 (Nashville: Broadman & Holman, 1994), 194.

16. Dwight David Eisenhower, quoted in Herbert Schlossberg, *Idols for Destruction* (Wheaton, IL: Crossway, 1990), 251.

him from denying Christ. Nor could it remove the stain of his guilt. Only Jesus Christ could do that, and only through his saving death, which is why Peter trusted in him for salvation.

Note that justifying faith is a personal faith. Justification by faith is not simply a general principle about the way of salvation; it is a call to make a personal commitment to Jesus Christ. The question is: Have you renounced all of your own efforts to save yourself, asking instead for God to save you through Jesus Christ?

Finally, Paul states the doctrine of justification in *universal* terms. His argument has built to this climax: "by works of the law no one will be justified" (Gal. 2:16). What is generally true, and must become personally true, is also universally true.[17] What was true for Peter and Paul is true for everyone, especially for every Gentile. If anybody could be saved by the law, it would be a natural-born Jew. Therefore, if it was impossible for the apostles to be justified this way, Jews though they were, it must be impossible for *anyone* to be justified this way. How absurd it would be for a man like Peter to compel Gentiles to keep the very law he had stopped trusting for his own salvation!

This principle, that justification cannot come by works, is what distinguishes Christianity from other religions. Other religions try to achieve ultimate bliss by scaling God's throne through human effort, but the Bible says we cannot get to God this way. In fact, Martin Luther explained that if we try to merit grace by our works, we are simply "trying to placate God with sins."[18] Luther meant that even our best works are tainted by evil motives. Paul had learned this universal principle from the Old Testament, for he is virtually quoting one of the psalms of David: "Enter not into judgment with your servant, for no one living is righteous before you" (Ps. 143:2). Or, as Paul translates it, "By works of the law no one will be justified" (Gal. 2:16). Total depravity extends to all humanity.

Becoming a Christian, therefore, means admitting that you cannot be saved by the good things that you do. The Galatians were tempted to gain favor with God by getting circumcised. This is no longer a temptation for most

---

17. Stott, *Message of Galatians*, 63.
18. Martin Luther, *Lectures on Galatians, 1535*, trans. and ed. Jaroslav Pelikan, in *Luther's Works* (St. Louis: Concordia, 1963), 26:126.

Christians, but many other things are. Going to church, reading the Bible, taking communion, giving to charity—these things will never get us into heaven. Not even becoming a martyr for the cause of Christ will qualify.

There is no way to be made right with God except through faith in Christ. In Luther's words, "Now the true meaning of Christianity is this: that a man first acknowledge, through the Law, that he is a sinner, for whom it is impossible to perform any good work. . . . If you want to be saved, your salvation does not come by works; but God has sent His only Son into the world that we might live through Him. He was crucified and died for you and bore your sins in His own body."[19]

Anyone who believes this is a Christian. And anyone who is a Christian has to live like one, and this includes having fellowship with everyone else who has been saved by the same grace. A beautiful illustration of this comes from the life and ministry of William Carey (1761–1834), the great Baptist missionary to India. Indian culture was dominated by the rigid Hindu caste system under which members of different social classes were not permitted to share a common meal. Carey's real breakthrough came when his first convert, a man named Krishna Pal, rejected his caste and began to eat dinner with the missionaries. One of Carey's co-workers exclaimed, "Thus the door of faith is open to the Gentiles. Who shall shut it? The chain of caste is broken; who shall mend it?"[20]

The door of faith is open anywhere and everywhere that Christians accept one another on the same basis that God has accepted them: by grace alone, through faith alone, in Christ alone.

19. Ibid., 126.
20. William Ward, quoted in Timothy George, *Faithful Witness: The Life and Mission of William Carey* (London: InterVarsity, 1991), 130–31.

6

DYING TO LIVE

Galatians 2:17–21

*I have been crucified with Christ. It is no longer I who live, but
Christ who lives in me. And the life I now live in the flesh I live by
faith in the Son of God, who loved me and gave himself for me.*
(Gal. 2:19–20)

hat Paul said in Galatians 2:16 bears repeating: "We know that
a person is not justified by works of the law but through faith
in Jesus Christ." This is the biblical doctrine of justification by
faith alone in Christ alone. As John Calvin (1509–1564) said, "we are justified in no other way than by faith, or, which comes to the same thing, . . .
that we are justified by faith alone."[1]

"Justification" is a legal term that refers to a person's standing before the
bar of God's justice. In order to be declared right with God, I must be righteous. But I am not righteous; I am a sinner. How, then, can I justify myself
to God? This is the question that the doctrine of justification answers.

RIGHTEOUS BY FAITH

It would be hard to think of a more important issue than how to be
accepted by God. Certainly it was important during the Reformation, when

1. John Calvin, quoted in R. C. Sproul, *Faith Alone: The Evangelical Doctrine of Justification* (Grand
Rapids: Baker, 1995), 173.

Protestants defended the doctrine of justification by faith alone over against the Roman Catholic doctrine of justification by faith plus works. Martin Luther claimed that "if the doctrine of justification is lost, the whole of Christian doctrine is lost."[2]

Justification remains a vital doctrine to this day, even if many evangelical Christians are not sure what it means or if it matters. The situation is reminiscent of the man who when asked to explain the difference between ignorance and apathy said, "I don't know and I don't care!" "Precisely!" came the reply. And ignorance and apathy are precisely the words to describe the church's present attitude. Christians do not know and do not care to know the doctrine of justification by faith. Yet there is no true Christianity without it. J. I. Packer once wrote, "The doctrine of justification by faith is like Atlas: it bears a world on its shoulders, the entire evangelical knowledge of saving grace." Packer went on to say what happens "when Protestants let the thought of justification drop out of their minds: the true knowledge of salvation drops out with it, and cannot be restored till the truth of justification is back in its proper place. When Atlas falls, everything that rested on his shoulders comes crashing down too."[3]

As crucial as justification is to Christianity, it is even more crucial to the Christian. It is of paramount personal importance to get into a right relationship with God. How can a righteous God accept an unrighteous individual like me?

Part of the answer is contained in the last phrase of Galatians 2:16: "By works of the law no one will be justified." In the previous chapter we noted that this phrase is a quotation from the Old Testament. It is important to realize that the New Testament writers did not simply quote a verse here and a verse there. Rather, they quoted verses in their original biblical contexts. Often, a single phrase is intended to call to mind an entire passage from the Old Testament.

This is what Paul does in Galatians 2. The psalm from which he quotes begins with a problem. David is pursued by enemies and tormented by guilt.

2 . Martin Luther, *Lectures on Galatians, 1535*, trans. and ed. Jaroslav Pelikan, in *Luther's Works* (St. Louis: Concordia, 1963), 26:9.

3. J. I. Packer, "Introductory Essay," in James Buchanan, *The Doctrine of Justification: An Outline of Its History in the Church and of Its Exposition from Scripture* (Edinburgh: Banner of Truth, 1961), vii.

He asks God to deliver him even though he knows that what he really deserves is divine judgment:

> Hear my prayer, O LORD;
>   give ear to my pleas for mercy!
> In your faithfulness answer me,
>   in your righteousness.
> Enter not into judgment with your servant,
>   for no one living is righteous before you. (Ps. 143:1–2)

David did not want to be brought before the bar of God's justice, where no living person can be acquitted, least of all himself. Yet David still appealed to God for his salvation, and the basis for his appeal was God's own righteousness. David asked God to come to his relief, not because he was righteous, but because *God* was righteous. He makes the same appeal at the end of the psalm: "For your name's sake, O LORD, preserve my life! In your righteousness bring my soul out of trouble" (Ps. 143:11). David asked to be saved by a righteousness that comes from God.

Psalm 143 is a psalm for the justified sinner, for an unrighteous man saved by the gift of God's righteousness. By quoting from this psalm, Paul showed that God's ultimate answer to David's prayer came through Jesus Christ. No one can be made right with God by obeying the law, for no one is righteous. But Jesus Christ the Righteous One makes us right with God.

It happens like this. When we put our faith in Jesus Christ, God treats us as if we were as righteous as Jesus is. God credits us with his righteousness. To use the proper term for this, God "imputes" Christ's righteousness to us, so that what Jesus did through the cross and the empty tomb counts for us. Justification is the judicial act in which God pardons sinners, considering them righteous because of the righteousness of Christ. When he justifies a sinner, God declares that as far as he is concerned, that sinner is as righteous as his own Son.

This doctrine of imputed righteousness is so important that it is worth taking the time to define. Martin Luther explained it like this: " 'Because you believe in me,' God says, 'and your faith takes hold of Christ, whom I have given to you as your Justifier and Savior, therefore be righteous.' Thus God accepts you or reputes you righteous solely on account of Christ, in whom you believe."[4] Calvin wrote: "It is entirely by the intervention of Christ's righteousness that we obtain justification before God. This is equivalent to saying that man is not just in himself, but that the righteousness of Christ is communicated to him by imputation, while he is strictly deserving of punishment."[5] Similarly, the Westminster Shorter Catechism defines justification as "an act of God's free grace, wherein he pardoneth all our sins, and accepteth us as righteous in his sight, only for the righteousness of Christ imputed to us, and received by faith alone" (Answer 33). An even fuller explanation comes from the Heidelberg Catechism, which asks, "How art thou righteous before God?" The answer is:

> Only by a true faith in Jesus Christ; so that, though my conscience accuse me that I have grossly transgressed all the commands of God, and kept none of them, and am still inclined to all evil; notwithstanding God, without any merit of mine, but only of mere grace, grants and imputes to me the perfect satisfaction, righteousness, and holiness of Christ; even so, as if I never had had, nor committed any sin; yea, as if I had fully accomplished all that obedience which Christ hath accomplished for me; inasmuch as I embrace such benefit with a believing heart. (A. 60)

OBJECTION: THE PROBLEM OF SIN

The doctrine of justification by faith alone raises an obvious problem. If by his free grace God has already declared us righteous, then why bother to become a better person? What incentive do we have to live for God? The doctrine of justification seems irresponsible. It sounds, in fact, like winning the spiritual lottery. If God gives righteousness away for free, who will ever work for him again?

Paul anticipates this objection by making it part of his argument. "But if, in our endeavor to be justified in Christ, we too were found to be sinners, is Christ then a servant of sin?" (Gal. 2:17). This is a fair question, and from the way he poses it, Paul seems to have something specific in mind. The clue is the word "sinners," which Paul used back in verse 15 to indicate the Jew-

---

4. Martin Luther, quoted in Mark A. Seifrid, "Paul, Luther, and Justification in Gal. 2:15–21," *Westminster Theological Journal* 65.2 (Fall 2003): 221.

5. Calvin, quoted in Sproul, *Faith Alone*, 93.

ish attitude toward Gentiles. The Gentiles were "sinners," not so much because they were immoral, but because they lived outside the boundaries of the law. According to the Judaizers, this was precisely the problem with Peter and Paul: they had become outlaws. In their personal habits, they were living like Gentile sinners rather than like Jews. They used to keep the law in all its detail. Now they were doing things like eating unholy food with uncircumcised Gentiles.

Hence the accusation that they were making Jesus a servant of sin, almost as if he were doing promotional work for the devil. Peter and Paul had sought to be justified by faith in Christ. This included giving up on the law as a way to get right with God. Whereas before they had always been law-abiding Jews, they were sinking to the level of pagans. When the Judaizers discovered that Peter and Paul were living like "Gentile sinners," they reached the obvious conclusion: being justified by faith causes people to sin in the name of Christ. And if Peter and Paul were guilty of this charge, then so were the Gentiles. They had come to faith in Christ, but they were still living like so-called sinners. Someone needed to hold them to a higher moral standard, and the Judaizers were just the men to do it!

What is the best way to answer this line of thinking? It must be admitted that Christians do not always make good advertisements for Christianity. When this is the case, it helps to remember that by definition, all Christians are sinners. Martin Luther said, "A Christian is not someone who has no sin or feels no sin; he is someone to whom, because of his faith in Christ, God does not impute his sin."[6] This is the crucial difference. Christians are sinners too, but their sins do not count against them. Therefore, with the possible exception of the prison system, the church is the only institution in the world for bad people.

This does not mean, however, that God himself is in the business of sin. "Certainly not!" Paul says (Gal. 2:17). God forbid! Or to put it in the vernacular, "No way!" Perish the thought that Christ is a "servant of sin," as if his grace is somehow to be blamed for my guilt. When God justifies sinners by faith, he is not aiding and abetting their sin. The very suggestion is blasphemous. God cannot sin (James 1:13), nor can he be held responsible for

6. Luther, *Galatians*, 26:133.

my sin. If I am still a sinner after I become a Christian, it is no one's fault but my own.

The doctrine that really does promote sin is justification by the law rather than by faith. Paul shows this by using his opponents' argument against them: "For if I rebuild what I tore down, I prove myself to be a transgressor" (Gal. 2:18). As we shall see, when Paul spoke of rebuilding what he tore down, he was referring to the Old Testament law that he had torn down by preaching the gospel of Jesus Christ. So what would happen if someone tried to rebuild the law? This was exactly what Peter was trying to do in Antioch. At first, he had destroyed the law by welcoming Gentiles into the church as full-fledged Christians. But then he allowed himself to be pressured into separating himself from them. In effect, Peter was rebuilding with one hand what he had destroyed with the other. First he told the Gentiles that they were saved by faith, not by works, but then he made the works of the law a test of Christian fellowship.

Not only is this what Peter did, but it is also what the Galatians were tempted to do. Some Jews had come to urge them to rebuild the law in place of the gospel. If the Galatians did that, they would become lawbreakers all over again. The law's purpose is to show that we are sinners, so the more of it that gets rebuilt, the more sinful we become! In the words of F. F. Bruce, "Any one who, having received justification through faith in Christ, thereafter reinstates law in place of Christ makes himself a sinner all over again."[7] To rebuild the law is actually to transgress it, because we cannot keep the law in its perfection.

DEAD TO THE LAW

In Christ the law has been destroyed as a way of getting right with God. And now that it has been knocked down, it has to stay down. This has profound personal implications. "For through the law I died to the law," wrote Paul, "so that I might live to God" (Gal. 2:19).

The first question to ask about this verse is, What does it mean to "die to the law"? Notice that the law is not what does the dying. Rather, Paul is the

7. F. F. Bruce, *The Epistle to the Galatians: A Commentary on the Greek Text*, New International Greek Testament Commentary (Grand Rapids: Eerdmans, 1982), 142.

one who dies with respect to the law. This is a remarkable thing for a former Pharisee to say. When Paul was a Pharisee he lived for the law, but now that he is a Christian he is dead to it. That is to say, he is no longer under its power. Calvin said, "*To die to the law* is to renounce it and to be freed from its dominion, so that we have no confidence in it and it does not hold us captive under the yoke of slavery."[8]

But then another question arises: How can someone die to the law *through the law*? It would seem to make more sense for Paul to say something like this: "Through the *gospel* I died to the law so that I might live for God." Instead he says that it was the law itself that persuaded him to abandon the law.

There are several ways to understand this. Perhaps Paul was saying that the law "did him in" by showing him that he was a sinner. This is certainly a point he makes elsewhere (Rom. 7:9–11). The law cannot save. All it can do is condemn us by proving that we cannot keep it. In the words of the old Scottish commentator John Brown (1784–1858), the Christian must therefore cease "to expect justification and salvation by obedience to its requisitions."[9] The law cannot promise life; it can only threaten death. Thus it is through the law that one dies to the law.

There is another possibility, however, which is based on the law's penalty. Remember that the law came with a deadly curse. Anyone who failed to keep everything God's law required (and note that in Galatians 2:19 Paul is referring to the whole law of God, not just the ceremonial law, as the New Perspective on Paul and the law would have it) was condemned to die. So the worst the law could do to a man was kill him. However, once the law had exacted its death penalty, there was nothing else it could do. A man can be executed only once, and once he has been executed, the law has no further claim on him. Perhaps this is why Paul considered himself dead to the law: because the law had already put him to death.

Now as far as the Christian is concerned, the penalty of the law has already been carried out. The law's demand of death was satisfied in the death of

8. John Calvin, *The Epistles of Paul the Apostle to the Galatians, Ephesians, Philippians and Colossians*, Calvin's New Testament Commentaries, trans. T. H. L. Parker, ed. David W. and Thomas F. Torrance (Grand Rapids: Eerdmans, 1996), 42.

9. John Brown, *An Exposition of the Epistle of Paul the Apostle to the Galatians* (Edinburgh, 1853; repr. Evansville, IN: Sovereign Grace, 1957), 96.

Christ. It was the law that put Christ to death on the cross. When Christ died, Paul died too, at least as far as the law was concerned. He died to the law in the death of his substitute. Hence his triumphant statement: "Through the law I died to the law" (Gal. 2:19).

ALIVE IN CHRIST

Having written his own obituary, Paul proceeds to explain the circumstances of his demise: "I have been crucified with Christ. It is no longer I who live, but Christ who lives in me" (Gal. 2:19–20). Here the apostle indicates when he died to the law: he died to the law when Christ died on the cross.

This text reveals something very surprising about the cross. It shows that at least four things were nailed to the cross of Calvary. The most obvious, of course, was Jesus himself, through his hands and feet. As the records plainly show, he was put to death by being nailed to the cross. Also fastened to the cross with a hammer and a nail was the public announcement that read: "Jesus of Nazareth, the King of the Jews" (John 19:19). The third thing that was nailed to the cross was the debt of our sin. Paul explained this to the Colossians: God forgave "all our trespasses, by canceling the record of debt that stood against us with its legal demands. This he set aside, nailing it to the cross" (Col. 2:13–14). The record of debt was the law of God, which condemns us by listing all our sins and which God canceled by nailing it to the cross.

But here is the surprise: if you are a follower of Christ, then *you* were nailed to the cross too! The crucifixion is not just a fact about the life of Christ and a momentous event in human history, but is also part of every Christian's personal life story. The Cambridge Puritan William Perkins (1558–1602) said, "We are in mind and meditation to consider Christ crucified: and first, we are to believe that he was crucified for us. This being done, we must go yet further, and as it were spread ourselves on the cross of Christ, believing and withall beholding ourselves crucified with him."[10]

Do not misunderstand this. Jesus Christ died once for all. He alone was the God-man, so he alone could atone for the sins of the world by offering

---

10. William Perkins, *A Commentary on Galatians*, Pilgrim Classic Commentaries, ed. Gerald T. Sheppard (London, 1617; repr. New York: Pilgrim, 1989), 124.

73

his life in our place. Yet the Scripture also says that the Christian *has been crucified* with Christ. It uses the perfect tense to show that this is something that really and truly happened, as if we were nailed to the very tree of Calvary. This is not a subjective experience in the life of the believer, but an objective reality that is based on the believer's relationship to Christ. Mark Seifrid writes, "Paul does not have merely his inward life in view, but his whole person and history, which has now been manifestly taken up in the cross and resurrection of Christ."[11]

The surprising truth that the Christian has been crucified in Christ rests on the most magnificent of all doctrines: union with Christ, which the Scottish theologian John Murray (1898–1975) called "the central truth of the whole doctrine of salvation."[12] We encounter it everywhere in the New Testament. Again and again, the Scripture teaches that the Christian is *in Christ.* To use the proper theological category, the Christian is united to Christ.

The way anyone becomes united to Christ is by faith. Paul said this in verse 16: "we also have believed in Christ Jesus." Once we put our faith in Christ, then *we* are in Christ. Our union with Christ becomes a spiritual reality. Martin Luther said, "By [faith] you are so cemented to Christ that He and you are as one person, which cannot be separated but remains attached to Him forever."[13]

The reason union with Christ is such a magnificent doctrine is that once we get into Christ by faith, then everything Christ has ever done becomes something we have done. It is as if we had lived his perfect life and died his painful death. It is as if we were buried in his tomb and then raised up to his glorious heaven (Rom. 6:3–5). God attaches us to the events of Christ's life so that they become part of our lives. His story—the story of the cross and the empty tomb—becomes our story.

The only way to get what Christ has to offer is to be united to him by faith. Calvin said, "We must understand that as long as Christ remains outside of us, and we are separated from him, all that he has suffered and done for the salvation of the human race remains useless and of no value for us."[14] But once we get into Christ, then we get everything he has to offer, especially his

---

11. Seifrid, "Paul, Luther, and Justification in Gal. 2:15–21," 221.

12. John Murray, *Redemption Accomplished and Applied* (Grand Rapids: Eerdmans, 1955), 161.

13. Luther, *Galatians*, 26:168.

14. John Calvin, *Institutes of the Christian Religion*, trans. Ford Lewis Battles, 2 vols., Library of Christian Classics 20–21 (Philadelphia: Westminster, 1960), 1:537 (3.1.1).

righteousness. When we are in Christ, God considers us as righteous as his own Son, not because we are righteous, but because we are in Christ.

The doctrine of union with Christ explains why the Christian is dead to the law. We were united to Christ in his crucifixion. As far as God is concerned, we were really and truly nailed to the cross with Christ. It was on the cross that the law carried out its death penalty against us. Therefore, as far as the law is concerned, we are now dead. There is nothing the law can do to improve our standing before God. We can live for Christ because we are dead to the law.

Not only are we dead to the law, it is almost as if we have stopped living altogether: "I have been crucified with Christ. It is no longer I who live, but Christ who lives in me" (Gal. 2:19–20). Paul is saying something like this: "I no longer have a life of my own. The only life I have is the life that God puts into me through Jesus Christ."

It would be hard to imagine a text more antithetical to our contemporary culture. Consider these words from the actress Shirley MacLaine:

> The most pleasurable journey you take is through yourself. . . . The only sustaining love involvement is with yourself. . . . When you look back on your life and try to figure out where you've been and where you are going, when you look at your work, your love affairs, your marriages, your children, your pain, your happiness—when you examine all that closely, what you really find out is that the only person you really go to bed with is yourself. The only person you really dress is yourself. The only thing you have is working to the consummation of your own identity.[15]

MacLaine's words capture the spirit of this selfish age. Moderns and postmoderns alike are obsessed with themselves. Self-esteem, self-improvement, self-fulfillment, self-indulgence—whatever you want, as long as it begins with your "self."

In these self-absorbed times, the Bible announces the death of the self: "It is no longer I who live" (Gal. 2:20). The world no longer revolves around me. I am no longer dominated by thoughts of my own pleasure and prestige. If I have a life at all, it is only the life that Christ lives in me.

---

15. Shirley MacLaine, quoted in Henry Fairlie, *The Seven Deadly Sins Today* (Washington: New Republic, 1978), 31–32.

This does not mean that becoming a Christian is a kind of suicide. We still have a normal physical existence, of course, what Paul calls "the life I now live in the flesh" (Gal. 2:20). Since it is the life *I* live, I even have a self. But the only self I have is the one that is united to Christ by faith. My life is the life that Christ "lives in me," the life "I live by faith in the Son of God" (Gal. 2:20).

This is the mystery of Christ's indwelling presence by the Holy Spirit. Theologians have tried to explain this mystery in various ways. Calvin said that the Christian "does not live by his own life but is animated by the secret power of Christ, so that Christ may be said to live and grow in him."[16] The Scottish theologian Henry Scougal (1650–1678) called it "the life of God in the soul of man."[17] One thing this means is that becoming a Christian is the best and only way to discover our identity. We will never find our true selves until we find ourselves in Christ. Our identity is established by our union with Christ. We have no self, except the self that we have in him. To have a "healthy self-image," then, is to see ourselves as we are in Christ.

CHRIST DIED FOR SOMEONE

Union with Christ provides the answer to the question we posed earlier: If God justifies bad people, then why be good? Isn't justification by faith alone a dangerous doctrine that encourages people to be immoral?

The answer is "Certainly not!" The reason the doctrine of justification by faith does not promote sin is that justifying faith is what gets us into Christ, and when we are in Christ we become new people. We are not simply justified by faith; we also *live* by faith. By faith we are in the crucified Christ. By the same faith Christ lives in us. Since we live in Christ, we no longer live in sin. We live in Christ, by Christ, and through Christ for the glory of God.

The Christian life is like life after death. We were crucified with Christ, dead both to the law and to ourselves. But we are still united to Christ by faith. Therefore, our story did not end at the cross, but went on to the empty tomb. Just as Jesus was brought back to life in his resurrection, so we also have been raised from the dead. God has given us a whole new life to live for him, a life of faith responding to love.

---

16. Calvin, *Galatians, Ephesians, Philippians and Colossians*, 42.
17. Henry Scougal, *The Life of God in the Soul of Man* (London, 1677; repr. Fearn, Ross-shire: Christian Focus, 1996).

If this is not Christianity, then there is no such thing as Christianity, which is the point with which Paul concludes the first major part of his letter: "I do not nullify the grace of God, for if justification were through the law, then Christ died for no purpose" (Gal. 2:21). J. Gresham Machen identified this as

> the key verse of the Epistle to the Galatians; it expresses the central thought of the Epistle. The Judaizers attempted to supplement the saving work of Christ by merit of their own obedience to the law. *That*, says Paul, is impossible; *Christ will do everything or nothing: earn your salvation if your obedience to the law is perfect, or else trust wholly to Christ's completed work; you cannot do both; you cannot combine merit and grace; if justification even in slightest measure is through human merit, then Christ died in vain.*[18]

For the sake of argument, assume that there is another way to be justified, apart from the work of Christ. Suppose that there is some other procedure for getting right with God. Imagine, for example, that what Paul's opponents were saying was true, that God will accept us only if we keep the law of Moses, getting circumcised and all the rest of it. Now explain why Christ died on the cross. Obviously not to justify sinners, because this is something that sinners must do for themselves. The cross is necessary only if it has the power to bring sinners into a right relationship with God.

Paul's point is that if it is possible to be justified by working the law, then there was no reason for Christ to be crucified. His death was pointless. His work was in vain. His cross was unnecessary. For if our own works can save us, then Christ's death was superfluous. Or perhaps Christ's death was insufficient, so that when he hung, dying on the cross, and said, "It is finished" (John 19:30), it wasn't really finished after all. Either salvation comes through the finished work of Jesus Christ, or it comes through human effort, but not both. If we can be saved by our own works, then Jesus was a false Messiah who died a worthless death on a meaningless cross.[19]

---

18. J. Gresham Machen, *Machen's Notes on Galatians*, ed. J. Skilton (Philadelphia: Presbyterian and Reformed, 1973), 161.

19. It is hard to see how Galatians 2:21 is compatible with the New Perspective on Galatians. The claim that "if justification were through the law, then Jesus died for no purpose" makes sense only when justification deals with our standing before God, and not when it relates primarily to Jewish acceptance of Gentiles in the church.

The notion that Christ died for nothing is scandalous, of course. Luther considered it "an intolerable and horrible blasphemy to think up some work by which you presume to placate God, when you see that He cannot be placated except by this immense, infinite price, the death and the blood of the Son of God, one drop of which is more precious than all creation."[20] In fact, anyone who tries to add works to faith is treating Jesus exactly the way his enemies treated him when he was dying on the cross. Timothy George writes that "if we add works of the law to the sacrifice of the cross, then indeed we make a mockery of Jesus' death just as the soldiers who spat upon him, the thieves who hurled insults at him, and the rabble who shouted, 'Come down from the cross!' "[21]

This is exactly what the Judaizers were doing. They were adding works to faith as their basis for being justified before God. By doing this they were saying that Christ died for nothing. They were nullifying the grace of God. But the one thing the apostle Paul absolutely refused to do was to nullify the grace of God. He had come to Christ by faith, not by works. He understood that to go back now and argue that the law can save sinners would be to deny the saving power of the cross. All by itself the cross proves that justification comes by grace, through faith, and not by works. If the righteousness of the crucified Christ is not accepted, then the grace of God must be abrogated. For in order for salvation to be by grace alone, through faith alone, it must come from Christ alone. Otherwise, Christ died for nothing.

Christ did die for something, of course. Or to put it more accurately, Christ died for *someone.* He died for me. Notice the intensely personal terms that Paul uses to describe his relationship to Jesus Christ. Although Jesus is the very Son of God, he "loved *me* and gave himself for *me*" (Gal. 2:20). The same God who loved the world loves me, specifically and individually. He not only loves me, but also gave himself for me when he died for my sins on the cross. Jesus freely and willingly volunteered to be my Savior. I, personally, was crucified with the Christ who died, personally, for me. Divine love is not some abstract concept. It is a passionate affection that has been expressed through sacrificial action.

20. Luther, *Galatians,* 26:176.
21. Timothy George, *Galatians,* New American Commentary 30 (Nashville: Broadman & Holman, 1994), 201.

When John Wesley (1703–1791) was coming to faith in Christ, this truth made a deep and lasting impression upon him. In his journal he describes what it was like to come to the end of the second chapter in Luther's *Commentary on Galatians:* "I laboured, waited, and prayed to feel 'who loved *me* and gave himself for *me.*'"[22] Wesley found that these verses were well worth the effort. So does everyone who comes to Christ by faith, becoming united to him in his crucifixion, and thereby receiving the free grace of the loving God.

22. John Wesley, *Journal* (London, 1849), 1:90.

7

By Faith Alone

Galatians 3:1–5

O foolish Galatians! Who has bewitched you? It was before your eyes that Jesus Christ was publicly portrayed as crucified. Let me ask you only this: Did you receive the Spirit by works of the law or by hearing with faith? (Gal. 3:1–2)

How can God accept me? Only if I trust in Jesus Christ. This is the biblical doctrine of justification by faith that Paul taught the Galatians. I cannot be saved by anything I do; I can be saved only by what Jesus did when he died on the cross and rose from the dead. There is no way for me to make myself right with God because I am unrighteous. But Jesus made things right through his crucifixion and resurrection. All that is left for me to do is receive the gift of God's free grace by putting my faith in God's Son.

This doctrine of justification by grace alone, through faith alone, in Christ alone has always had its detractors. If justification comes by grace, then all the glory goes to God. But people want to keep some of the glory for themselves. Thus they seek to justify themselves before God by their own works.

Martin Luther encountered this problem when he began preaching the gospel in his native Germany. According to Luther, "The doctrine of justification is this, that we are pronounced righteous and are saved solely by faith in Christ, and without works."[1] Yet when Duke George of Saxony heard this teaching, he complained that it was "a great doctrine to die by, but a lousy one to live with!"[2] The duke recognized that justification by faith is a great comfort in death. It guarantees that when the sinner stands before God's throne, all his sins will be pardoned. Instead of having to defend his life, the sinner will be defended by the life of the crucified Christ. But Duke George wanted to know what there was to do in the meantime. If the sinner is saved ultimately by God's grace rather than by his own works, how or why should he live for God?

The answer Paul gives at the beginning of Galatians 3 is that justification is not only a great doctrine to die with, but also a wonderful doctrine to live by. The biblical doctrine of justification by grace alone, through faith alone, in Christ alone is a doctrine for the whole Christian life from beginning to end.

BEWITCHED!

It may be helpful to review Paul's argument to this point. In chapters 1–2 he used his spiritual autobiography to prove that he was a genuine apostle of the one true gospel. Now in chapters 3–4 he explains the theology of that gospel, beginning with a rebuke.

Paul's rebuke must have caused quite a stir when his letter was first read in Galatia: "O foolish Galatians! Who has bewitched you?" (Gal. 3:1). Paul was upset. Although to this point his language has been forceful, it has not been quite so personal. Yet here he practically splutters with indignation. And rightly so! The Galatians were in danger of nullifying the grace of God. The so-called Judaizers had come from Jerusalem to persuade them that works of the law were necessary for their justification. But in that case, what was the point of the cross? Why would someone else have to die for my sins if I could take care of them myself? The logical implication of justification by works is that "Christ died for no purpose" (2:21).

With this thought in mind, Paul's subsequent outburst becomes completely understandable. "For when we hear," wrote Calvin, "that the Son of God, with

1 . Martin Luther, *Lectures on Galatians, 1535*, trans. and ed. Jaroslav Pelikan, in *Luther's Works* (St. Louis: Concordia, 1963), 26:233.

2. Timothy George, *Galatians*, New American Commentary 30 (Nashville: Broadman & Holman, 1994), 197.

all His blessings, is rejected and that His death is esteemed as nothing, what godly mind will not break out into indignation?"[3] As far as Paul was able to tell, the Galatians were guilty of sheer spiritual stupidity. J. B. Phillips paraphrases him to say: "O you dear idiots of Galatia . . . surely you can't be so idiotic!" Paul was at a loss to know how people could believe such nonsense.

The Galatians were behaving so foolishly that the apostle suspected some kind of witchcraft. "Who has bewitched you?" he demanded (Gal. 3:1). The Greek term *ebaskanen* means "to give someone the evil eye, to cast a spell over, to fascinate in the original sense of holding someone spellbound by an irresistible power."[4] It was as if a sorcerer had cast an evil spell on them, or as if a magician had them under his hypnotic influence.

Paul knew, of course, that the Galatians were not really enchanted. They were under the influence of false teachers who wanted to add the law of Moses to faith in Jesus Christ to produce a "Jesus plus" gospel. But the language he uses suggests that there was some kind of demonic influence at work. One of the devil's favorite stratagems is to distort the truth so that people can no longer tell the difference between the one true gospel and all the false alternatives.

Doctrinal error has two primary sources: human ignorance and demonic malevolence. The church in Galatia faced both problems. The Galatians themselves were so foolish as to abandon the gospel, but as we shall see, they were doing so because they were under spiritual attack. Even to this day, theological nonsense always comes from the same two sources. A family member becomes entranced with a cult, for example. Parents refuse, on religious grounds, to give a child proper medical care. The leaders of the church are either unable or unwilling to discriminate between justification by faith and justification by works. In part, these errors may be due to sheer human folly. But if this seems like an inadequate explanation, remember that Christian doctrine is the battlefield where the most intense spiritual warfare takes place.

This does not mean, of course, that Satan is to be blamed for our own foolishness. A good illustration of this comes from Germany after the Sec-

3. John Calvin, *The Epistles of Paul the Apostle to the Galatians, Ephesians, Philippians and Colossians*, Calvin's New Testament Commentaries, trans. T. H. L. Parker, ed. David W. and Thomas F. Torrance (Grand Rapids: Eerdmans, 1996), 46.

4. G. Delling, "Baskainō," in *Theological Dictionary of the New Testament*, ed. Gerhard Kittel, trans. Geoffrey W. Bromiley, 10 vols. (Grand Rapids: Eerdmans, 1964–1976), 1:594–95.

ond World War. A group of ministers met to discuss why the church had failed to take a stand against the evils of the Third Reich. Some of them tried to justify their actions by appealing to the "demonic forces" that had led them astray. But another minister stood up to reproach them. "Gentlemen," he said, "we have all been very foolish."[5] When it comes to theological error, we should beware the wiles of Satan without overlooking our own seemingly boundless capacity for folly.

CHRIST ON DISPLAY

In order to "break the spell" that they were under, the Galatians needed to look to the cross. Paul follows his rebuke with a reminder: "It was before your eyes that Jesus Christ was publicly portrayed as crucified" (Gal. 3:1). The fact that Paul specifically mentions the eyes is intriguing, because the ancients generally thought that enchantment came through "the evil eye." Now that they were bewitched, the Galatians needed to fix their eyes back on the cross of Christ.

The Galatians had seen the cross before, when Paul came to them preaching the gospel. The word "portrayed" comes from the world of advertising. The Greeks used it to refer, for example, to the kind of public notice posted to show that a property was up for sale. What the Galatians had seen, then, was a graphic public display of the crucified Christ. Jesus Christ had been placarded before them, as if on a giant billboard or a large canvas. This does not mean that Paul used visual aids in his preaching, like a sketch pad or a flannelgraph. Nor does it mean that he hired an ad agency to market the gospel in Asia Minor. He is referring instead to his proclamation of the gospel. It is often said that a picture is worth a thousand words. But if there is time for a thousand words, people can see the picture for themselves, which is what happened when Paul presented the gospel. Whether he preached standing out in the streets or sitting down in people's homes, he always publicized the same thing: Jesus Christ, and him crucified.

When people visit Tenth Presbyterian Church in Philadelphia, where I serve as senior minister, they sometimes wonder where the cross is because

5. The story is told by R. Alan Cole in *The Epistle of Paul to the Galatians: An Introduction and Commentary*, Tyndale New Testament Commentaries (Leicester: Inter-Varsity, 1965), 86.

there is no physical representation of a cross in the sanctuary. Indeed, part of the church's beauty is that it has no icons to distract the congregation from the worship of God. But there *is* a cross. Every time the Scriptures are opened and Christ is preached, the message of the cross is lifted high for all to see. Calvin said: "Let those who want to discharge the ministry of the Gospel aright learn not only to speak and declaim but also to penetrate into consciences, so that men may see Christ crucified and that His blood may flow. When the Church has such painters as these she no longer needs wood and stone, that is, dead images, she no longer requires any pictures."[6] This is the power of preaching. It takes the mighty acts of God in history and displays them to minds and hearts in the present. By the time Paul was finished preaching to them, the Galatians felt they had seen the crucifixion with their own eyes, watching the living body of Jesus nailed bloody to the cross.

When Paul and the other apostles preached the gospel, they began with the person of Jesus Christ, the incarnate Son of God. Jesus was and is true God and true man, one person in two natures, human as well as divine. The apostles first identified Jesus as the God-man. Because he was a man, he was able to enter into our situation and suffer for our sins. Because he was also God, he was able to live in perfect obedience and offer a sacrifice of infinite value.

The apostles preached that this Christ had been crucified. To preach is to portray the cross. Paul always preached what he called "the word of the cross" (1 Cor. 1:18). He said, "We preach Christ crucified" (1 Cor. 1:23). Or again, he resolved "to know nothing among you except Jesus Christ and him crucified" (1 Cor. 2:2). Paul's gospel was the gospel of the crucified Christ. It centered on the death of God's own Son on the cross, and on the implications of that death for the salvation of the world.

It is significant that in Galatians Paul speaks of the crucifixion in the perfect tense. He used the perfect form of the verb "crucify" back in chapter 2 when he said, "I have been crucified with Christ" (2:19). He uses it again at the beginning of chapter 3. Literally, Jesus Christ was portrayed not "as crucified," but "as *having been* crucified" (Gal. 3:1).

6. John Calvin, *Calvin's New Testament Commentaries*, trans. T. H. L. Parker, ed. David W. and Thomas F. Torrance (Grand Rapids: Eerdmans, 1974), 147.

The perfect tense denotes a past event that continues to have significance in the present. And if ever there was an event that called for the perfect tense, it was the crucifixion of Jesus Christ. Jesus was crucified on a particular day, by particular men, outside a particular city, on a particular tree. If we had been there to witness his crucifixion, we could have reached out to touch the cross and picked up a splinter in our fingers. The crucifixion was a factual event in human history. On the cross, Jesus gave his life as the once-and-for-all atonement for sin. According to God's strict standard of justice, sin demanded the death penalty, which Jesus paid. By God's mercy, the sacrifice Jesus made was accepted as the full price for sin. This is what it means to portray Jesus Christ as crucified.

But there is more. God proved that he accepted the sacrifice Jesus made by raising him from the dead. Therefore, to preach Christ *having been crucified* is not simply to preach him crucified; it is also to preach him risen. Jesus is no longer on the cross. At this very moment he is a risen and living Savior who is able to grant forgiveness to everyone who believes in him. This forgiveness goes all the way back to the cross, a past event with a present consequence.

Paul was upset with the Galatians because they were forgetting all of this. He had laid out for them Jesus Christ having been crucified. But then some other teachers had come along to write some graffiti on his billboard. Unwilling to accept salvation in Christ alone, they wanted to add their own finishing touches to the work of Christ.

What the Galatians needed, then, was a reminder that on the cross Jesus did everything necessary for their salvation. Jesus is, in the words of John Brown, "the only and all-sufficient Saviour."[7] His cross is the only and all-sufficient atonement for sin. Thus our faith in him is the only and all-sufficient way to be justified before God. And since Jesus is the only and all-sufficient Savior, it would be totally senseless to try to add anything to what he did on the cross. In particular, it would be utter and complete folly to try to get God to accept us by keeping his law. The only way to be justified is by faith alone.

---

7. John Brown, *An Exposition of the Epistle of Paul the Apostle to the Galatians* (Edinburgh, 1853; repr. Evansville, IN: Sovereign Grace, 1957), 103.

IN THE BEGINNING

Deep down, the Galatians knew that they were justified by faith alone, for this is how they had come to Christ in the first place. In order to stop them from going back to the law, Paul made a personal appeal to their spiritual experience.

This appeal came in a series of rapid rhetorical questions—four of them in all:

1. A question about *initiation*, in which Paul took the Galatians back to the moment of their conversion: "Did you receive the Spirit by works of the law, or by hearing with faith?" (Gal. 3:2).
2. A question about *completion*, or how the Christian makes it to the end of the Christian life: "Having begun by the Spirit, are you now being perfected by the flesh?" (Gal. 3:3).
3. A question about *persecution*, the cost of following a crucified Christ: "Did you suffer so many things in vain—if indeed it was in vain?" (Gal. 3:4).
4. A question about *miracles* and their meaning for the Christian life: "Does he who supplies the Spirit to you and works miracles among you do so by works of the law, or by hearing with faith?" (Gal. 3:5).

Essentially, all these questions boiled down to a single issue: Does the Christian obtain the Holy Spirit by working the law or by hearing with faith? This question was meant to be rhetorical, for the Galatians could not possibly deny their experience of the Holy Spirit. If they were Christians at all—as Paul assumed they were—they had received the Holy Spirit when they came to Christ.

Paul's mention of the Spirit is a reminder of God's triune being. There is one God, who exists in three persons: the Father, the Son, and the Holy Spirit. Each person of the Trinity is involved in the salvation of the sinner. The Father sent the Son to be the Savior, and now the Father and the Son send the Spirit to convert the sinner.

The Galatians knew something about the work of the Holy Spirit, the third person of the Trinity, for they had come under his regenerating influence. They had received his gifts, such as teaching and prophecy. They were starting to display his fruit—love, joy, peace, and all the rest (Gal. 5:22–23). The Holy Spirit even worked miracles among them, as he often does when the gospel first penetrates a culture. The apostles cast out demons and healed the sick. Perhaps the Galatians themselves had performed mighty works of divine power, at least for a time. Having had all these memorable experiences, the Galatians could never forget what the Holy Spirit had done in their churches. They had irrefutable evidence of his work and presence.

Paul wanted to know the *cause* of this work of the Spirit among the Galatians. He recognized the life-shaping power of spiritual experience. He understood that people often make decisions based on their encounter with God. But he also understood that it is Christian doctrine that explains religious experience, and not the other way around. So he wanted to know how the Galatians had received the Holy Spirit.

There were and are only two possibilities: the Spirit comes either by "works of the law" or by "hearing with faith." As we saw back in chapter 5, the phrase "works of the law" refers to law-keeping in general, and not simply to the Old Testament ceremonial law. So here two principles are set in opposition: law and faith. If the Spirit comes by working the law, then there is something I must *do* to get the Spirit. If I keep Torah and follow the regulations of the Old Testament law, then God will give me his Spirit. Thus the blessing of the Holy Spirit is God's reward for my spiritual achievements.

Left to themselves, people want exactly that: some method that will guarantee a good spiritual experience. Show us where the bar of obedience is so we can press it and get the religious cheese. But God is not a mechanism. The only way to know him is by entering into a trusting relationship with him. The indwelling presence of his Spirit comes by faith alone. A group of Chinese Christians had this truth clearly in mind in 1998 when they drafted a confession of faith for their house churches, in which they wrote: "For by grace we are saved through faith; we are justified by faith; we receive the Holy Spirit through faith; and we become the sons of God through faith." Justification and the Spirit come by faith.

There is another sense, of course, in which the Holy Spirit precedes faith, for it is the Holy Spirit who enables a sinner to believe in Christ in the first place. But the work of the Spirit does not become fully evident until the sinner actually believes, as the Galatians knew from their own experience. The question Paul asked them was a real "no-brainer." They did not have to *do* anything to get the Holy Spirit. In fact, they had received the Spirit long before the Judaizers came to tell them they had to keep the law. They simply trusted in what Jesus had done on the cross and through the empty tomb. The Galatians received the Spirit when they came to faith in Christ. As Paul puts it, they received the Spirit "by believing what [they] heard" (Gal. 3:2 NIV), namely, the law-free gospel of the crucified Christ. For the Christian, hearing is believing. Faith in Christ comes by hearing the gospel, and the Spirit comes along with the faith. Thus the Spirit's work is not a reward based on a person's own spiritual achievement, it is a gift granted to those who believe in Christ's achievement.

In case the Galatians had any doubts as to where the Spirit came from, Paul gave them a hint: "Did you receive the Spirit by works of the law or by hearing with faith?" (Gal. 3:2). The gift of the Holy Spirit was not something they gained; it was something they were given. This is hinted at again in verse 5, where Paul makes it clear that God is the one who generously supplies the Spirit—not to those who observe the law, but to those who believe the gospel of his Son.

What Paul says here helps to clarify several important truths about the person and work of the Holy Spirit. Some Christians teach that the Holy Spirit is a gift Christians receive sometime *after* they come to Christ. This "second blessing" suggests that Christians come in two varieties: with and without the Spirit. What Paul says here obviously rules this idea out. The gift of the Spirit is received by the same faith that lays hold of Christ. The works, gifts, and fruit of the Holy Spirit belong to the very beginning of the Christian life. Thus the whole Christian life is lived in the Spirit.

Notice also that the Spirit is not opposed to sound doctrine. Indeed, the two belong so closely together that we cannot live by the Spirit unless we are orthodox in our theology. A church that does not have sound doctrine does not experience the true blessing of the Holy Spirit. The converse is equally true: a church without the Spirit is not as orthodox as it thinks it is.

FROM START TO FINISH

Once the Galatians were forced to admit that they had received the Holy Spirit by faith alone, the argument was over. This is why Paul said he wanted to ask them only one question. Grant him that the Spirit comes by faith alone, and the whole matter is settled.

This truth—that the Holy Spirit comes by faith alone—has profound implications for the Christian life. It means that the Christian life finishes exactly the way it starts. The way *into* the Christian life is also the way *on* in the Christian life. "Are you so foolish?" Paul asks. "After beginning with the Spirit, are you now trying to attain your goal by human effort?" (Gal. 3:3 NIV), or, more literally, "by the flesh"? The term "flesh" calls to mind the physical rite of circumcision. What it means is human nature apart from God's Spirit, in all its weakness and sin. So Paul's question is this: Are you trying to be perfected by your own (sinful) efforts?

The very suggestion is absurd, of course, yet it is precisely what the Judaizers were telling the Galatians. They said that faith was fine as far as it went, but justification was completed through works. John Stott summarizes their theology as follows: "They did not deny that you must believe in Jesus for salvation, but they stressed that you must be circumcised and keep the law as well. In other words, you must let Moses finish what Christ has begun. Or rather, you yourself must finish, by your obedience to the law, what Christ has begun. You must add your works to the work of Christ. You must finish Christ's unfinished work."[8] However, there is never any need to refinish the finished work of Christ. In fact, trying to do so would ruin his priceless work altogether. It would be something like retracing Babe Ruth's signature on a baseball. Rather than adding to its value, doing so would completely destroy it.

Paul understood that only God can complete what God has begun, so that the completion must come by faith rather than by works. He said as much to the Philippians, using exactly the same word to say it: "he who began a good work in you will bring it to completion [i.e., perfection] at the day of Jesus Christ" (Phil. 1:6). And if it is true that God is going to complete his work in us by faith, it would be sheer folly to go back to the law: "The gospel of Christ crucified, as Paul saw it, so completely ruled out the law as a means of getting right with God that it was scarcely credible that people who had once embraced such a gospel should ever turn to the law for salvation."[9]

8. John R. W. Stott, *The Message of Galatians: Only One Way*, The Bible Speaks Today (Downers Grove, IL: InterVarsity, 1968), 22.

9. F. F. Bruce, *The Epistle to the Galatians: A Commentary on the Greek Text*, New International Greek Testament Commentary (Grand Rapids: Eerdmans, 1982), 148.

One of the reasons it would have been especially foolish for the Galatians to return to the law has to do with all the hardships they had faced: "Did you suffer so many things in vain—if indeed it was in vain?" (Gal. 3:4). The word "suffered" (*epathete*) may refer to actual suffering, such as the kind of persecution that Paul and Barnabas endured when they first came to Galatia (Acts 13–14). Perhaps the Galatians themselves had come under attack for their faith in Christ. But if the cross is unnecessary, then why bother to be persecuted for it?

There is another option, however. The Greek word is also a word for "experience." Thus it might simply refer to all the spiritual experiences the Galatians had been through. The Holy Spirit had done a gracious, even a miraculous work among them, but now Paul wondered whether it had all been in vain. He sincerely hoped not. In fact, his words at the end of verse 4—"if indeed it was in vain"—seem almost hopeful. Perhaps all is not yet lost.

At first glance, these verses seem to be about sanctification rather than justification. Sanctification is the process by which a sinner becomes more holy. Christians usually think of sanctification as everything that happens after justification (which comes at the beginning of the Christian life). Their thinking goes something like this: "I was justified by faith when I first came to Christ. Now that I am justified, I must move on to my sanctification."

It is true enough that sanctification follows justification, but justification never gets left behind. We will *never* stand before God on the basis of our own righteousness. We can stand before God only on the basis of the righteousness of Jesus Christ. Once and forever, we are justified before God by the righteousness we have received by faith. To be sure, we are becoming more holy all the time. Having been justified, we are now becoming sanctified. But we cannot use our obedience—as imperfect as it is—to establish our righteousness before God. To put this another way, we cannot base our justification on our sanctification.

From start to finish, the whole Christian life is by grace through faith. A new life in Christ commences with faith, continues by faith, and will be completed through faith. To put this another way, the gospel is for Christians just as much as it is for non-Christians. We never advance beyond the good news of the cross and the empty tomb. There is nothing else to add to faith as the ground of our salvation because faith unites us to Jesus Christ. Works have no part in establishing the basis for our salvation, but are added to faith in much the same way that a building rests upon and rises from its foundation. Therefore, the Christian always looks back to the gospel and never to the law as the basis for his righteousness before God.

Recently some scholars have argued that justification by faith alone is *not* the main subject of this letter. This is part of a so-called New Perspective on Paul and the law. According to this viewpoint, justification is only "brought into the discussion about how the Galatians should behave as Christians and whether they should 'add' obedience to the Mosaic Law, to their faith in Christ," but it is not presented as the basis for the salvation of sinners.[10] These scholars are certainly right about what Paul's opponents were saying. Remember the situation. Some Jews who identified themselves as Christians had gone to Galatia to improve Paul's gospel. They said that his doctrine of justification was just an "entry-level gospel."[11] If the Galatians wanted a promotion, they needed to add something to faith alone. Although they had come into a saving relationship with Christ by grace, they could maintain that relationship only by obedience.[12]

What the Judaizers were saying really amounted to self-justification. They wanted the Galatians to justify themselves before God (and man) by adding works to faith. In particular, they wanted the Galatians to be circumcised. But for Paul the issue was not really circumcision; his concern was the very idea of merit-based religion, which is precisely why justification by faith alone is the main subject of his letter. Paul attacked the Judaizers over circumcision not simply because he wanted to promote better Jewish-Gentile relations, but because he was concerned for their very souls.

There is no such thing as performance-based Christianity. Having begun by faith, we must continue by faith. Justification is a doctrine for the whole Christian life from start to finish. It is not simply a doctrine for coming to Christ in the first place, although we are justified the moment we trust in

10. Ben Witherington III, *Grace in Galatia: A Commentary on Paul's Letter to the Galatians* (Edinburgh: T & T Clark, 1998), 175.
11. George, *Galatians*, 213.
12. This is the way that E. P. Sanders and other advocates of the New Perspective generally characterize first-century Judaism: "getting in by grace, staying in by obedience." In their view, this formulation preserves the graciousness of God in salvation. But what these scholars fail to recognize is that this theology contains a grace-destroying legalism: if we continue with God by obedience, then even if we begin by grace we are ultimately thrown back on ourselves and our own ability to keep the law. This was precisely Paul's concern in Galatians, as it later was for the Protestant Reformers.

Christ. Nor is it merely a great doctrine to die with, although God will justify us through faith in Christ at the final judgment.

Justification is a doctrine to live by each and every moment. It is a doctrine for the *damned*. There comes a day when every man, woman, and child must admit to being a hardened sinner, rotten to the very core, and deserving of God's just wrath. When that day comes, the only hope is to come to Christ by faith alone.

Justification is also a doctrine for the *doubtful*. There are days in the life of every Christian when the whole thing seems rather implausible. Is it true that God loves me and has a wonderful plan for my life? Does he really care about me? When the doubts come, the believer goes back to the cross where Christ died to justify sinners and holds on to it by faith alone.

Justification is a doctrine for the *discouraged*, too. At times, things seem rather gloomy and hopeless. In fact, sometimes they seem altogether impossible, so that we wonder how we can make it through another day. But this is exactly why we need to preach the gospel to ourselves every day. As we get out of bed we say, "I know what my real problem is: I am a sinner living in a sinful world." Then as we step into the shower we say, "Although I am a great sinner, I have an even greater Savior, who loved me and gave himself for me." By breakfast time we are able to make it through the day, trusting in God's grace alone.

The good news of the gospel is that even though we are lost and needy sinners, if we know Christ, then we are and always will be justified. Justification is much more than a great doctrine to die with, although it certainly is that. Justification by grace alone, through faith alone, in Christ alone is also a wonderful doctrine to live by.

A painting by the Flemish painter Hendrik Leys (1815–1869) illustrates what happens when Christians lose sight of the crucified Christ. The painting is called "Women Praying at a Crucifix near St. James in Antwerp." The women themselves are portrayed with painstaking detail. Careful attention is paid to every fold in the fabric of their gowns. Likewise, the background is painted to show the beauty of the garden by the church wall. There is one thing missing from the painting, however, and that is the cross itself. Leys shows the women at worship, but not the Christ they have come to adore. "So what do we see?" asks the Dutch art critic Hans Rookmaaker

(1922–1977). "People from a past period, full of faith, reverent, praying—but we do not see the object of faith, the crucified Christ."[13]

Often, this is precisely our problem in the Christian life. Recovering Pharisees that we are, we sometimes lose sight of the object of our faith: Christ having been crucified for our sins. But when we bring him back into the picture, and see him portrayed as the Savior who not only died, but also rose again, then we regain the vision to live for him by faith.

13. Hans Rookmaaker, *Modern Art and the Death of a Culture* (Wheaton, IL: Crossway, 1994), 69.

8

Father Abraham Has Many Sons

Galatians 3:6—9

Know then that it is those of faith who are the sons of Abraham.
And the Scripture, foreseeing that God would justify the Gentiles
by faith, preached the gospel beforehand to Abraham, saying, "In
you shall all the nations be blessed." (Gal. 3:7–8)

ome of the simplest Bible songs for children contain some of the soundest theology. Consider the chorus taken from Galatians 3:

Father Abraham had many sons,
And many sons had Father Abraham;
And I am one of them, and so are you,
So let's all praise the Lord!

The song gets sillier after that—turning into a sort of sanctified "Hokey Pokey"—but its basic theology is profound. It is so profound, in fact, that I had no idea what it meant when I was a child. I first heard the song at camp, and I thought to myself, "Father Abraham had many sons? I thought Jacob was the guy with all the kids!"

Father Abraham was an important figure to the Judaizers, the goody-two-shoes of the apostolic church who believed in justification by faith plus the works of the law. If the Judaizers taught any Bible songs when they went to Galatia, they probably taught one that went like this:

Father Abraham had many sons,
And many sons had Father Abraham;
And I am one of them, but you are not,
So let's all get together for a little procedure we like to call circumcision.

The Judaizers were serious about this. Belonging to God meant being a child of Abraham. So, for example, when the Jews wanted to prove to Jesus that they were children of God, they said, "We are offspring of Abraham. . . . Abraham is our father" (John 8:33, 39). Therefore, if the Gentiles wanted to belong to God, they had to become children of Abraham.

The only way to become a true child of Abraham, said the Judaizers, was to be circumcised as he was. This was taught right in the Scriptures. God said to Abraham, "This is my covenant, which you shall keep, between me and you and your offspring after you: Every male among you shall be circumcised" (Gen. 17:10). What could be plainer? Until the Gentiles were circumcised, they had no right to call Abraham their father—or to call God their Father, for that matter.

THE MAN OF FAITH

Undoubtedly the reason the apostle Paul has so much to say about Abraham in Galatians 3 and 4 is that the Judaizers made such a fuss over him. They claimed that Father Abraham and all his children belonged to God, not by faith alone, but by works of the law.

In addition to misunderstanding the gospel, the Judaizers were also guilty of misunderstanding the Old Testament. Therefore, in order to refute their performance-based version of Christianity, Paul had to go back to the Hebrew Scriptures. In verses 1 through 5, his argument for justification by faith alone appealed to experience—the Galatian experience of the Holy Spirit. In verses 6 and following, he argues for faith alone on the basis of biblical history, using Abraham as a test case: "Abraham believed God, and it was counted to him as righteousness" (Gal. 3:6).

Paul's choice of an Old Testament text was inspired. The Judaizers loved to go back to Genesis 17, where God's covenant with Abraham was signified by circumcision. But Paul went back even further, to God's promise of a child in Genesis 15.

God made Abraham quite a few promises in his time: "Now the LORD said to Abram, 'Go from your country and your kindred and your father's house to the land that I will show you'" (Gen. 12:1). Then God promised to make him into a great nation, to bless him, and to make his name great (Gen. 12:2–3). Abraham believed God's promises. No sooner had he received his instructions than he "went, as the LORD had told him" (Gen. 12:4). In its short biographical summary of this period in Abraham's life, the book of Hebrews says: "By faith Abraham obeyed when he was called to go out to a place that he was to receive as an inheritance. And he went out, not knowing where he was going. By faith he went to live in the land of promise, as in a foreign land, living in tents with Isaac and Jacob, heirs with him of the same promise. For he was looking forward to the city that has foundations, whose designer and builder is God" (Heb. 11:8–10). So Abraham left the land of his fathers and journeyed by faith to the Promised Land.

Some years later, God came to Abraham with another promise. This time it was the promise of a son. Frankly, it was hard to believe. In the past, God had promised him land, but Abraham still did not own any property. Now he was promised an heir, but he still didn't have any children. And he wasn't getting any younger either! In fact, he was pushing one hundred. Abraham, a father, at that age?

To show Abraham what he had in mind, God took him outside and showed him the stars. He said, "Look toward heaven, and number the stars, if you are able to number them." Then he said, "So shall your offspring be" (Gen. 15:5). What God promised to do for Abraham was impossible. Yet Abraham believed that God would make it so. He took the promise the way every divine promise ought to be taken: by faith. As the Scripture says, "He believed the LORD, and he counted it to him as righteousness" (Gen. 15:6). Or, as Paul quoted it for the Galatians, "Abraham believed God, and it was credited to him as righteousness" (Gal. 3:6).

What Paul emphasized was the result of Abraham's faith. His faith was "counted" or "credited" (*elogisthē*) to him as righteousness. When Abraham believed, God reckoned that he was righteous. To put it in financial terms, he accounted him righteous. Trusting God was like opening a bank account. Immediately, God transferred righteousness into Abraham's account.

This does not mean that Abraham was actually righteous, only that he was declared righteous. He was considered to have a right standing before God. To use the proper theological term, God "imputed" righteousness to Abraham. God is the one who has the legal right to state whether a man is righteous or unrighteous, and in this case, he considered Abraham righteous through his faith.

A good example of what it means to be declared righteous comes from the life of the astronomer William Herschel (1738–1822). As a young boy growing up in Hanover, Germany, Herschel loved listening to military music. Eventually he joined a military band. But when the nation went to war, he found himself marching into battle, totally unprepared for the horrors of war. During a period of intense fighting he deserted his unit and fled from the field of battle. The penalty for desertion was death, so Herschel could no longer remain in Germany. He fled to England to pursue further studies in music and science. Eventually he became a famous man, renowned throughout Europe for his musical abilities as well as his scientific discoveries.

William Herschel had left his past behind him, and for many years he gave little thought to the death sentence that remained over him. But then another German arrived in Britain: George, head of the House of Hanover, crowned King of England. King George knew the secret of Herschel's past and summoned him to appear before the royal court. With great trepidation, the scientist arrived at the palace, where he was told to wait in a chamber outside the throne room. Finally, one of the king's servants brought Herschel a document. Anxiously, he opened it and read the following words: "I George pardon you for your past offenses against our native land."[1]

---

1. Ben Witherington III, *Grace in Galatia: A Commentary on Paul's Letter to the Galatians* (Edinburgh: T & T Clark, 1998), 195.

Herschel had received a royal pardon. The fact of his desertion was not overlooked, yet he was acquitted, and therefore he was justified in the eyes of the law. In a similar way, Abraham received a royal pardon from the King of all kings. He was declared righteous. Unrighteous though he was, his faith was counted for righteousness by God.

Although everyone agrees that Abraham was righteous, not everyone agrees how he got that way. Some Jewish writings—outside the Bible—depict him as a man whose righteousness was a reward for his obedience. His right standing before God was not a gift; it was something he had to earn. According to the book of Sirach (44:19–21), for example, the promises God made were a response to Abraham's faithfulness. Other rabbis said he had to pass through ten trials in order to merit God's favor.[2] Thus the first book of Maccabees asks, "Did not Abraham prove steadfast under trial, and so gain credit as a righteous man?" (1 Macc. 2:52). Paul's answer to this question was a resounding "No!" Abraham was steadfast under trial, true enough, but he never gained any credit from God for his works of obedience. God counted him righteous by faith, and nothing else.

The striking thing about Abraham is that he was justified *before* he did any works. If Abraham had been justified by works, then he would have had something to brag about. But "what does the Scripture say?" Paul asks in his letter to the Romans. Simply this: "Abraham believed God, and it was counted to him as righteousness" (Rom. 4:3). He was justified not as a worker, but as a believer. Faith was the instrumentality of his justification.

In particular, Abraham did not have to get circumcised to be justified. This is the genius of Paul's argument against the Judaizers: God counted Abraham righteous before he had even heard of circumcision! In Romans, Paul asks if the blessing of God's forgiveness is "only for the circumcised, or also for the uncircumcised" (Rom. 4:9). His answer is: "We say that faith was counted to Abraham as righteousness. How then was it counted to him? Was it before or after he had been circumcised? It was not after, but before he was circumcised" (Rom. 4:9–10). In other words, the great patriarch was justified while he was still an uncircumcised Chaldean!

---

2. Timothy George, *Galatians*, New American Commentary 30 (Nashville: Broadman & Holman, 1994), 218.

LIKE FATHER, LIKE SON

The fact that Abraham was justified as a Gentile made him the perfect example to use for the Galatians, who had been wrestling with two questions: Whom does God accept, and on what basis? For his answer, Paul took Abraham's history and applied it to their situation, and to ours: "Know then that it is those of faith who are the sons of Abraham" (Gal. 3:7).

No doubt this statement enraged the Judaizers when they heard it. Their claim to fame was that they were the children of Abraham, while others were not. "We have been circumcised," they gloated, "so we are the sons of Abraham!" Paul picked up their vocabulary and smacked them with it, declaring that the only real children of Abraham are those who believe. Paul not only taught this; he insisted on it. Grammatically, verse 7 reads like this: "The ones of faith, *these* are the sons of Abraham." All who believe—and only those who believe—are children of Abraham. Membership in Abraham's family is not hereditary. Father Abraham's true sons and daughters are not the people who keep the law, but the people who live by faith. Their family resemblance is spiritual rather than physical.

Practically speaking, this means that God will accept us only on the same basis he accepted Abraham. Like father, like son. If Abraham was justified by faith, then his children have to be justified by faith too. Therefore, we will never become children of God by what we do, but only by what we believe.

What, then, must we believe? Notice the object of Abraham's faith: he put his trust in God. "Abraham believed God" (Gal. 3:6), and this was credited to him as righteousness. What Abraham believed was not simply God's promises, which he could hardly believe, but God himself. Abraham put his faith in the faithful God—the God who made him the promise. When Abraham didn't know where he was going, or how he was going to get there, he trusted God to get him where he needed to be. When he didn't have any children, or any reason to think he ever would, he believed that God would make good on his promise. Against all hope and beyond all doubt, Abraham committed himself and his whole life to God. The Scripture says, "No distrust made him waver concerning the promise of God, but he grew strong in his faith as he gave glory to God, fully convinced that God was able to do what he had promised. That is why his faith was 'counted to him as righteousness'" (Rom. 4:20–22).

If we are to become children of Abraham, and therefore children of God, we must have the same faith, and we must put it in the same place. We must trust the God who keeps every promise he has ever made. We trust him for guidance, believing that he will show us the way we should go. We trust him for providence, believing that he will take care of whatever we need. We trust him for deliverance, believing that he will bring us through times of trial. We trust him for everything, just as Abraham did. But most of all we trust him for salvation through his Son. Now that God the Son has come into the world, to believe God is to accept the gospel of Jesus Christ, "receiving and resting upon him alone for salvation, as he is offered to us in the gospel."[3]

To have faith is to believe the good news of the cross and the empty tomb. It is to accept what the Bible says about the crucifixion and resurrection of Jesus of Nazareth. It is to trust in "Jesus Christ as crucified," as Paul said back in verse 1. It is to believe that Jesus died on the cross for our sins and was raised from the dead to give us eternal life.

These are the things we must believe if we want God to accept us the way he justified Abraham: "But the words 'it was counted to him' were not written for his sake alone, but for ours also. It will be counted to us who believe in him who raised from the dead Jesus our Lord, who was delivered up for our trespasses and raised for our justification" (Rom. 4:23–25). When we place all our trust and confidence in the God who raised the crucified Christ from the dead, then God credits Christ's righteousness to our account. He imputes Christ's righteousness to us, so that we are righteous in his sight by faith. Thus we become true children of Abraham, and of God.

THE SAME AS IT EVER WAS

This faith is not just for Abraham and the Galatians, but for everyone. In verse 6 Paul proved that justification by faith was God's plan for Abraham. In verse 7 he showed that people like the Galatians could become Abraham's children by the same faith. Then in verse 8 he proves that justification by faith alone has always been God's plan for all people everywhere: "And the Scripture, foreseeing that God would justify the Gentiles by faith, preached

---

3. Westminster Shorter Catechism, Answer 86.

the gospel beforehand to Abraham, saying, 'In you shall all the nations be blessed'" (Gal. 3:8).

This quotation takes us even further back in Abraham's story, to the very first promise God ever made to him: "And I will make of you a great nation, . . . and in you all the families of the earth shall be blessed" (Gen. 12:2–3). There is also an echo in Galatians from Genesis 18:18, where God said, "Abraham shall surely become a great and mighty nation, and all the nations of the earth shall be blessed in him."

By quoting from Genesis in this way, Paul teaches something important about the Bible. The promises in Genesis come from the mouth of God, but for Paul, what the Bible says and what God says are one and the same. So Paul says, "The Scripture . . . preached" (Gal. 3:8), even though God was the one doing the talking. This is one place where, as the great Princeton theologian Benjamin Breckinridge Warfield (1851–1921) put it, "God and the Scriptures are brought into such conjunction as to show that in point of directness of authority no distinction was made between them."[4] The Bible is God's word written. This is why the Scripture is alive. It has the power to announce because God speaks in it with a living and powerful voice. The words on the pages of the Bible come straight from the mouth of God.

Because it was written by God—through human authors, of course—the Bible speaks with one mind and one message. That one message is justification by faith alone. God's plan of salvation, the covenant of grace, runs from Abraham right through to Christ: "The Scripture . . . preached the gospel beforehand to Abraham" (Gal. 3:8). What God said to Abraham was nothing less than a proclamation of the gospel. Christians sometimes sing about "the old, old story of Jesus and his love." The story is older than some people realize. It goes back at least to the days of Abraham. Indeed, it goes all the way back to Adam and Eve (Gen. 3:15), who were the first to hear it. Ultimately, the good news of the Old Testament is the good news about Jesus Christ.

The gospel is the good news about God forgiving sins and granting eternal life. These are the very things Abraham believed. He did not know Jesus Christ by name, but he trusted him nonetheless. He believed that God would

---

4. Benjamin Breckinridge Warfield, *The Inspiration and Authority of Scripture* (Philadelphia: Presbyterian and Reformed, 1948), 299.

forgive his sins and grant him eternal life. He had faith, in other words, in both the atonement and the resurrection.

Consider Abraham's actions on Mount Moriah, where God told him to offer his beloved son Isaac as a sacrifice. Children love to question their parents about travel arrangements, and Isaac was no exception. As they hiked up the mountain, it dawned on him that something was missing. "Behold, the fire and the wood," Isaac said, "but where is the lamb for a burnt offering?" (Gen. 22:7). Abraham believed that God would provide the atoning sacrifice. So he answered, "God will provide for himself the lamb for a burnt offering, my son" (Gen. 22:8). Abraham was right: God provided a ram, caught in the thicket, which Abraham offered in place of his son (Gen. 22:13). He had faith in God's gift of an atoning sacrifice.

Abraham also had faith in the resurrection. Before he went up the mountain with Isaac, he "said to his young men, 'Stay here with the donkey; I and the boy will go over there and worship and come again to you'" (Gen. 22:5). Abraham went up the mountain, knife in hand, fully intending to sacrifice his son. Yet there was not the slightest doubt in his mind that Isaac would walk back down the mountain with him. How could this be? The Scripture tells us what Abraham was thinking: "He considered that God was able even to raise him from the dead, from which, figuratively speaking, he did receive him back" (Heb. 11:19). Father Abraham believed in God's power over death. He trusted God to forgive sins and grant eternal life. Thus the gospel according to Abraham included both the atonement and the resurrection.

All Abraham's children believe the same gospel. His true sons and daughters are the people of faith. If the gospel was good enough for Abraham, it is good enough for us. We trust the atoning death and the bodily resurrection of Jesus Christ, as God planned from the very beginning. His way of dealing with us in our sin is eternally the same.

One of the implications of this is that the doctrine of justification by faith is not some kind of theological novelty. In their fascination with Rome, some evangelical Christians now question the importance of Reformation theology. In particular, they wonder if it was really necessary to divide the church over the doctrine of justification. What does it matter, they wonder, whether I am saved by faith alone or by faith plus works? Who cares whether God makes me righteous or declares me righteous, as long as I am righteous in the end?

102

To those who doubt the necessity of the Reformation doctrine of justification, we testify—with Paul as well as Abraham—that justification has always come only by faith. Justification by grace alone, through faith alone, in Christ alone has always been the very heart of God's plan for the salvation of sinners. Thus Ernst Käsemann has rightly concluded that "justification remains the centre, the beginning and the end of salvation history."[5]

Paul could not have expressed this point more forcefully than he did in these words: "the Scripture, foreseeing that God would justify the Gentiles by faith" (Gal. 3:8). The Old Testament had the foresight to predict the coming of Jesus Christ, the Savior of the world. The Scriptures not only predicted that he would come, but also prophesied the precise way that he would save. He would justify sinners by faith, exactly as God justified Abraham.

So Let's All Praise the Lord!

This plan of salvation is for all people everywhere. It is universal. It is for all nations. The blessing of justification was never for the Jews alone; it was always intended for the whole world. In Galatians 3:8 Paul refers to the "Gentiles" and to the "nations." In fact, these are two different translations for the same term. The word does not refer to political states, but to people groups. Through Abraham, God's blessing would come to every ethnic community in the world, to every tribe, people, and language. This was the agenda that Jesus established for the church, to "go therefore and make disciples of all nations" (Matt. 28:19). It later became Paul's agenda for world missions. This explains why he went to places like Galatia to proclaim the good news about Jesus Christ that God had first announced to Abraham.

Preaching the gospel to every people group remains the church's agenda to this very day. To think and to act biblically is to think and to act globally. We preach the whole gospel to the whole world, knowing that it is the will of God for Jesus Christ to stake his claim on every ethnic community on the face of the earth. In the words of another children's song, which is also profound in its theology:

---

5. Ernst Käsemann, *Perspectives on Paul*, trans. Margaret Kohl (Philadelphia: Fortress, 1971), 76.

> Jesus loves the little children,
> All the children of the world;
> Red and yellow, black and white,
> They are precious in his sight;
> Jesus loves the little children of the world.

If the little children of the world want to become sons and daughters of Abraham, they must come to Jesus Christ by faith. The gospel we preach to the nations is the gospel of justification by faith.

In verse 9 Paul summarizes what he has been saying to this point: "So then, those who are of faith are blessed along with Abraham, the man of faith" (Gal. 3:9). This verse speaks of a common blessing. We are blessed *with* Abraham, so that all his blessings become our blessings. By faith, we become the object of the blessing God promised to Abraham. Thus he becomes our brother as well as our father. This is part of the doctrine of the communion of the saints. God offers one salvation in one Christ, to be shared by one people, Abraham included.

The blessing Paul has in mind is the gospel blessing God announced to Abraham: to be justified, or accepted as righteous in God's sight. Timothy George asks, "What was it that the Scriptures 'foresaw' and 'preached beforehand' to Abraham? Simply this: the good news of salvation was to be extended to all peoples, including the Gentiles, who would be declared righteous by God, just like Abraham, on the basis of faith."[6]

Abraham received many blessings from God in his time. He obtained an inheritance in the Promised Land. He was given a child, and through the child, he became the father of many nations. But the greatest blessing he ever received was to be justified.

Earlier I mentioned the pardon that William Herschel was granted by King George of England. There is more to the story. The document the king gave to Herschel began by pronouncing him "not guilty," but it went on to say that for his outstanding service to humanity as a musician and scientist, Herschel would be granted a knighthood. From that point on he was one of King George's knights, honored throughout the United Kingdom as Sir

---

6. George, *Galatians*, 225.

William Herschel. When Herschel was justified, not only was he declared righteous, but he also became a friend of the king.

This was Abraham's experience too, and it can become our experience. We can receive the same blessings that Abraham experienced. We can be made right with God. We can become a personal friend of the Creator of the universe, and live with him for all eternity. All that is required is faith in Jesus Christ. If we want the same blessing Abraham received, we have to receive it the same way. Abraham was justified as a man of faith. He was not justified as a circumcised Jew, but as a believer. Therefore, the legacy of Father Abraham is inherited by faith: "those who are of faith are blessed along with Abraham, the man of faith" (Gal. 3:9).

We do not have to be circumcised in order to be justified before God. We do not have to keep the law. We do not have to become culturally Jewish. We do not have to *do* anything, only believe. It is those who believe in Jesus Christ who receive the blessing God promised to Abraham. Thus it is by faith alone that anyone sings the words of the song, so profound in its theology:

> Father Abraham has many sons,
> And many sons has Father Abraham;
> And I am one of them, and so are you,
> So let's all praise the Lord!

9

THE OLD CURSED CROSS

Galatians 3:10—14

Christ redeemed us from the curse of the law by becoming a curse
for us—for it is written, "Cursed is everyone who is hanged
on a tree." (Gal. 3:13)

*I*magine the scene: An entire nation gathers on the sides of two mountains to worship. Half the people stand on one mountainside, half on the other. They worship responsively, alternating their praise. First one group cries out to God, and then the other, with every man, woman, and child shouting in unison.

This was the scene when the people of God crossed the Jordan River and entered the Promised Land. According to the command of Moses, six tribes stood on Mount Gerizim and six on Mount Ebal to form an antiphonal choir. Rather than singing in harmony, they recited a litany of blessings and curses. The tribes on Mount Gerizim blessed the people of God, while the tribes on Mount Ebal cursed them.

What curses they were! "Cursed be the man who makes a carved or cast metal image" (Deut. 27:15). "Cursed be anyone who dishonors his father or his mother" (Deut. 27:16). "Cursed be anyone who perverts the justice due to the sojourner, the fatherless, and the widow" (Deut. 27:19). "Cursed be anyone who does not confirm the words of this law by doing them" (Deut. 27:26). The Levites recited a dozen curses in all, and after each one, all the people said, "Amen!"

THE PROBLEM WITH THE LAW

The apostle Paul knew these curses well. He had read them in the book of Deuteronomy, of course, but he had also heard them recited on five memorable occasions. Five times Paul was punished by the Jews for preaching the gospel, and each time he received the standard punishment: "forty lashes minus one" (2 Cor. 11:24). The synagogue manuals of that time required someone to read out the curses of the law while the prisoner was being whipped.[1] Thus as Paul received the final stripe on his back, he may well have heard the very words that he later quoted to the Galatians: "Cursed be everyone who does not abide by all things written in the Book of the Law, and do them" (Gal. 3:10).

This verse pronounces God's solemn judgment against sinful humanity. God's standard is perfect. He requires nothing less than total obedience to the entire law. God's perfect law is for everyone, for Jew and Gentile alike. Some recent commentators argue that Paul was referring to the disobedience of Israel as a nation, and not to the sin of individuals. However, in the context of Deuteronomy, God's curse clearly falls on individuals who fail to keep the law. Others suggest that these verses refer only to the Jews, but this is to overlook the fact that *everyone* is obligated to obey God. God's law is not just for Jews as Jews; it is for human beings as human beings.

Not only must we keep God's law, but we must also continue to keep it. God requires consistent, constant obedience to his revealed will. Furthermore, the law must be kept in its entirety. Everyone must continue to do *everything* written in God's law, down to the last detail.

The Scripture refers here to God's moral law, and not merely to the rituals that separate Jews from Gentiles, as the New Perspective on Paul and the law would have it. This makes a critical difference to our interpretation of Galatians, and indeed to our whole understanding of the gospel. The New Perspective maintains that when Paul wrote about abiding by all things written in the book of the law, he did not have the whole Old Testament law in mind. What he meant instead were the ceremonial regulations that marked Israelites off from Gentiles, such as circumcision and the rules for table

---

1. Richard N. Longenecker, *Galatians*, Word Biblical Commentaries (Dallas: Word, 1990), 117.

fellowship, not the moral code that people might use to justify their righteousness before God.

E. P. Sanders first articulated this view in his book *Paul, the Law, and the Jewish People.*[2] According to Sanders, Paul did not mean to emphasize the word "all," but merely employed it as part of Deuteronomy 27:26, which he wished to cite for polemical reasons. But as Andrew Das points out in his critique of Sanders and others who hold this view, "all" is central to the meaning of that Old Testament verse, which concludes an extended condemnation of every possible violation of God's law, and of those who break it. The word "all" is equally central to Paul's argument. As Das explains, "Deuteronomy 27:26 is cited in Galatians 3:10 to provide a reason why those relying on the works of the law are under a curse: the law demanded that all its precepts be obeyed."[3]

At stake in the recent dispute over this verse is Paul's purpose in writing Galatians and, by extension, his understanding of the doctrine of justification. Is Paul only concerned to challenge Jewish Christians not to refuse table fellowship with Gentile Christians, as the New Perspective maintains? Or, in keeping with the classic Protestant understanding of Paul and the law, is he more fundamentally concerned with the way in which sinners might hope to have a saving relationship with a righteous God?

In citing Deuteronomy 27:26, Paul supplies the answer. This verse wraps up an exhaustive catalog of the demands that God makes in his law (nearly all of which fall under the category of moral law) and his curse on anyone who violates any one of these demands. When Paul writes, "All who rely on observing the law are under a curse" (Gal. 3:10 NIV), he is defending the doctrine of justification through faith alone, insisting that no one can be accepted by God through the law unless it is kept in all its perfection. As it is written, "Whoever keeps the whole law but fails in one point has become accountable for all of it" (James 2:10; cf. Heb. 2:2).

The punishment for failing to keep God's perfect standard is God's righteous curse. Every lawbreaker is subject to divine condemnation. "What does every sin deserve?" asks the Westminster Shorter Catechism. The answer is,

2. E. P. Sanders, *Paul, the Law, and the Jewish People* (Philadelphia: Fortress, 1983), 21–22.
3. A. Andrew Das, *Paul, the Law, and the Covenant* (Peabody, MA: Hendrickson, 2001), 164.

"Every sin deserves God's wrath and curse, both in this life, and that which is to come" (Q. & A. 84).

This means that we ourselves are under the same curse that was shouted down from Mount Ebal. There is a hidden premise in Galatians 3:10, a premise so obvious that it remains unspoken: *We* are lawbreakers.[4] We are sinners living in rebellion against God. To quote again from the Shorter Catechism, "No mere man since the fall is able in this life perfectly to keep the commandments of God, but doth daily break them in thought, word, and deed" (A. 82). This is the doctrine of total depravity: not that we are as sinful as we can possibly be, but that we are all sinful all the way through. There is no part of us—body, soul, or spirit; mind, heart, or will—that is not corrupt.

The doctrine of depravity is taught everywhere in Scripture: "There is no one who does not sin" (1 Kings 8:46); "All we like sheep have gone astray; we have turned every one to his own way" (Isa. 53:6); "None is righteous, no, not one" (Rom. 3:10); "for all have sinned and fall short of the glory of God" (Rom. 3:23). What the Bible says about human nature is confirmed by human history, which is a sordid tale of war and woe. It is confirmed by our neighbors, by the lies of our co-workers and the self-centeredness of the people on our street. It is confirmed by the petty disagreements within our families and even our churches. But the doctrine of total depravity writes its most compelling proof on our own hearts. Your own guilty conscience ought to be enough to convince you that you are unworthy of God. Do you ever stretch the truth? Do you ever take something that doesn't exactly belong to you? Do you ever speak an unkind word? If so, then God's law condemns you as an accursed liar, thief, and murderer.

If it is true that everyone, without exception, is condemned by the curse of the law, then why would anyone ever try to base salvation on keeping the law? This is Paul's point. Everyone who depends on the law is under a curse because the law curses everyone who breaks it, which everyone does. Ironically, by advocating obedience to the law the Judaizers were not escaping God's curse but actually incurring it!

The apostle refers specifically to "all who rely on works of the law" (Gal. 3:10). It is the same phrase he used back in chapter 2 when he contrasted

4. Or as Andrew Das states it, "All who rely on the works of the law do not observe and obey all the things written in the book of the law" (ibid., 146). Das also points out that omitting a self-evident premise was common in ancient rhetoric.

those who are "justified by works of the law" with those who are "justified by faith" (Gal. 2:16). Those who "rely on works of the law" are people who want to be accepted on their own merits. They expect God to justify them because they do the right things. But this is a legalistic perversion of the law. Anyone who tries to be justified by working the law is attempting the impossible. God did not give us the law to make us good. Part of the law's purpose, in fact, is to show us how bad we really are. Therefore, it is completely hopeless to get right with God by keeping the law; "the law is a matter of performance, but a performance that is beyond human possibility."[5] If justification did come by the law, we could not be justified, because we cannot keep the law. The Puritan William Perkins explained it like this: "If we could fulfill the law, we might be justified by the law: but no man can be justified by the law, or by works: therefore no man can fulfill the law."[6]

The problem with the law, then, is not the law; the problem with the law is our sin. Since we cannot keep the law, the law cannot bless us. All it can do is curse us, placing us under the condemnation of divine wrath.

THE PRINCIPLE OF THE LAW

If the law cannot bless us, then how can we receive God's blessing? This is the question Paul has been wrestling with throughout this letter. How do I stand in right relationship with God? How can God accept me? What must I do to gain his favor? In a word, how can I be justified?

There are two possibilities: Either I am justified by works of the law or I am justified by faith in Jesus Christ. Paul's answer, of course, is that justification comes only by faith and not by works. He has stated this before, but here he repeats it: "Now it is evident that no one is justified before God by the law, for 'The righteous shall live by faith.' But the law is not of faith, rather 'The one who does them shall live by them' " (Gal. 3:11–12). Justification cannot come by works of the law; it must come by faith.

Faith and works operate according to different principles. They are two entirely different ways to live: by believing and by doing. If we live by faith,

5. Donald A. Hagner, "The Law in Paul's Letter to the Galatians," *Modern Reformation* 12.5 (Sept./Oct. 2003): 34.

6. William Perkins, *A Commentary on Galatians*, Pilgrim Classic Commentaries, ed. Gerald T. Sheppard (London, 1617; repr. New York: Pilgrim, 1989), 163.

we trust God to justify us through Jesus Christ. As Paul preached on another occasion, "by him everyone who believes is freed from everything from which you could not be freed by the law of Moses" (Acts 13:38–39). On the other hand, if we live by works, we count on our own contribution to make us fully acceptable to God. But we cannot have it both ways. Believing and doing are mutually exclusive. Either we trust God to justify us through faith or we try to justify ourselves by works.

Faith and works, then, are like a man who has one foot on the dock and one foot in his boat. As the boat starts to pull away from the dock, he will have to make a choice, or else end up in the water. As Calvin explained, they are two contrary ways to live: "The law justifies him who fulfils all its commands, whereas faith justifies those who are destitute of the merit of works and rely on Christ alone. To be justified by our own merit and by the grace of another are irreconcilable."[7]

Paul illustrates these two life-principles from the Old Testament. In verse 11 he quotes from the prophet Habakkuk: "The righteous shall live by faith." To quote the entire verse: "Behold, his soul is puffed up; it is not upright within him, but the righteous shall live by his faith" (Hab. 2:4). This must have been an important verse to Paul, since it also shows up as the theme verse of Romans (Rom. 1:17).

In their original context, Habakkuk's words condemned the pride of the Babylonians who conquered Jerusalem. The prophet accused them of proud self-confidence. They were "not right in relation to God: instead of trusting in him they held aloof in a spirit of self-sufficiency, trusting in themselves."[8] But this is not how God wants his people to live. He wants them to live by faith. They are the justified ones, the ones who have been declared righteous by God. Now they must live by faith, as Abraham did. Instead of trusting in themselves, they must trust God. Faith must characterize their relationship with God from beginning to end.

This verse from Habakkuk had a tremendous influence on the life of Martin Luther. Luther encountered it in the monastery at Erfurt, although at

---

7. John Calvin, *The Epistles of Paul the Apostle to the Galatians, Ephesians, Philippians and Colossians,* Calvin's New Testament Commentaries, trans. T. H. L. Parker, ed. David W. and Thomas F. Torrance (Grand Rapids: Eerdmans, 1996), 54.

8. F. F. Bruce, "Habakkuk," in *The Minor Prophets: An Exegetical and Expository Commentary,* ed. Thomas Edward McComiskey, 3 vols. (Grand Rapids: Baker, 1993), 2:860.

first he was uncertain what it meant. Later he went through a dark period of illness and depression during which he imagined that he was under the wrath of God. Lying on a bed in Italy, and fearing that he was soon to die, Luther found himself repeating the words over and over again: "The righteous will live by his faith. The righteous will live by his faith."

Not long after he recovered, Luther went on to Rome, where he visited the church of St. John Lateran. The pope had promised an indulgence forgiving the sins of any pilgrim who mounted its staircase, which was alleged to have come from the judgment hall of Pontius Pilate. Believing that the steps were stained with blood of Christ, pilgrims mounted the stairs on their knees, pausing frequently to pray and kiss the holy staircase.

The story continues in the words of Luther's son, from a manuscript preserved in the library of Rudolstadt: "As he repeated his prayers on the Lateran staircase, the words of the prophet Habakkuk came suddenly to his mind: 'The just shall live by faith.' Thereupon he ceased his prayers, returned to Wittenberg, and took this as the chief foundation of all his doctrine." Luther no longer believed that there was anything he could do to gain favor with God, and he began to live by faith in God's Son. As Luther himself later said, "Before those words broke upon my mind I hated God and was angry with him. . . . But when, by the Spirit of God, I understood those words— 'The just shall live by faith!' 'The just shall live by faith!'—then I felt born again like a new man; I entered through the open doors into the very Paradise of God."[9]

Martin Luther rightly understood that the works of the law cannot justify the way faith can. The law is a different way of living entirely, and it operates according to a completely different principle. To illustrate the life-principle of the law, Paul quoted from the book of Leviticus: "The one who does them shall live by them" (Gal. 3:12). To quote the original passage in its entirety: "You shall follow my rules and keep my statutes and walk in them. I am the LORD your God. You shall therefore keep my statutes and my rules; if a person does them, he shall live by them: I am the LORD" (Lev. 18:4–5).

9. See James Montgomery Boice, *The Minor Prophets: An Expositional Commentary*, 2 vols. (Grand Rapids: Kregel, 1996), 2:91–92.

The law, as found in Leviticus and elsewhere, operates on a different basis from faith. The only blessings it has to offer are for those who keep it. As far as justification is concerned, the law is not for believers; it is only for doers. Therefore, the law is based on works. Thomas Schreiner offers this paraphrase to explain what Paul means: "Salvation by works of the law is contrary to faith, for salvation by works of law means that the one who does the law will live by his obedience."[10] This is the principle of the law: Just do it. If you do the law, you will be legally righteous, and you will live.

This implies that the law could save us if we could keep it. The trouble is—and this takes us back to the problem with the law in verse 10—that no one can keep it. If we could keep the law, we would be justified by the law; but we can't, so we won't. The principle of the law is living by doing; the problem with the law is that we cannot live up to it.

This is well illustrated by the Christian man who went out to dinner with a friend. While they were waiting for their meal, they began to talk about spiritual things. The man's friend happened to mention that he had not sinned for twenty years. It was such an outrageous boast that the Christian man hardly knew what to say. While he was trying to think of a reply, the waitress arrived with their food, and in her carelessness, she managed to dump the entire meal on his friend's lap. Immediately the man's friend began to curse the waitress. When the commotion finally died down, the Christian man said, "Well, I guess your streak is over!"

There are two ways to be justified. One is by works of the law. But this is doomed to fail because no one can continue to do everything written in the law, not even a man who says he hasn't sinned in twenty years. The other way to be justified is by faith, which alone can make a sinner righteous before God. Martin Luther explained God's true way of justifying sinners like this: "If you wish to placate Me, do not offer Me your works and merits. But believe in Jesus Christ, My only Son, who was born, who suffered, who was crucified, and who died for your sins. Then I will accept you and pronounce you righteous."[11]

10. Thomas R. Schreiner, *The Law and Its Fulfillment: A Pauline Theology of Law* (Grand Rapids: Baker, 1993), 60.

11. Martin Luther, *Lectures on Galatians, 1535*, trans. and ed. Jaroslav Pelikan, in *Luther's Works* (St. Louis: Concordia, 1963), 26:231.

THE PENALTY OF THE LAW

Luther rightly understood that only Christ can justify a sinner, and only through his cross. The apostle Paul explained it to the Galatians like this: "Christ redeemed us from the curse of the law by becoming a curse for us— for it is written, 'Cursed is everyone who is hanged on a tree' " (Gal. 3:13).

This verse is a reminder of the penalty first mentioned in verse 10. The penalty of the law is the wrath of God. God's law pronounces a curse on everyone who fails to keep it—a curse, remember, that we are all under. Therefore, if we are to be saved, the curse must be removed. And this is what Christ was doing on the cross: redeeming his people from the law's accursed penalty.

The word "redemption" comes from the marketplace. It refers to the payment of a price, as it sometimes does today. For example, the coupon on the top of a cereal box can be "redeemed" for a prize. In Paul's world, the word "redeemed" was most often used at the slave market, where it referred to the purchase price for a slave. Sometimes a friend or a relative would buy a slave back from captivity and set him free. The slave would thus be liberated through the payment of a ransom.

Ordinarily, a ransom price is paid by the highest bidder. In the case of the redemption of God's children, bound in slavery to sin, the price was the highest ransom of all. In the triumphant words of an ancient hymn by Venantius Honorius Fortunatus (530–609): "The royal banners forward go, / The cross shows forth redemption's flow. / Where He, by whom our flesh was made, / Our ransom in His flesh has paid." We have been redeemed by the very lifeblood of Jesus Christ.

When the New Testament speaks of the redemption of sinners, it customarily emphasizes redemption's costly price: "the Son of Man came not to be served but to serve, and to give his life as a ransom for many" (Matt. 20:28); "you were ransomed from the futile ways inherited from your forefathers, not with perishable things such as silver or gold, but with the precious blood of Christ, like that of a lamb without blemish or spot" (1 Peter 1:18–19).

In order to pay this priceless ransom, Jesus had to endure God's curse. To understand what this means, it helps to know the Old Testament law for the execution of a criminal: "And if a man has committed a crime punishable by death and he is put to death, and you hang him on a tree, his body shall not remain all night on the tree, but you shall bury him the same day, for a hanged man is cursed by God. You shall not defile the land that the LORD your God is giving you for an inheritance" (Deut. 21:22–23). The point of hanging a criminal in this way was to expose his capital crime to public shame. Hoisting his body onto a tree demonstrated that he was under God's curse. But he was not to be left on the tree overnight, for this would be an offense to God.

God's people took these regulations seriously. When Joshua defeated five Canaanite kings at Makkedah, he had their corpses displayed on five trees and taken down at sunset (Josh. 10:26). The same thing was done with seven sons of Saul at Gibeah (2 Sam. 21:6). Remember, too, that the Jewish leaders wanted to be sure to get Jesus down from the cross before sundown (John 19:31), so as not to desecrate the Sabbath. To hang on a tree was the ultimate curse.

Imagine, then, how offensive Christianity was to the Jews, because at the very heart of its message was a man hanging on a tree! The apostolic message was about a man who was so cursed by God that he was crucified. Yet rather than concealing this fact, the apostles drew attention to it. When Peter preached to the Jewish leaders in Jerusalem, he said, "The God of our fathers raised Jesus, whom you killed by hanging him *on a tree*" (Acts 5:30). Peter used the same word in his first letter: "He himself bore our sins in his body *on the tree*" (1 Peter 2:24). Or again, when Paul spoke in the synagogue at Pisidian Antioch, he described how Jesus was taken down "*from the tree*" (Acts 13:29).

The apostles almost went out of their way to call the cross a "tree." At the same time, they claimed that the crucified Jesus was also the Christ. To the Jews, this was absolute blasphemy: a cursed Messiah on a cursed cross. No wonder the cross was such a stumbling block to them! To put it in the most shocking and yet perhaps the most accurate way, the apostolic message was about a God-damned Messiah.

Jewish hostility to this idea is documented in several ancient texts. Writing in the second century, Justin (c. 100–165) recounts a conversation with Trypho the Jew, who refused to believe that God's Messiah could die on a tree. He said, "But whether Christ should be so shamefully crucified, this we are in doubt about. For whosoever is crucified is said in the law to be accursed, so that I am exceedingly incredulous on this point."[12] Another writer from the same period, Aristo of Pella, recorded a similar dispute between a Christian and a Jew concerning the crucifixion. When he realized what the Christian was claiming, the Jew, whose name was Papiscus, dismissed Jesus entirely, saying, "The execration of God is he that is hanged."[13] What could be more blasphemous than an alleged Messiah nailed to an accursed tree?

Perhaps Paul himself struggled with this question. He knew that Jesus was Lord when he met the risen Christ on the road to Damascus. But what could account for Christ's death on the cross? It seemed to be a real dilemma. How could the only man who ever continued to do everything written in the book of the law be subjected to its curse? Either through his study of the Scriptures or by direct revelation, Paul was given this amazing resolution: "Christ redeemed us from the curse of the law by becoming a curse for us" (Gal. 3:13). "The language here is startling, almost shocking," wrote A. W. F. Blunt. "We should not have dared to use it. Yet Paul means every word of it."[14]

Paul meant every word because he understood what Christ was doing on the cross. His death was a substitution; he was crucified in our place. As Paul wrote to the Corinthians, "[God] made him to be sin who knew no sin" (2 Cor. 5:21). And when he took our sins upon himself, Christ also had to bear God's curse, becoming "a curse for us" (Gal. 3:13). The death penalty for breaking the law was executed on Jesus Christ. He was condemned by the very curses that were once shouted from Mount Ebal.

The law's accursed penalty did not apply to Jesus personally because he never broke the law, but God imputed our sins to his Son. Martin Luther's explanation is worth quoting at length:

> The whole emphasis is on the phrase "for us." For Christ is innocent so far as His own Person is concerned; therefore He should not have been hanged from the tree. But because, according to the Law, every thief should have been hanged, therefore, according to the Law of Moses, Christ Himself should have

---

12. Justin Martyr, *Dialogue with Trypho, a Jew*, in *Ante-Nicene Fathers*, ed. Alexander Roberts and James Donaldson, 10 vols. (New York, 1885; repr. Peabody, MA: Hendrickson, 1994), 1:244.

13. Aristo of Pella, *Disputation of Papiscus and Jason*, in *Ante-Nicene Fathers*, ed. Alexander Roberts and James Donaldson, 10 vols. (New York, 1886; repr. Peabody, MA: Hendrickson, 1994), 8:749.

14. A. W. F. Blunt, *The Epistle of Paul to the Galatians*, The Clarendon Bible (Oxford: Oxford University Press, 1925), 96–97.

been hanged; for He bore the person of a sinner and a thief—and not of one but of all sinners and thieves. For we are sinners and thieves, and therefore we are worthy of death and eternal damnation. But Christ took all our sins upon Himself, and for them He died on the cross. . . .

He is not acting in His own Person now. Now He is not the Son of God, born of the Virgin. But He is a sinner, who has and bears the sin of Paul, the former blasphemer, persecutor, and assaulter; of Peter, who denied Christ; of David, who was an adulterer and a murderer, and who caused the Gentiles to blaspheme the name of the Lord. In short, He has and bears all the sins of all men in His body—not in the sense that He has committed them but in the sense that He took these sins, committed by us, upon His own body, in order to make satisfaction for them with His own blood.[15]

When Christ took our sins upon himself he was accursed, not for his own sins, but for ours. The curse we deserved was legally transferred from us to him. Luther described this as the "fortunate exchange" in which we trade our sin and the curse it deserves for Christ's righteousness: "So long as sin, death, and the curse remain in us, sin damns us, death kills us, and the curse curses us; but when these things are transferred to Christ, what is ours becomes His and what is His becomes ours. Let us learn, therefore, in every temptation to transfer sin, death, the curse, and all the evils that oppress us from ourselves to Christ, and, on the other hand, to transfer righteousness, life, and blessing from Him to us."[16]

Now perhaps we can begin to understand the meaning of Christ's cry of dereliction from the cross: "My God, my God, why have you forsaken me?" (Matt. 27:46). When he hung on the tree, God the Son was accursed by God the Father. The law's curse is God's curse because the law is God's law. Thus, Christ became an object of divine reprobation, cursed both by God and by his law.

In that old cursed cross we see the wrath of God against the sin of humanity. The cross is a public demonstration for all time of his condemnation. Having seen the God-man on the cursed tree, who can doubt the sinfulness of sin or the wrath of God?

15. Luther, *Galatians*, 26:277.
16. Ibid., 26:284.

Yet in the same cursed cross we see more clearly than anywhere else the power of divine grace. God endured God's own curse to save us from our sins. This is expressed beautifully in the words of the old American folk hymn:

> What wondrous love is this,
>   O my soul, O my soul,
> What wondrous love is this,
>   O my soul!
> What wondrous love is this,
>   that caused the Lord of bliss
> To bear the dreadful curse
>   for my soul, for my soul,
> To bear the dreadful curse for my soul!

THE PROMISE OF THE GOSPEL

The love of Christ is wondrous. He was crucified to remove the curse. Since we are no longer subject to the death penalty of the law, we can receive the promise of the gospel, "that in Christ Jesus the blessing of Abraham might come to the Gentiles, so that we might receive the promised Spirit through faith" (Gal. 3:14).

Here Paul summarizes everything he has been saying in this chapter. He reminds us of the blessing given to Abraham: a right standing with God. He reminds us that this blessing is for all the nations of the Gentiles. He reminds us that God's blessing includes receiving the Holy Spirit, with all his gifts and graces.

All these blessings could never come by works of the law. They come only "in Christ Jesus." This is the doctrine of union with Christ—that all of God's blessings come to us when we get into Jesus Christ. And the way to get into Jesus is by faith. All of God's blessings come only through faith in the cross of Christ. Through the old cursed cross the nations of the world receive forgiveness for their sins. Through the old cursed cross we are accepted by God's justifying grace. Through the old cursed cross we receive the promised Holy Spirit.

We receive all these things by faith in the crucified Christ. Faith deserves to have the last word because it is the last word in Galatians 3:14. What was a curse for Christ becomes a blessing to us *by faith.*

10

THE PROMISE BEFORE THE LAW

Galatians 3:15—18

This is what I mean: the law, which came 430 years afterward,
does not annul a covenant previously ratified by God, so as to
make the promise void. For if the inheritance comes by the law,
it no longer comes by promise; but God gave it to Abraham
by a promise. (Gal. 3:17–18)

woman died and left all her property to a Christian university. Or so it seemed. According to the precise terms of her will, all her "worldly goods" were "bequeathed" to a particular educational institution. The woman's children, who lived on the other side of the country, were surprised to discover that they had been left out of their mother's estate. "Surprised" is hardly the word for it. They were outraged that the college had "taken advantage" of their mother in this way.

The children decided to contest the will in a court of law. They tried to claim that their mother's bequest applied only to personal effects and not to real estate. But in the end they lost their case and, with it, any chance of gaining an inheritance. There was nothing they could do to change the terms of the will. As far as the law was concerned, the matter had been settled when the old woman died.

THE PERMANENCE OF THE COVENANT

This is the kind of legal situation Paul has in mind in Galatians 3:15. Throughout this chapter he has been proving that justification and the Holy Spirit come by faith and not by works. First he argued from experience—the experience the Galatians had when they received the Holy Spirit (Gal. 3:1–5). Next he argued from Scripture—the biblical record about Abraham, the man of faith (Gal. 3:6–14). But when it comes to making a theological point, it always helps to have a good illustration, so next Paul takes "a human example" (Gal. 3:15). His illustration comes from the world of jurisprudence. According to standard legal practice, "with a man-made covenant, no one annuls it or adds to it once it has been ratified" (Gal. 3:15). The covenant is permanent.

By "covenant," Paul does not have in mind a legal contract for a business transaction. He refers instead to a covenant for an inheritance, what today might be called a "last will and testament." Whereas the Greek word *diathēkē* usually means "covenant," it can also mean "testament," and in this passage the latter is the better translation. A will is not a contract. It does not set terms that various parties are obligated to fulfill. Instead, it simply declares what one party intends to do. A last will and testament is a legal arrangement in which one party bestows his or her estate on someone else. It is a grant rather than a bargain.

The kind of human covenant Paul has in mind is also irrevocable. Once it is signed, sealed, and delivered, it cannot be changed. There is no way to set it aside or add to it. It cannot be abrogated or annulled. It cannot be amended or adjusted. It is legally binding exactly as it stands.

There is some debate as to which legal system Paul had in mind when he spoke about this human covenant. Roman law was like English law. Roman covenants *could* be annulled or added to. A man (usually property owners were men) could tear up his old will and write a new one at any time. Or he could add a codicil to change the terms of his original will. Among the Romans, it was only when the man died that his testament could no longer be altered. If Paul was thinking in terms of Roman law, this is what he meant by "ratified." A last will and testament was permanently settled at death. American jurisprudence works the same way. Once an estate has gone through probate, it cannot be redivided.

Greek law was slightly different from Roman law. According to the Greeks, a will could *not* be repealed or revoked. It could not even be modified. Once it had been properly registered and deposited at the public-record office, a Greek testament could never be altered.[1] This practice would fit Paul's point exactly: once the covenant was made, it was irrevocable.

But perhaps the apostle was thinking in terms of Jewish inheritance law. The Jews had a special procedure for making an irrevocable testament prior to death.[2] This was called *mattenat bari,* and there is a good example in the story Jesus told about the prodigal son: "There was a man who had two sons. And the younger of them said to his father, 'Father, give me the share of property that is coming to me'" (Luke 15:11–12). The younger son asked for his inheritance before his father died. In other words, he was asking for *mattenat bari,* an irrevocable testament that could be neither added to nor annulled.

It is not certain which legal system is intended in Galatians 3, but it hardly matters. In any legal system, there comes a time when a testament is settled once and for all, either by death or by some official action. After that point, nothing can be done to change the terms in any way.

If this is true at the human level, it is all the more true when it comes to the covenant God established through Abraham: "Just as no one can set aside a human covenant that has been duly established, so it is in this case" (Gal. 3:15 NIV). Paul's argument is from the lesser to the greater. What holds true in a human court has even greater force in the courtroom of Almighty God.

The analogy of a last will and testament is a good one because it has several points of comparison with the Abrahamic covenant. Consider the conditions of that arrangement, which the Scripture repeatedly calls a "covenant" (Gen. 15:18; 17:2; etc.). And since it was a covenant, Paul was able to compare it to the covenants of his day. As far as covenants go, what God proposed to Abraham was more like a testament. It was not a contract set up between relative equals. On the contrary, it contained a long list of things God promised to grant as his legacy to Abraham.

1. F. F. Bruce, *The Epistle to the Galatians: A Commentary on the Greek Text,* New International Greek Testament Commentary (Grand Rapids: Eerdmans, 1982), 170–71.
2. Timothy George, *Galatians,* New American Commentary 30 (Nashville: Broadman & Holman, 1994), 246.

The Abrahamic covenant was properly established. In those days, legal agreements were not based on a handshake or a piece of paper. Instead, they were sealed in blood by a covenant ceremony:

> [God] said to him, "Bring me a heifer three years old, a female goat three years old, a ram three years old, a turtledove, and a young pigeon." And he brought him all these, cut them in half, and laid each half over against the other. . . .
>
> When the sun had gone down and it was dark, behold, a smoking fire pot and a flaming torch passed between these pieces. On that day the LORD made a covenant with Abram. (Gen. 15:9–10, 17–18)

The animals were sacrificed and God passed between them, thus validating his covenant in a legally binding way.

Paul's point is that what God covenanted to do for Abraham that night would remain in force forever: "Paul regards the promise to Abraham as a divinely ratified settlement or covenant and argues from its considerable priority to the law that its provisions cannot be made null and void by the later introduction of the law."[3] One cannot adjust the terms of a human testament, much less a divine one. Therefore, once God duly established his covenant, it could never be annulled or amended. It was permanent.

THE PARTY TO THE COVENANT

What does all this have to do with the Galatians, or with us? Paul answers this question by identifying the party to the covenant: "Now the promises were made to Abraham and to his offspring. It does not say, 'And to offsprings,' referring to many, but referring to one, 'And to your offspring,' who is Christ" (Gal. 3:16).

Here again Paul proves to be a careful student of the Old Testament. God repeated his promises to Abraham on several occasions. Often he made his promise to Abraham's offspring as well as to Abraham himself: "Then the LORD appeared to Abram and said, 'To your offspring I will give this land'" (Gen. 12:7); "all the land that you see I will give to you and to your offspring forever" (Gen. 13:15); "To your offspring I will give this land" (Gen. 24:7).

---

3. Ronald Y. K. Fung, *The Epistle to the Galatians*, New International Commentary on the New Testament (Grand Rapids: Eerdmans, 1988), 157.

In Galatians, what Paul wishes to emphasize about the word "offspring" is that it occurs in the singular. The Bible says "offspring," not "offsprings."

By resting his case on the ending of a noun, the apostle teaches something important about the authority of the Bible. How could he make such a precise point from the Hebrew text of the Old Testament unless he believed that the Bible is God's Word written? Even though he did not use these precise words, Paul obviously believed that the Bible is infallible and inerrant from beginning to end.

Some scholars argue that at this point Paul is reading too much into the grammar of the Old Testament. For example, as part of his New Perspective on Paul and the law, E. P. Sanders claims that Paul "was not concerned with the meaning of biblical passages in their own ancient context. He had in Scripture a vast store of words, and if he could find passages which had the right combination of words, and stick them together, he scored his point."[4] In this particular instance, Sanders and other scholars point out that "offspring" is actually a collective noun. In other words, although its form is singular, it can refer to a plurality. Another example of a collective noun is the word "family." Although "family" appears in the singular, it actually refers to more than one individual. In the same way, the word "offspring" can refer either to an individual child or to all of a man's descendants.

The truth is that Paul and the other inspired authors of the New Testament paid careful attention to the grammar and context of the Old Testament passages they quoted, and this is a perfect example. Paul knew full well that "offspring" was a collective noun. In fact, he uses the word that way several times, including later in this very chapter (Gal. 3:29). He also knew that the offspring God promised to Abraham would be as numerous as the sand and the stars. But Paul wanted to explain that God's covenant promises referred to someone in particular. In Galatians 3:16 he is not so much making an argument based on Old Testament grammar as he is explaining what the Old Testament really means. The promise of the offspring referred first of all to Abraham's son Isaac. Ultimately it referred to all of God's children, but especially to God's Son, Jesus Christ.

Jesus Christ is the true offspring. He is the party to the covenant that God made with Abraham. The covenant was all about Jesus Christ. It looked for-

---

4. E. P. Sanders, *Paul* (Oxford: Oxford University Press, 1991), 56.

ward to his coming. This is why Paul could claim, just a few verses earlier, that the Scripture "preached the gospel beforehand to Abraham" (Gal. 3:8). What God promised to Abraham was the good news about Jesus Christ, for it is in him that all nations on earth are blessed.

This shows how God's covenant with Abraham has something to do with us. As Paul explained earlier in the chapter, we do not have to be biologically related to Abraham to claim his inheritance. All we need is faith in Jesus Christ. The true sons of Abraham are not identified biologically, but Christologically.[5] The covenant promise was really for Christ, and when we belong to Christ, the promise belongs to us.

Once we understand that God's promise to Abraham is a promise to Christ, then the fact that the word "offspring" is a collective noun makes perfect sense. A collective noun can refer either to a single individual, or to a group of individuals, or to both. So it is with the offspring of Abraham. The promise refers first of all to a single individual, Jesus Christ. But it also refers to a collection of individuals, namely, everyone who belongs to Christ. The party to the covenant is Christ and all who are in him. God gave the promise to Abraham. The promise was Christ. Since we are in Christ, the promise is for us. In the words of the Puritan William Perkins, "The promises made to Abraham are first made to Christ, and then in Christ to all that believe in him."[6]

Here we are reminded again of the doctrine of union with Christ, which is so central to Galatians and to Paul's theology in general. The Christian is *in* Christ. We participate in him. By faith we are incorporated into him. We have covenant solidarity with him. We are so united to Christ that what is his becomes ours. To quote again from Perkins, "The right way to obtain any blessing of God, is first to receive the promise, and in the promise Christ: and Christ being ours; in him, and from him, we shall receive all things necessary."[7]

It is almost as if there is only one party to the covenant: Jesus Christ. But this is exactly what the Galatians were in danger of forgetting. By trusting in the works of the law, they were dividing the church along racial lines: Jews on one side, Gentiles on the other. They were not united in Christ. Paul used

---

5. George, 247.

6. William Perkins, *A Commentary on Galatians*, Pilgrim Classic Commentaries, ed. Gerald T. Sheppard (London, 1617; repr. New York: Pilgrim, 1989), 184.

7. Ibid., 186.

the promise to the offspring, therefore, to remind them that God's eternal plan is for one family in one Christ. By the time he gets to the end of chapter 3, this will be the climax of his argument: "in Christ Jesus you are all sons of God through faith. . . . And if you are Christ's, then you are Abraham's offspring, heirs according to promise" (Gal. 3:26, 29).

THE PROMISE OF THE COVENANT

"Promise" is a key word in Galatians 3, appearing eight times in the last fifteen verses. What Paul says about the promise of the covenant is that it comes before the law.

Perhaps this is a good place to review the apostle's argument: Verse 15 described the *permanence* of the covenant, which was established once and for all when God gave it to Abraham. Verse 16 identified the *party* to the covenant. God's promise to Abraham was also made to Christ, and to everyone who is in him. Next Paul clarifies the *promise* of the covenant, saying, "This is what I mean: the law, which came 430 years afterward, does not annul a covenant previously ratified by God, so as to make the promise void" (Gal. 3:17).

The promise and the law are two separate, though complementary, arrangements. They operate on entirely different principles: faith and works. The promise is about what God will do, while the law is about what we must do. The difference between the promise and the law is evident from the vocabulary God used when he first gave them. When he made the promise to Abraham, God said, "I will, I will, I will." But in the law of Moses God said, "Thou shalt, thou shalt, thou shalt."

The law and the promise operate in entirely different ways, a difference John Stott explains as follows: "The promise sets forth a religion of God— God's plan, God's grace, God's initiative. But the law sets forth a religion of man—man's duty, man's works, man's responsibility. The promise (standing for the grace of God) had only to be believed. But the law (standing for the works of men) had to be obeyed."[8] And when we say that the promise

---

8. John R. W. Stott, *The Message of Galatians: Only One Way*, The Bible Speaks Today (Downers Grove, IL: InterVarsity, 1968), 86–87.

had to be believed, we do not mean a belief that is bare assent, but a firm and trusting grasp of God and all that he has promised in Christ.

These two different principles—promise and law—are not on equal terms. One has the priority. Within God's covenant of grace, it is the promise that takes precedence over the law. The law is secondary within the history of redemption, not primary. The law principle is subordinate to the promise principle.

For one thing, the promise came first in time. God gave Abraham the promise long before he gave Moses the law. In keeping with the length of Israel's captivity in Egypt (Ex. 12:40–41), Paul says that the law came almost half a millennium later, 430 years after the promise. Some might argue that the law therefore superseded the promise. Or that the law supplemented the promise, which is what the Judaizers were trying to teach the Galatians. They wanted to add works to faith as the basis of their standing before God. In other words, they were trying to make the law an addendum to the promise.

This is exactly why Paul introduced his legal illustration. God's promise to Abraham was an irrevocable covenant. It had the same status that a will has after it has gone through probate. There was no way it could be invalidated. The law could not replace the promise. It could not even supplement the promise. Once God made his covenant, it could never be annulled or added to.

This means that the gospel has more to do with Abraham than it does with Moses. The Judaizers were fond of Moses, which is why they tried to introduce a legalistic version of Christianity. They said that the law was necessary to make the promise complete. It took works to finish what faith had started. By the time the Judaizers were finished with them, the Galatians needed to be reintroduced to the doctrine of justification by faith alone. For as far as justification is concerned, the law is just a Moses-come-lately. It did not change the terms of God's promise, as if God had signed a contract with Abraham and then changed his mind by adding some fine print for Moses.

Besides, if the law had been necessary for salvation, it would have come too late to do Abraham any good! When God gave Moses the law, Abraham had been dead for centuries. Fortunately, he had been justified by faith long before the law of Moses was even introduced. Abraham's salvation was not based on anything Abraham did. The covenant did not establish any legal requirements that he had to satisfy. It all came free, the way an inheritance always does. God's covenant with Abraham came with no strings attached—no ifs, ands, or buts. The covenant was entirely a matter of promise, received by faith.

HEIRS OF THE PROMISE

If the covenant was based on promise, then it could not come through the law. This is the conclusion of Paul's argument: "For if the inheritance comes by the law, it no longer comes by promise; but God gave it to Abraham by a promise" (Gal. 3:18). This is the way inheritance law always operates. A beneficiary receives an inheritance on the basis of a binding legal promise. Therefore, if God has promised an inheritance, it must come by way of promise, and not by works of the law.

This brings us back to the point Paul has been trying to make all through this letter, the point recovering Pharisees keep needing to hear: God deals with us according to his promise, and not according to our performance. We are justified by faith only and not by works: "If God's covenant was established by faith and not by works of the law, then the covenantal relationship God has with the Galatians through Christ is also by faith and not by works of the law."[9] It was the same for the Galatians as it was for Abraham, and it is also the same for us: we are justified by grace through faith.

To see why this is so, it helps to remember how promises work. It is impossible to earn a promise. The only way to receive a promise is to trust in it. If a wealthy benefactor promises to give me a house in Laguna Beach, there is nothing I can do to fulfill the promise. The only thing I can do is to trust him to keep his promise (or not, as the case may be). I may decide it is prudent to secure my own housing, just in case my would-be benefactor fails to make good on his promise. But I cannot fulfill his promise to me on his behalf.

So it is with the promises of God's covenant. Only God can fulfill them. Therefore, when he promises us salvation, it follows that we cannot earn it for ourselves: "For the promise to Abraham and his offspring that he would

9. Scot McKnight, *Galatians*, NIV Application Commentary (Grand Rapids: Zondervan, 1995), 165–66.

be heir of the world did not come through the law but through the righteousness of faith. For if it is the adherents of the law who are to be the heirs, faith is null and the promise is void" (Rom. 4:13–14).

This brings us to a very practical conclusion: God deals with us according to his promises, not according to our works. Everything God has to offer comes through a promise. And so, writes John Stott, "every sinner who trusts in Christ crucified for salvation, quite apart from any merit or good works, receives the blessing of eternal life and thus inherits the promise of God made to Abraham."[10] As it was for Abraham, so it is for everyone who is in Christ.

Salvation in Christ does not rest on a law that we inevitably break; it rests on a promise that God *cannot* break. God has promised forgiveness of sins through the death and resurrection of Jesus Christ. He has promised eternal life to everyone who comes to Christ in faith. God will not—indeed, he cannot—go back on his promise. His covenant is an irrevocable will and testament. It stands firm forever.

Salvation in Christ is not a commercial transaction. My relationship with God is not based on my ability to make a deal or strike a bargain. The Christian life is not a quid pro quo, so that if I do what God wants, then God will do what I want. God simply does not operate this way. Instead, my relationship with God is based entirely on believing his gracious promise.

What God promises is an inheritance, and it is the right of whoever bestows an inheritance to set his own terms. God can do what he wants with his spiritual blessings. His legacy includes forgiveness of sins, fellowship with Christ in the Spirit, and the free gift of eternal life. What God has decided to do with his legacy is to give it clear away. As the Scripture says, "God gave it to Abraham by a promise" (Gal. 3:18). The word "gave" appears in the perfect tense to show a past action with present results. It means that salvation is a gift given once and for all and then kept forever.

Since salvation is a matter of God's free grace, we do not have to work to obtain it. No one ever works for an inheritance! It is a gift, not a paycheck. We receive our inheritance from God the same way Abraham received it: by faith. We simply believe that God will make good on his promise to save us through the death and resurrection of Jesus Christ. And then, of course, we

10. Stott, *Message of Galatians*, 89.

act on our faith, living like the true heirs of God that we have become through his covenant in Christ.

A good illustration of what this means in practical terms comes from a professor on a university campus in the Far East. One of his students came to him in despair and confided that he was a practicing homosexual. "I feel like a slave," the young man lamented. The professor responded with the loving truth. "You are a slave," he said, and then he began to teach him about gaining freedom from sin through faith in Jesus Christ.

This was so attractive to the student that he wanted to become a Christian himself. But there was one thing that held him back: the thought that he was not good enough for God. How could God forgive him for everything he had done? So he said to his professor, "First I must become a Christian like you. Then God will love me."

The professor responded by saying, "*I'm* not a Christian like me, either. I'm no better than you are, except for the love and power of God. He loves you now as you are." This is the grace of God, that he does not deal with us on the basis of our performance, but on the basis of his promise. No matter what we have done, our sins are covered by the covenant righteousness of Christ. And now that we are in Christ, our standing before God does not fluctuate with the inconsistency of our daily obedience. On the basis of the promise that he made before the law, God loves us with an unconditional love.

11

THE LAW LEADING TO CHRIST

Galatians 3:19—25

*So then, the law was our guardian until Christ came, in order
that we might be justified by faith. But now that faith has come,
we are no longer under a guardian.* (Gal. 3:24–25)

or two glorious summers, the Chicago Cubs taught baseball
fans the fundamentals of Reformation theology. First the Cub-
bies made a trade for Vance Law and started him at third base.
Then a few months later, marvelous to say, they brought first baseman Mark
Grace up from the minor leagues. There they were, right next to each other
in the batting order: Law and Grace. They were in the proper order, too, first
Grace, batting in the fifth position, and then Law. For as Paul explained to
the Galatians, God gave grace to Abraham before he gave Moses the law. And
there they stood on the baseball diamond—Grace and Law—holding down
the opposite corners of the infield. Opposing batters would smash the ball
to third, where Law would knock it down and throw it over to first for the
out. Reformation theology in action: Law to Grace to retire the side.[1]

The apostle Paul never had to suffer through a long losing season at
Wrigley Field, but he would have loved Chicago's theology. Law and grace
are not opponents; they are teammates working together for the salvation

1. This illustration was first presented by Mark A. Noll in "Diamond Devotional," *Reformed Journal*, July 1989, 6–7.

of God's people. The law leads to grace, which is to be found only in Christ. This is what Paul demonstrated as he answered the question: "Why then the law?" (Gal. 3:19).

THE LAW REVEALS SIN

This question was an obvious one to raise. In Galatians 3 Paul has been arguing that God's blessings come by grace through faith, and not by the law. He has appealed to experience, to Scripture, and to daily life to prove that justification and the Holy Spirit come through a promise. But if everything God has to offer comes by way of promise, then who needs the law? Does the law serve a purpose, or is it superfluous?

The law, because it is God's law, has a place in God's plan. In the first place, it reveals sin: "Why then the law? It was added because of transgressions" (Gal. 3:19). This statement raises as many questions as it answers. We already know that the law was added. God gave it 430 years after he gave Abraham the promise. But what does it mean that the law was added "because of transgressions"? Of the several uses of God's law, which one is in view here?

One possibility is that the law was added to deal with bad behavior, either through its system of sacrifices or through its penalties. Because the law has consequences, it has some ability to control transgression. In addition to showing the difference between right and wrong, it shows how wrongdoers ought to be punished, and the fear of that punishment helps to restrain evil. The law thus has a deterrent effect within human society. Calvin called this "the second use of the law." The power of the law in government helps restrain evil. So when Paul said that the law was added "because of transgressions," perhaps he meant that God gave it to help people avoid sin.

It is more likely, however, that he meant exactly the opposite. Sometimes the law restrains sin, but this is not why God gave Moses the law with all its regulations and requirements. He did not give it to decrease transgression, but actually to *increase* it. The law exposes sin for what it really is, namely, a violation of God's holy standard. That is what transgression means: the crossing of a legal boundary or the breaking of a specific law.

The law has a way of making people want to break it. Paul explained this effect of the law to the Romans. "If it had not been for the law," he wrote, "I would not have known sin" (Rom. 7:7). And as soon as Paul found out what

131

sin was, he wanted to try it: "The law came in to increase the trespass" (Rom. 5:20). Or, to paraphrase what Paul said to the Galatians, the law was given "in order that there might be transgressions."[2] Sometimes the law serves as a stimulus to sin.

One purpose of the law, then, is not preventive but provocative.[3] Rather than preventing transgression, the law actually provokes people to sin. By doing so, it does not make things better, but makes a bad situation even worse: "For by works of the law no human being will be justified in his sight, since through the law comes knowledge of sin" (Rom. 3:20). God did not give the law to reveal the way to be justified; he gave it to disclose the evil power of sin. "Therefore," wrote Martin Luther, "the true function and the chief and proper use of the Law is to reveal to man his sin, blindness, misery, wickedness, ignorance, hate and contempt of God, death, hell, judgment, and the well-deserved wrath of God."[4]

Yet this is a good thing. When the Scripture says that the law was "added," it literally says that the law came in by a side road. The law feeds into the promise; it is the on-ramp to the gospel highway. The more we know the law, the more we see our sin, and the more we see this, the more we confess that we need a Savior. "The law was given," wrote Calvin, "in order to make transgressions obvious, and in this way to compel men to acknowledge their guilt."[5] And it is only when we see our guilt that we see how much we need Jesus. The law is the law so that Christ can become our Savior.

THE LAW HAS ITS LIMITS

Calvin called the law's ability to reveal sin the "first use of the law." This is not the law's only use, of course. As we have seen, its second use is to restrain evil. There is also a "third use of the law." Paul will introduce this use in chap-

2. F. F. Bruce, *The Epistle to the Galatians: A Commentary on the Greek Text*, New International Greek Testament Commentary (Grand Rapids: Eerdmans, 1982), 175.

3. Timothy George, *Galatians*, New American Commentary 30 (Nashville: Broadman & Holman, 1994), 253.

4. Martin Luther, *Lectures on Galatians, 1535*, trans. and ed. Jaroslav Pelikan, in *Luther's Works* (St. Louis: Concordia, 1963), 26:309.

5. John Calvin, *The Epistles of Paul the Apostle to the Galatians, Ephesians, Philippians and Colossians*, Calvin's New Testament Commentaries, trans. T. H. L. Parker, ed. David W. and Thomas F. Torrance (Grand Rapids: Eerdmans, 1996), 61.

ter 5, where the law shows the Christian how to live for Christ. But first the law has to reveal our sin.

The first use of the law is temporary. The law reveals sin for only a certain period of time. As far as its first use is concerned, the law is a sort of parenthesis between the promise given to Abraham and the fulfillment of the promise in Jesus Christ.

In one sense God's law is eternal. God has a perfect, permanent moral standard for his people. This standard was made known already to Adam, and it will last for all eternity because it is based on the very character of God.[6] There is another sense, however, in which God's law is temporary. The specific administration of the law given to Moses—with all its ceremonies, curses, and sacrifices—had its limits. As far as the history of salvation is concerned, its usefulness as a preparation for the gospel was only temporary. It was in force only "until the offspring should come to whom the promise had been made" (Gal. 3:19).

Paul explained what "the offspring" meant back in verse 16. God's eternal, unbreakable covenant promise was made to Abraham and to his offspring, in the singular. The promise was made in the singular because it referred to a specific individual, namely, God the Son. When the Son came, the work of the law was finished. The law was thus limited in its duration. The time for it to reveal sin and increase transgression lasted only from Mount Sinai to Mount Calvary.

The law had another limitation, too, and this had to do with the way it was given: "it was put in place through angels by an intermediary" (Gal. 3:19). It is difficult to know precisely what this means, or quite how it fits into Paul's argument. Angels are not specifically mentioned in Exodus 19, where God gave the law to Moses in a thick cloud, with thunder and lightning, fire and smoke, and earthquakes and trumpets. Yet Moses mentioned the angels shortly before he died. As he blessed God's people, he looked back on the way God had given him the law and said:

The Lord came from Sinai
and dawned from Seir upon us;
he shone forth from Mount Paran;

6. See Philip Graham Ryken, *Written in Stone: The Ten Commandments and Today's Moral Crisis* (Wheaton, IL: Crossway, 2003), 11–25.

> he came from the ten thousands of holy ones,
>> with flaming fire at his right hand. (Deut. 33:2)

When God gave Moses the law, he was accompanied by countless hosts of angels.

This is confirmed elsewhere in Scripture. David sang, "The chariots of God are twice ten thousand, thousands upon thousands; the Lord is among them; Sinai is now in the sanctuary" (Ps. 68:17). Not only were the angels with God when he gave the law, but the law was actually given through them. So when Stephen preached the gospel to the Jewish leaders, he said that the law was "delivered by angels" (Acts 7:53). Similarly, the writer to the Hebrews called it "the message declared by angels" (Heb. 2:2).

The fact that God gave the law through angels must have fascinated the Judaizers. They were trying to convince the Galatians that they had to keep the law to fulfill the gospel. Perhaps they used the fact that God spoke through angels to give the law added authority.

As far as Paul was concerned, however, the role of the angels did nothing to enhance the law. Quite the opposite. When compared with the promise, coming through angels put the law at a decided disadvantage. This is what Paul is hinting at when he says that the law was put into effect "by an intermediary" (Gal. 3:19). The promise had no such mediator. God gave it immediately to Abraham on the basis of his own eternal, immutable will.[7] But the law came to God's people indirectly, through angels and by a mediator, meaning Moses. Moses served as the go-between, for "an intermediary implies more than one, but God is one" (Gal. 3:20). God spoke to the people through Moses, and Moses spoke for the people to God.

Having a mediator distinguishes the law from the promise and shows how sin put human beings at a disadvantage. The promise came unmediated, straight from God to Abraham. However, the law required a mediator because sinners cannot come directly into God's presence; we stand at a dis-

---

7. Steven Baugh writes: "The mediation of the law through angels by the hand of Moses was not an 'eternal ordinance ordained and written in the heavenly tablets' and thereby representing an intractable principle of inheritance of God's promises overthrowing faith in Christ. Rather, the promises of God to a fallen world are rooted in his sovereign, intratrinitarian counsel, traditionally called the *pactum salutis*, which Moses did not and could not mediate, for God is one" ("Galatians 3:20 and the Covenant of Redemption," *Westminster Theological Journal* 66.1 [Spring 2004]: 69–70).

tance. As Stephen Neill comments, "The promise came to Abraham first-hand from God; and the law comes to the people *third-hand*—God—the angels—Moses the mediator—the people."[8]

These verses show the danger of giving angels more attention than they deserve. In these postmodern times, angels have become trendy. They have their own books, calendars, movies, and television programs. There are even angels in the outfield, at least in Anaheim, where the Angels play baseball. But real angels have no interest in being worshiped themselves. They are totally absorbed with God, and all they would have us do is join them in adoring him.

But to return to the main argument, the law has its limits. It had a limited function, for a limited time. Unlike the promise, it was delivered by angels, which made it secondary. And since eventually it gave way to the promise, it was only temporary.

The Law Cannot Give Life

The more Paul talks about the limits of the law, the more it sounds as if the law stands in contradiction to the promise. Throughout this chapter Paul draws a sharp contrast between working the law and trusting in the promise. Law and promise are two entirely different principles, of which the law is clearly inferior. So the apostle asks the obvious question: "Is the law then contrary to the promises of God?" (Gal. 3:21). This is a variation on the question raised in verse 19. If the law does have a purpose, isn't that purpose somehow at odds with God's promise?

That question is so thoroughly reasonable that Paul's answer comes as a total surprise. The law is opposed to the promise, right? "Certainly not!" (Gal. 3:21). Paul takes what seems to be the logical conclusion of his argument and utterly rejects it. God forbid that the law should stand against the promise!

The reason that the law was not at odds with the promise is that it had a totally different purpose. Unlike the promise, it could not give life. If it could have done so, then the promise would have been unnecessary: "For if a law had been given that could impart life, then righteousness would certainly

8. Stephen C. Neill, *Paul to the Galatians* (Lutterworth, UK: World Christian Books, 1958), 44.

have come by the law" (Gal. 3:21 NIV). This is what the Judaizers had been telling the Galatians, that the way to get a righteous life was by keeping the law. They probably would have agreed with these popular sayings from the Mishnah: "Lots of Torah, lots of life"; "If he has gotten teachings of Torah, he has gotten himself life eternal."[9]

This way of looking at the law is tempting for former Pharisees, with their performance-based approach to Christianity. But the law cannot give life. Remember the principle on which it operates: "The one who does them shall live by them" (Gal. 3:12). In other words, the law offers God's blessing only to those who are able to keep it. And the problem, of course, is that no one (except Jesus Christ) is able to keep it.

The problem with the law is not the law, but the fact that we break it every day. Therefore, as Paul has said before, and will say again, no one can be justified by works of the law. The law can prove that we are sinners, but it cannot make us right with God. It is not life-giving; it is transgression-increasing, and therefore death-producing. As Paul confided to the Romans, "I was once alive apart from the law, but when the commandment came, sin came alive and I died. The very commandment that promised life proved to be death to me. For sin, seizing an opportunity through the commandment, deceived me and through it killed me" (Rom. 7:9–11).

The law is something like chemotherapy.[10] When chemotherapy is used to treat cancer, it does not give life. Actually, it is an instrument of death. The chemicals that are poured into the body destroy healthy tissue as well as cancer cells. During the course of treatment, chemotherapy actually makes the patient feel much worse. But it is all necessary for the patient's long-term health. In much the same way, the law makes us worse so that Christ can make us better.

THE LAW DRIVES US TO FAITH

Paul set out in verse 19 to explain the purpose of the law. By verse 22 we are still waiting to discover what it is. So far the apostle has said more about what the law *cannot* do than what it can. It cannot give life; all it can do is

---

9. Mishnah Aboth 2:8, quoted in Scot McKnight, *Galatians*, NIV Application Commentary (Grand Rapids: Zondervan, 1995), 181.

10. This analogy is suggested in George, 260.

reveal sin. It does not come straight from God; it was mediated by angels. And it will not last forever; it lasted only until the coming of Christ. Yet even in its apparent failure, the law was doing God's work. It was not merely temporary; it was also preparatory. It was leading the way for something else: "But the Scripture imprisoned everything under sin, so that the promise by faith in Jesus Christ might be given to those who believe" (Gal. 3:22). The law itself cannot justify, but what it can do is drive us to faith, which *does* justify.

By "the Scripture," Paul means especially the law. As we have seen, one purpose of the law is to reveal sin, and in fact to increase it, so that the whole world becomes imprisoned by it. This is true for the Jews, who have the law of Moses, and also for the Gentiles, who have God's law written on their hearts (see Rom. 2:14–15). Therefore the whole world is under the law, convicted of sin and captive to its guilt.

By making this declaration of depravity, the law performs a valuable public service and proves that it still has a valuable place in the plan of salvation. The law is powerless to make anyone right with God. It cannot justify; it can only condemn. It cannot make us righteous; it can only lock us up in the prison of sin. But by showing that it cannot save, the law helps us to look for a Savior. And when the world starts looking for a way out of sin, it discovers that God's mercy is the only escape.

This is how the law leads to Christ. It cannot save, in and of itself, but it leads us to Christ, and he can save. Martin Luther explained it like this:

> The Law with its function does contribute to justification—not because it justifies, but because it impels one to the promise of grace and makes it sweet and desirable. Therefore we do not abolish the Law; but we show its true function and use, namely, that it is a most useful servant impelling us to Christ . . . ; for its function and use is not only to disclose the sin and wrath of God but also to drive us to Christ. . . . Therefore the principal purpose of the Law in theology is to make men not better but worse; that is, it shows them their sin, so that by the recognition of sin they may be humbled, frightened, and worn down, and so may long for grace and for the Blessed Offspring.[11]

11. Luther, *Galatians*, 26:315, 327.

When the law is used properly, therefore, it is not opposed to the promise. Rather than contradicting the promise, it is actually complementary to it. The law points to the promise by showing that only faith can justify. Thus it leads us to Christ, and when we believe in Christ, we receive all the blessings God promised to Abraham.

THE LAW IS LIKE A GUARDIAN

The apostle Paul concludes his argument with two illustrations that show how the law leads to Christ. The first comes from the prison system: "Now before faith came, we were held captive under the law, imprisoned until the coming faith would be revealed" (Gal. 3:23). In this analogy, the law is a prison warden to keep us locked up in sin's penitentiary. We are the inmates, and the law is our jail-keeper, or perhaps our prison cell. The law, with its penalties, restrains and punishes us.

It should be noted that although nobody likes to be a prisoner, it is not always a bad thing to be in prison. A good example comes from the life of the apostle himself. Many years after he wrote Galatians, Paul was arrested in Jerusalem and placed in a Roman garrison. While he was imprisoned, a group of enemies conspired not to eat or drink until Paul was assassinated (Acts 23:12). When this nefarious plot was uncovered, the Roman commander called out a detachment of 200 soldiers, 70 horsemen, and 200 spearmen to escort Paul to Caesarea. The apostle was still a prisoner, of course, but his captors actually saved his life. By placing a guard around him, they were eventually able to deliver him safely to Rome.

In much the same way, the law kept the Jews under its protective custody. It watched over them, keeping them safe until it could lead them to Christ. An old commentary by G. G. Findlay describes the situation like this:

> The law was all the while standing guard over its subjects, watching and checking every attempt to escape, but intending to hand them over in due time to the charge of faith. The law posts its ordinances, like so many sentinels, round the prisoner's cell. The cordon is complete. He tries again and again to break out; the iron circle will not yield. The deliverance will yet be his. The day of faith approaches. It dawned long ago in Abraham's promise. Even now its light shines into his dungeon, and he hears the word of Jesus, "Thy sins are

forgiven thee; go in peace." Law, the stern jailor, has after all been a good friend, if it has reserved him for this. It prevents the sinner escaping to a futile and illusive freedom.[12]

The law is a guardian, refusing to let go until it hands us directly over to Christ.

Paul then uses another illustration to make the same point, only this time it comes from the nursery: "So then, the law was our guardian until Christ came, in order that we might be justified by faith. But now that faith has come, we are no longer under a guardian" (Gal. 3:24–25). What Paul means by "guardian" is literally a "pedagogue"—a slave appointed to serve as a child's protector. In wealthy Greek families, children were individually raised by pedagogues. From age six until late adolescence, the child was under constant care and supervision. The pedagogue was part babysitter and part chaperone. Since he was in charge of discipline, the pedagogue was also part probation officer. Ancient drawings usually depict him holding a rod or a cane to administer corporal punishment.[13]

The pedagogue was not primarily a teacher, although sometimes he helped a child review his lessons. Thus the King James Version is somewhat misleading when it translates the word as "schoolmaster." The pedagogue did have to make sure that his pupil made it to and from school. He helped to feed and dress the child, and also to carry the child's educational tools (tablet and stylus, book or scroll, musical instrument).[14] Once at school, there was a special room where pedagogues waited for their young students until their lessons were finished. But the pedagogue was not the educator; he was the disciplinarian.

A pedagogue served the best interests of the child in many ways, and a close bond of affection often developed. Discipline was not necessarily severe, and the pedagogue provided protection as well as punishment. He also served as a moral tutor, shaping the child's ethics.

12. G. G. Findlay, quoted in George, 264.
13. John R. W. Stott, *The Message of Galatians: Only One Way*, The Bible Speaks Today (Downers Grove, IL: InterVarsity, 1968), 97.
14. Ben Witherington III, *Grace in Galatia: A Commentary on Paul's Letter to the Galatians* (Edinburgh: T & T Clark, 1998), 265.

In the plan of salvation, the law is the pedagogue that raised the Jews from childhood through adolescence. It was not a schoolmaster to teach them how to get better and better until God finally accepted them. On the contrary, the law was for discipline. It told God's people what to do, and then it punished them for failing to do it. There were times when the Jews chafed under this discipline (chaperones never have been very popular!). But all the while, the law was preparing God's children to enter their majority.

Like any pedagogue, the law eventually worked its way out of a job. When a child comes of age, it no longer needs constant supervision. The ancient Greek writer Xenophon (c. 428–c. 354 B.C.) explained, "When a boy ceases to be a child, and begins to be a lad, others *release* him from his 'pedagogue' and from his teacher; he is then *no longer under them*, but is allowed to go his own way."[15] In much the same way, the law was needed only until the coming of Christ.

This is what Paul means when he speaks of the coming of faith. In one sense, faith had already come, since God had always told his people to trust him. But what they trusted in was the Savior to come. The true object of their faith was Jesus Christ, and when he came on the scene, the time for the law was over and the era of faith had begun.

These two illustrations—the prison and the pedagogue—show that the law had the legitimate purpose of keeping us safe until Christ came to save us. God used the law "to shut us up in prison until Christ should set us free, or to put us under tutors until Christ should make us sons."[16]

This is true not just in the history of salvation, but also at the personal level. The law does the same things for us that it did for the Jews before the time of Christ. It reveals sin by showing that our misdeeds are transgressions of God's law. Sinners that we are, sometimes it actually increases our sin, thus imprisoning us in our guilt. The more the law imprisons us in our sin, however, the more it shows us our need for grace and thus it drives us to Christ: "Now the law came in to increase the trespass, but where sin increased, grace abounded all the more, so that, as sin reigned in death, grace also might reign through righteousness leading to eternal life through Jesus Christ our Lord" (Rom. 5:20–21). By itself, the law cannot save, but it can

15. Xenophon, *State of the Lacedaemonians* 3.1, quoted in Witherington, 265.
16. Stott, *Message of Galatians*, 98.

lead us to the Savior. "The true use of the Law is this," wrote Martin Luther: "that I know that by the Law I am being brought to an acknowledgment of sin and am being humbled, so that I may come to Christ and be justified by faith."[17]

This is why people need to know God's law. This is why the church must call a sin a sin, whatever the sin may be. People do not want to hear this, of course. They do not want to be told that lust, greed, gluttony, and injustice are sins. Whenever anyone suggests that there is such a thing as sin, they immediately become defensive. They complain that Christians are being judgmental. Sometimes, to their shame, Christians *are* judgmental. However, that is usually not the real issue. The real issue is that sinners do not want to be judged for their sins.

Yet if Paul was right about the purpose of the law, then people must hear its judgments in order to be saved:

> Not until the law has bruised and smitten us will we admit our need of the gospel to bind up our wounds. Not until the law has arrested and imprisoned us will we pine for Christ to set us free. Not until the law has condemned and killed us will we call upon Christ for justification and for life. Not until the law has driven us to despair of ourselves will we ever believe in Jesus. Not until the law has humbled us even to hell will we turn to the gospel to raise us to heaven.[18]

We need the law to lead us to Christ. For only when the law reveals our sin will we ever start to look for the free grace that God has for us in the gospel.

17. Luther, *Galatians*, 26:348.
18. Stott, *Message of Galatians*, 93.

12

ALL GOD'S CHILDREN

Galatians 3:26—29

For in Christ Jesus you are all sons of God, through faith. For as many of you as were baptized into Christ have put on Christ. There is neither Jew nor Greek, there is neither slave nor free, there is neither male nor female, for you are all one in Christ Jesus. And if you are Christ's, then you are Abraham's offspring, heirs according to promise. (Gal. 3:26–29)

Sometime in the late 1990s Philadelphia motorists were startled to read a prominent billboard that asked: "WHO'S THE FATHER?" The ad was sponsored by Precise Paternity—a company that uses DNA testing to establish identity. It was a sign for postmodern times, when people are unsure who they are or where they came from.

Human beings have always needed to know their identity. The Christian answer to humanity's search for meaning is given at the end of Galatians 3, which explains who the Christian is in relation to God (Gal. 3:26–27), humanity (Gal. 3:28), and history (Gal. 3:29).

SONS OF GOD

When it comes to personal identity, the first thing to know is who the father is. So the apostle Paul establishes the Christian's paternity: "for in

Christ Jesus you are all sons of God, through faith" (Gal. 3:26). If you know Jesus Christ, then you know who you are, because you know to whom you belong. A Christian is a child of God. Back in verse 7 Paul said that every believer is a child of Abraham. Now he takes it one step further: every believer is a son or a daughter of the Most High God.

This is the climax of Paul's argument. He has just finished explaining how the law is a pedagogue for underage children. But eventually children outgrow their need for a guardian, so the law lasts only until the coming of Christ. Now we have the full rights of sons and daughters. We are no longer "minors, under the restraint of a tutor, but sons of God and heirs of His glorious kingdom, enjoying the status and privileges of grown-up sons."[1]

This was a message that the Galatians especially needed to hear. Remember what the Judaizers were saying. Since they were Jews, they had always thought of themselves as God's only children, so they treated Gentile Christians like second-rate members of the family. Until they got circumcised, Gentiles could not be siblings; at most, they were only cousins.

Paul responded to this teaching by welcoming the Gentiles within the full embrace of God's family: "in Christ Jesus you are all sons of God, through faith" (Gal. 3:26). His emphasis falls on what is the first word of the verse in Greek: "all," meaning both Jews and Gentiles. The gospel is for Gentiles as much as for Jews, and therefore the privilege of sonship is for all God's children.

The way anyone becomes a member of God's family is by legal adoption, which the Westminster Shorter Catechism defines as follows: "Adoption is an act of God's free grace, whereby we are received into the number, and have a right to all the privileges of the sons of God" (A. 34). Legally speaking, an adopted child is a true son or daughter. He or she has the same rights and privileges as a natural-born child. There is someone to call "Father." There is someone to care for every need. There is someone to give fatherly affection and discipline. In addition, the adopted child will receive a full share of the family inheritance.

The Christian gains all these rights and privileges by becoming a child of God. There is someone to call "Father," for we pray to our Father in heaven

1. John R. W. Stott, *The Message of Galatians: Only One Way*, The Bible Speaks Today (Downers Grove, IL: InterVarsity, 1968), 99.

(Matt. 6:9). There is someone to care for us, for our heavenly Father knows exactly what we need (Matt. 6:32). He loves us with tender affection. "See what kind of love the Father has given to us," marveled the apostle John, "that we should be called children of God; and so we are" (1 John 3:1).

Our Father loves us so much that he refuses to let us go our own way. Instead, he disciplines us to make us holy: "It is for discipline that you have to endure. God is treating you as sons. For what son is there whom his father does not discipline?" (Heb. 12:7). Best of all, God has promised his children a full share of his infinite and eternal inheritance. If we are God's children, Paul reasoned with the Romans, then we are heirs—"heirs of God and fellow heirs with Christ" (Rom. 8:17). A good father gives everything he is and everything he has to his children. God, who has the most to give, is the best Father of all. Thus there is no higher status a human being can ever achieve than to be called a son or a daughter of the Most High God.

The way to gain this high status is simply through faith in Jesus Christ: "for in Christ Jesus you are all sons of God, through faith" (Gal. 3:26). Throughout this letter Paul has argued that God's blessings come only by faith: justification is by faith (Gal. 2:16; 3:6); union with Christ is by faith (Gal. 2:20); the blessings of Abraham come by faith (Gal. 3:9); and the promise of the Holy Spirit is received by faith (Gal. 3:14). Everything God has to offer comes by faith, and adoption is no exception. This blessing, too, comes through faith in Christ. In the words of the apostle John, "But to all who did receive him, who believed in his name, he gave the right to become children of God" (John 1:12).

Adoption shows the contrast between faith and works in the most vivid way, for no one ever works his way into a family. The highest position one can achieve simply by working in a household is servant. A servant may live with a family. A servant may do the family's laundry, cook the family's meals, clean the family's house, and feed the family's dog. But the servant could do all these things day after day for decades without ever becoming a member of the family (in much the same way that someone who is not a relative could not expect to rise to the top of a family business). In such a case, the only way to become a son or a daughter is by adoption. This can be granted only by the will of the father; it can never be gained by the works of the servant. And when it comes to God's family, the Father is willing to adopt anyone who believes in his Son, Jesus Christ.

The New Perspective on Paul and the law has once again raised an old question as to the precise meaning of the relationship between faith and Christ in the book of Galatians. Several times Paul has mentioned "faith in Jesus Christ" (Gal. 2:16; 3:22). But there is another way to interpret this phrase. It could mean "the faith *of* Jesus Christ," that is, his own faithfulness to God. The question is, Who is doing the trusting: Christ or the Christian? Is Paul talking about faith *in* Christ or the faithfulness *of* Christ? And if it is the latter, does Galatians really teach the Reformation doctrine of justification by faith after all?

Grammatically speaking, either translation is possible. It is true that Jesus was faithful. In fact, our salvation depends on his faithfulness to obey the law and suffer the punishment for our sins. But even if Christ is the one who is faithful, we still need to put our faith in his faithfulness. Galatians 3:26 leaves no question as to the kind of faith that Paul is talking about: "You are all sons of God through faith in Christ Jesus" (Gal. 3:26 NIV). Here there is no ambiguity because Paul explicitly uses the preposition "in." The only way to get into God's family is by personally trusting in Jesus Christ. This confirms the truth and indeed the necessity of justifying faith. It is by putting our own personal faith in Christ that we are saved into the family of God.

Liberal theology used to teach "the fatherhood of God and the brotherhood of man." The idea was that since every single human being is a son or a daughter of God, we are all brothers and sisters. In one sense this is true. God exercises his care over all his creatures, and we all belong to a common humanity. Yet sonship is a privilege granted specifically to those who come to God through faith in Jesus Christ. Although God is Creator of all, Ruler of all, and Judge of all, he is the Father only of his Son Jesus Christ and of those who are in Christ by faith.

BAPTIZED INTO CHRIST

Those who do come to Christ in faith are to be baptized: "For as many of you as were baptized into Christ have put on Christ" (Gal. 3:27). Here Paul is referring to the inward reality of spiritual cleansing by faith, and not simply to the outward sign of water baptism.

Water baptism is a sacrament instituted by the Lord Jesus Christ. It is administered with water, in the name of the Father, the Son, and the Holy

Spirit (Matt. 28:19). It is a sign in which the washing with water signifies cleansing from sin. It is also a seal, like the official mark on a public document, visibly confirming that we belong to God by faith. But this does not mean that believers are saved merely by the act of water baptism. This needs to be said because some Christians (including some Presbyterians as well as some Baptists, Lutherans, and Episcopalians) place so much emphasis on the objectivity of baptism that they make the sacrament itself the thing that saves. Yet this is precisely the kind of thinking that Paul was warning against. The Judaizers were treating circumcision as a method for gaining salvation. What good would it do simply to replace one method (circumcision) with another (baptism)? The truth is that neither circumcision (the sign of the old covenant with Abraham) nor baptism (the sign of the new covenant in Christ) effects salvation, but both signify the salvation that comes by grace through faith.

There is, of course, a strong connection between circumcision and baptism (see Col. 2:11–12). Both sacraments are for believers and their children, who receive the sign of the covenant from faithful parents in the hope that God will bring them to faith. Under the old covenant, most people entered the covenant community by birth. Yet they belonged to the family of God by faith, just like father Abraham. The sacrament connected with their adoption was circumcision, which was administered to every son on the eighth day of life, as well as to adult converts to Judaism. So were the Israelites then adopted by circumcision? No, circumcision was the sign and the seal of their membership in God's family, which they had to receive by faith, whether before (in the case of adult converts) or after (in the case of children) their circumcision.

What is the situation under the new covenant? The same in nearly every respect except the outward sign. We enter the family of God the same way: by faith. We are given a sign and a seal of our adoption, namely, baptism. This sacrament is not the method of our salvation, any more than circumcision ever was. By itself, water baptism—whether administered to children or to adults—does not make us children of God. But it is an outward sign of our adoption, which we receive by faith in Jesus Christ.

Faith and baptism go together. Often, but not always, they occur in close proximity. Paul himself is a good example. His initiation came after his conversion. He was saved when he called Jesus "Lord" on the Damascus road

(Acts 9:5), but he was baptized several days later (Acts 9:18). What elsewhere he calls "the washing of regeneration and renewal of the Holy Spirit" (Titus 3:5) was part of his becoming a child of God. Paul was saved by the baptism of the Holy Spirit, not water baptism; yet baptism was the sign of his salvation.

In effect, baptism grants the Christian his or her adoption papers. Perhaps this is why many churches give baptismal certificates to children and adults who receive this sacrament. It also explains why baptism is so important, even if it is not absolutely necessary. The thief who was converted on the cross went to paradise without ever getting baptized. But baptism is the sign and seal of being a child of God, and therefore under ordinary circumstances it is unthinkable for a Christian not to be baptized.

What baptism especially symbolizes is the believer's union with Christ. As Paul told the Galatians, "you . . . were baptized into Christ" (Gal. 3:27). Here again we encounter one of the central doctrines of Paul's theology: union with Christ. The Christian really is joined to Christ. Christ is in the Christian; the Christian is in Christ. The way we get into Christ is by faith, and the sign and seal of our being in him is baptism. This is why the first Christians were said to be baptized "in the name of Jesus Christ" (Acts 2:38). They were baptized into God's triune name, of course, but they were being incorporated into Christ.

Being united to Christ means that we are connected to everything Christ ever did for our salvation. We participate in his obedient life, his suffering death, and his glorious resurrection. This is all symbolized in baptism, which is the sign and seal of our union with Christ: "Do you not know that all of us who have been baptized into Christ Jesus were baptized into his death? We were buried therefore with him by baptism into death, in order that, just as Christ was raised from the dead by the glory of the Father, we too might walk in newness of life" (Rom. 6:3–4). The message of Galatians, like the message of Romans, is the gospel message of the cross and the empty tomb— Christ crucified and Christ risen. Baptism signifies our personal connection to Christ in these saving events. We are united to the Savior who died and rose again; we have a new identity in Christ.

Another way of describing this union is to say that we are clothed with Christ: "For as many of you as were baptized into Christ have put on Christ" (Gal. 3:27). It is sometimes said that the clothes make the man. This is espe-

cially true in baptism, where Jesus Christ becomes the garment of our righteousness. Here the apostle may have in mind one early Christian practice
for baptism. When adult converts came for baptism, they stripped off their
clothes. Once they had been baptized, they were handed a white robe to sym-
bolize their new life in Christ. Or Paul may have in mind the ritual for the
adoption of a slave, which also called for a new white robe. Either way, a
Christian is someone who has put on Christ, and now stands as a free, pure
child of God.

THE WALLS THAT DIVIDE

What is your relationship to God? If you are a Christian, then you are one
of God's sons or daughters. This family relationship has one rather obvious
implication: Everyone who belongs to God belongs to everyone else who
belongs to God. All of God's sons and daughters are brothers and sisters.

The Scripture emphasizes that within this new spiritual family no one is
excluded: "There is neither Jew nor Greek, there is neither slave nor free,
there is neither male nor female, for you are all one in Christ Jesus" (Gal.
3:28; cf. 1 Cor. 12:13; Col. 3:11). Being in Christ transcends and transforms
our social categories. To put it another way, union with Christ establishes
our communion as saints.

Here Paul mentions the very things that divide us most: race, rank, and
sex.[2] These three divisions polarized the ancient world. Consider the prayer,
sometimes attributed to Socrates, in which a Greek man gave thanks to God
"that I was born a human being and not a beast, next a man and not a woman,
thirdly, a Greek and not a barbarian."[3] Pagans generally despised their slaves
and mistreated their women. In some places slaves were forbidden to enter
pagan temples, while women were treated as chattel.

A similar prejudice often prevailed in Israel, where some men thanked
God every day that they were not Gentiles, slaves, or women. Listen to these
Jewish benedictions from the first century: "Blessed art thou, O Lord our
God, King of the universe, who hast not made me a foreigner. Blessed art
thou, O Lord our God, King of the universe, who hast not made me a slave.

2. Ibid., 100.
3. Diogenes Laertius, *Vitae Philosophorum* 1.33, quoted in Ben Witherington III, *Grace in Galatia:
A Commentary on Paul's Letter to the Galatians* (Edinburgh: T & T Clark, 1998), 270.

148

Blessed art thou, O Lord our God, King of the universe, who hast not made me a woman."[4]

Of these three distinctions—race, rank, and sex—ethnicity was the most divisive. As far as the Jews were concerned, the whole world was divided into two parts. The distinction between Jews and Gentiles governed worship, marriage, commerce, even table fellowship. F. F. Bruce writes, "The cleavage between Jew and Gentile was for Judaism the most radical within the human race. It was indeed possible for a Gentile to become a Jewish proselyte. . . . But a Gentile who became a proselyte crossed over to the Jewish side of the gulf; the gulf remained."[5]

This gulf is precisely what the Judaizers wanted to maintain. They were dividing the Galatian church along racial lines, forcing Gentile Christians to choose sides. Would they remain Greek or did they have to become culturally Jewish? There are signs of this struggle throughout the New Testament.

There are also signs of this struggle throughout human history. Jew against Greek. Slave against free. Man against woman. Timothy George writes: "Race, money, and sex are the primal powers in human life. No one of them is inherently evil; rather, they are the stuff of which life itself is made. . . . Yet each of these spheres of human creativity has become degraded and soiled through the perversity of sin. Nationality and ethnicity have been corrupted by pride, material blessings by greed, and sexuality by lust."[6] Much of what we call history is the story of these three conflicts. Consider the long, tragic history of the persecution of the Jews, or the lingering effects of slavery in the United States, or the oppression of women in so many places around the world. The history department at any local college or university will tell at least part of the truth about these evils. The multiculturalists will base everything on racial conflict. The Marxists will view history as a perpetual class struggle. The feminists will look at human relationships through the lens of gender.

Christians usually reject those worldviews because they are too simplistic, but each of them has correctly identified part of the problem. The greatest barriers to the harmony of humanity are ethnic, economic, and gender

4. Timothy George, *Galatians*, New American Commentary 30 (Nashville: Broadman & Holman, 1994), 285.

5. F. F. Bruce, *The Epistle to the Galatians: A Commentary on the Greek Text*, New International Greek Testament Commentary (Grand Rapids: Eerdmans, 1982), 188.

6. George, *Galatians*, 284–85.

distinctions. What color is your skin? What language do you speak? How much money do you earn, and how do you earn it? Do you have a Y-chromosome? These are the questions that have always divided us.

The walls are everywhere: race against race, class against class, gender against gender. Most armed conflicts around the globe have a strong ethnic component. In America, the reason the race card sometimes gets played is that it is still in the deck. Legislation has done all it can to achieve integration, but where is the reconciliation? Meanwhile, the battle of the sexes rages on: divorce, rape, abuse, sexual harassment, radical feminism.

The problems of race, rank, and sex also disturb our peace within the church. In Paul's day, the Jews hindered the apostolic mission to the Gentiles. But for the rest of church history, it has been the Gentiles who have discouraged the Jews from receiving the gospel. Our legacy includes not only anti-Semitism, but also slavery. To give just one example from Presbyterian history, consider these words of bigotry from a nineteenth-century sermon: "You slaves will go to heaven if you are good, but don't ever think that you will be close to your mistress and master. No! No! There will be a wall between you; but there will be holes in it that will permit you to look out and see your mistress when she passes by."[7] It is hard to say which is worse: the blatant racism of these words, or the deadly legalism. Then there are all the ways that women have been patronized and marginalized in the life of the church. We can recognize this and work against it without going to the unbiblical extreme of promoting women's ordination. All too often the gifts of women have been underutilized, and their contributions undervalued. All these problems persist to the present day, when racial, social, and sexual tensions boil just beneath the surface of church life.

UNITED IN CHRIST

The Bible teaches that divisions of race, rank, and gender can be overcome only in Christ: "There is neither Jew nor Greek, there is neither slave nor free, there is neither male nor female, for you are all one in Christ Jesus" (Gal. 3:28). More literally, "you are all one person in Christ." Here again the

7. Cited in John B. Cade, "Out of the Mouths of Ex-Slaves," *Journal of Negro History* 20 (July 1935): 329.

emphasis falls on the "all." Jews and Gentiles, slaves and free, men and women—we are *all* God's children. The church of Jesus Christ is our first family, and in that family there are no second-class children.

What God has established in Christ is nothing less than a new humanity. Our relationship to one another is based entirely on our relationship to him. As we are united to him, we become united to one another; union with Christ is the basis for our communion as saints. According to the seventeenth-century German Reformed theologian Johan Heidegger, the communion of saints is "the union, society and assembly of all believers who have some-thing in common with each other. Now this common thing is Christ the Head of the Church, as well as the gifts which flow down from Him as Head to the Body."[8]

When it comes to salvation, there are no differences among us. We are equal under the law and equal in the gospel. We are all equally in need of salvation and equally unable to save ourselves because of our sin. We all need the same cross and the same empty tomb. We all need the same atoning death and the same bodily resurrection. In a word, we all need the same Christ. Once we have come to him by the same faith, it is Christ for all and all in Christ.

This is one reason why Paul opposed the Judaizers so strenuously. They were drawing boundaries inside the church—Jews on one side, Gentiles on the other. By imposing circumcision, which was only for men, they were also excluding the women. Indeed, part of the wisdom of baptism is that it is a sacrament for everyone. *All* God's children are baptized into Christ.

Regardless of race, rank, or sex, we are all united in Christ. Jews and Gentiles are united in Christ. Christ has destroyed the barrier between Jew and Gentile, reconciling both to God through the cross (Eph. 2:15–17). Slaves and free citizens are also united in Christ: "For he who was called in the Lord as a slave is a freedman of the Lord. Likewise he who was free when called is a slave of Christ" (1 Cor. 7:22). The free person has become a slave for Christ, while in Christ the slave finds his freedom.

Men and women are united in Christ as well. The apostle Paul is often slandered for his attitude toward women, but he was no chauvinist. Under

---

8. Johan Heidegger, *Medulla Theologiae Christianae* (Zurich, 1696), quoted in Heinrich Heppe, *Reformed Dogmatics Set Out and Illustrated from the Sources* (London: Allen and Unwin, 1950), 659.

the inspiration of the Holy Spirit, he recognized that women were made in the image of God and could be remade in the image of Christ. He welcomed them as first-class members of God's family and praised them for their partnership in ministry. The remarkable thing about Paul was not what a chauvinist he was, but how much of a feminist he was, in the sense that he promoted the full recognition of the gifts and status of women in Christ. His teaching about gender created as much controversy then as it does now, but for exactly the opposite reason. Over against the common view that women were inferior, Paul liberated women within the life of the church. The radical edge of apostolic teaching on gender is the fundamental equality of all God's sons and daughters.

The kind of equality Paul has in mind is not the kind that obliterates every racial, social, or sexual distinction. Galatians 3:28 is sometimes misused so as to contradict what the New Testament says elsewhere about Jews and Gentiles, slaves and masters, or men and women. The church is not a raceless, classless, androgynous society. When we come to Christ, we do not cease to be Asians or Africans, bosses or employees, or girls and boys. With regard to our physical and social identity, we continue to be what we have always been, only now we are what we are in Christ.

Being in Christ establishes a fundamental unity within which our diversity can be cherished. Ethnic distinctions remain. Paul did not cease to be a Jew when he became a Christian, but continued to value his ethnic heritage. Economic differences remain, too. Although the New Testament forbids the kidnapping of someone into slavery (1 Tim. 1:10), it does not explicitly abolish slavery in all its forms. This is partly because slavery in the ancient world was sometimes voluntary. But whether slavery was voluntary or not, the important thing was for Christian slaves and Christian masters to treat one another as brothers and sisters in Christ (see Col. 3:22–4:1). So Philemon was to welcome the runaway Onesimus "no longer as a slave but more than a slave, as a beloved brother" (Philem. 16).

Gender differences remain as well. Here Paul's grammar is significant, for Galatians 3:28 reads literally, "There is neither Jew nor Greek, slave nor free, male *and* female." This may be a deliberate echo of Genesis 1:27: "male and female he created them." It reminds us that the difference between the male and the female goes back to the creation itself. Our God-given gender has implications for our unique spiritual responsibilities in the home and in the church, *without threatening our fundamental equality in Christ.* To be specific, God calls men to exercise servant leadership as husbands and as officers in the church, while he calls women to submit to this leadership as wives and as members of the church. But it is a mistake to think of our service as men or our submission as women in terms of status, for in Christ there is no status.

To summarize: Our ethnic, social, and sexual distinctions continue to exist. But since we are in Christ, these distinctions do not divide us. They do not determine our standing in God's family. Therefore, we should see our oneness in Christ

> not as a leveling and abolishing of all racial, social or gender differences, but as an integration of just such differences into a common participation "in Christ," wherein they enhance (rather than detract from) the unity of the body, and enrich the mutual interdependence and service of its members. In other words, it is a oneness, because such differences cease to be a barrier and cause of pride or regret or embarrassment, and become rather a means to display the diverse richness of God's creation and grace, both in the acceptance of the "all" and in the gifting of each.[9]

We have the best and the truest fellowship when we recognize our diversity, but see it as less important than our unity in Christ.

The church has a long way to go before becoming God's new humanity in Christ. By and large, the church remains racially and socially segregated. Evangelical churches, especially, are divided over the role of women in the church. Galatians 3:28 gives an indication of what our problem is: The reason we so often fail to treat one another as we should is that we are not yet far enough into Christ. There is no segregation in Christ. If there are still snobbery, prejudice, and even hatred in us, it is because we are not all the way into Christ.

It is only when we are in Christ that we become able to see people the way Jesus sees them and treat them the way he treats them. A good example is the way Jesus treated the woman at the well (John 4). She was a poor Samaritan woman, so Jesus was separated from her ethnically, socially, and sexu-

9. James D. G. Dunn, *The Epistle to the Galatians,* Black's New Testament Commentary (Peabody, MA: Hendrickson, 1993), 208.

ally. But that did not stop him from loving her and dying for her sins. Now we are called to reach out to those who are different from us with the love of Christ.

What would this look like? It would change the way we think and talk about one another. We could never refer to "those people"; we would always have to say "us." It would change the way we treat one another, too. Jews would love Gentiles (and vice versa). Blacks would show hospitality to whites (and vice versa). The disabled would seek friendships with the able-bodied (and vice versa). Internationals would welcome nationals (and vice versa). The poor would love the rich (and vice versa). Women would respect men (and vice versa). Then, rather than hindering our unity, differences of race, rank, and sex would become an opportunity to show the world what it means to be in Christ.

HEIRS OF THE PROMISE

God's new humanity in Christ is not just for the here and now; it is for all eternity: "And if you are Christ's, then you are Abraham's offspring, heirs according to promise" (Gal. 3:29). This verse establishes the Christian's identity in relation to history. In relation to God's deity, I am a son or a daughter—a child of God. In relation to humanity, I am a brother or a sister of all God's children. In relation to history, I belong to the one family God began in time and will keep for all eternity. John Stott explains that Christians "find their place in eternity (related first and foremost to God as His sons and daughters), in society (related to each other as brothers and sisters in the same family) and in history (related also to the succession of God's people down through the ages)."[10]

"If you are Christ's," Paul says. Literally, "if you are of Christ." To be *in* Christ is to be *of* Christ. It is to belong to him, so that once we come to him in faith, we have the right to wear a T-shirt that reads "Property of Jesus Christ."

To belong to Christ is to belong not only to one another, but also to Abraham. Remember that God made his promise to both Abraham and his offspring. The word "offspring" referred specifically to Abraham's true son Jesus

---

10. Stott, *Message of Galatians*, 101.

154

Christ (Gal. 3:16). If we are in Christ, then we are God's offspring—sons of Abraham. This is important because in the ancient world only the son received the inheritance. To say that we are all sons of God has nothing to do with being masculine. Sonship means that we will inherit everything God has ever promised to give his children—forgiveness of sin, heaven, eternal life, and all the rest of it.

The Judaizers understood that God intended to establish one people, in history, that would last for all eternity, but they were wrong about the entrance requirements. They told the Galatians that they could not become children of Abraham until they became Jews. Paul's response was that they were children of Abraham already, simply by coming to Christ. All it takes to become one of God's heirs is faith in Jesus Christ. This shows, incidentally, that the church is God's true Israel. When Gentiles come to faith in Christ, they become part of the only family God has ever had.

Are you a member of the family? If you are not sure who you are, it must be because you have not yet found your true self in Jesus Christ. Perhaps you have never come to him in faith, trusting him to save you from your sins and make you a child of God. Or perhaps you do trust in Christ, but you are still looking for your identity somewhere else.

The only way to find ourselves is to come to God in Christ. Those who are in Christ know exactly who they are. We know who our Father is, for we are sons and daughters of the Most High God. We know who our siblings are, for we are brothers and sisters of all God's children. If you are a Christian, that is who you are, and who you will be, forever.

13

FROM SLAVERY TO SONSHIP

Galatians 4:1–7

In the same way we also, when we were children, were enslaved to the elementary principles of the world. But when the fullness of time had come, God sent forth his Son, born of woman, born under the law, to redeem those who were under the law, so that we might receive adoption as sons. (Gal. 4:3–5)

*I*n the spring of 1999, the duke and duchess of Northumberland went to court to block their son from inheriting his fortune when he turned eighteen. Their son, the young Earl Percy, was only fourteen years old at the time, and his parents had his best interests in mind. One day the earl was to inherit a vast fortune, including Alnwick Castle, a one-million-pound inheritance, and almost half a million dollars in annual income. But his parents did not want him to inherit too much too soon. They were well aware that other British noblemen had squandered their fortunes on drugs and riotous living. So they set up a trust to manage the young earl's fortune until his twenty-fifth birthday.[1]

---

1. Maureen Johnson, "Earl won't have to face temptation very soon," *The Philadelphia Inquirer*, 31 May 1999, A26.

TREATED LIKE A SLAVE, BUT STILL A SON

What happened to young Percy is akin to the paradoxical situation the apostle Paul describes at the outset of Galatians 4. He has been drawing a contrast between the old covenant and the new, between the era of Moses and the time of Christ, between living under the law and living by faith. The law, he explained in chapter 3, is like a prison warden (Gal. 3:23) or a pedagogue (Gal. 3:24) to control God's people until they come to Christ. Now he makes a slightly different comparison: "I mean that the heir, as long as he is a child, is no different from a slave, though he is the owner of everything" (Gal. 4:1).

Here it helps to know something about Greek civil law, which seems to be what the apostle has in mind.[2] In those days, it was customary for a wealthy man to hand his heir over to the care of guardians. Throughout his childhood, the eldest son knew he would inherit his father's estate, but he did not own it yet.[3] The English Standard Version is somewhat misleading when it says that the child "is the owner of everything" (Gal. 4:1). More accurately, the heir apparent is "lord of all," meaning that his father's land belongs to him by title, but not yet by actual possession.

In the meantime, the heir had about as much liberty as a common slave. He had no legal or property rights. His guardian kept him under discipline. He was told when to wake up, when to go to school, what to wear, how to behave, and when to go to bed. He also had a trustee to manage his property, especially if his father was deceased. Until he came of age he was called "the young master"—"master" because one day he would inherit the estate, but "young" to keep him firmly in his place.

Under this system, the young master sometimes felt more like a slave than a son. But it was all for his own good. What seemed at times like bondage was necessary to bring him to full maturity. Nor did his minority last forever. Eventually he received his inheritance, in keeping with the date legally established by his father.

2. Ben Witherington III, *Grace in Galatia: A Commentary on Paul's Letter to the Galatians* (Edinburgh: T & T Clark, 1998), 282–83.
3. James D. G. Dunn, *The Epistle to the Galatians*, Black's New Testament Commentary (Peabody, MA: Hendrickson, 1993), 210.

The point of Paul's analogy is that the law plays a similar role in the story of salvation: "In the same way we also, when we were children, were enslaved to the elementary principles of the world" (Gal. 4:3). What makes this verse difficult to interpret is the phrase "the elementary principles of the world." It would seem that Paul is talking about the law given to Moses, for he will use the phrase "under the law" in both of the next two verses (Gal. 4:4–5).

Perhaps, then, "elementary principles of the world" is another way of describing the law. The laws of God are indeed the basic principles of the world. In Greek, "basic principles" means "essential components" or "elementary things." The term was sometimes used to refer to basic teachings like the ABCs (or the "alpha, beta, gammas," as they were called back then). This is one good way to describe God's law. To study the law is to learn the alphabet of God's will.

To follow the analogy through, the Old Testament law was like elementary school for the people of God. The Jews had specific rules to govern their conduct, what the writer to the Hebrews called "regulations for the body imposed until the time of reformation" (Heb. 9:10). When it came to worship, the Jews had to go to a particular place and offer particular sacrifices in a particular way. Keeping all these requirements was like being in grammar school, tracing the ABCs that were first written by the hand of God.

Eventually, schoolchildren outgrow their elementary education. They master the alphabet and move on to composition. In the same way, God raised his people on the law to prepare them for the gospel. The Puritan William Perkins thus described Israel as "a little school set up in a corner of the world; the law of Moses was, as it were, an ABC, or primer, in which Christ was revealed to the world, in dark and obscure manner, specially to the Jews."[4]

By calling the law an "elementary principle," Paul was giving the law teachers from Jerusalem a remedial education. Those Judaizers had been telling the Galatians that the law was a graduate school for the gospel. But Paul insisted that being under the law was actually a sign of spiritual immaturity. For the Galatians to go back to the law would be like a Ph.D. repeating kinder-

4. William Perkins, *A Commentary on Galatians*, Pilgrim Classic Commentaries, ed. Gerald T. Sheppard (London, 1617; repr. New York: Pilgrim, 1989), 243.

garten to work on his alphabet.[5] If they wanted to be spiritual grown-ups, they would have to advance beyond the law.

There is another way to interpret "elementary principles," however, which also includes the Gentiles, who "were just as enslaved in their pagan idolatry as the Jews had been in their servitude to the law."[6] The term "elementary principles" shows up again in Galatians 4:9, where Paul is clearly talking about pagan worship. Among the pagans, "elementary principles" could refer to spiritual beings, such as the elemental spirits of earth, air, fire, and water. So perhaps when Paul spoke of being "enslaved to the elementary principles of the world" (Gal. 4:3), he was referring to demonic powers. There was a time when the Galatians themselves were in bondage to precisely such gods and goddesses.

Whether the term "elementary principles" refers to God's law for the Jews (which seems more probable) or to Satan's control of the Gentiles, the point is that eventually God's people needed to grow up. For a time, they were no better off than slaves. Indeed, while they were children, they practically had to be treated as slaves. But in truth they had always been sons, so the day finally came when they left their religious infancy behind and grew into full spiritual maturity.

THE COMING OF GOD'S SON

What brought God's people from slavery to sonship was the death and resurrection of Jesus Christ. We were under the law until the coming of Christ, which Paul describes in these beautiful, almost poetic words: "But when the fullness of time had come, God sent forth his Son, born of woman, born under the law, to redeem those who were under the law, so that we might receive adoption as sons" (Gal. 4:4–5).

As these verses outline the plan of salvation, they give six central teachings about the coming of Christ. The first concerns the *timing* of his coming. Jesus came "when the fullness of time had come" (Gal. 4:4). Under ancient law, the father had the right to fix the time when his son would receive

---

5. Timothy George, *Galatians*, New American Commentary 30 (Nashville: Broadman & Holman, 1994), 296.
   6. Ibid., 295.

his estate.[7] In the same way, God the Father determined when God the Son would come to give all God's children their inheritance.

Jesus himself knew that he had come at just the right time: "Now after John was arrested, Jesus came into Galilee, proclaiming the gospel of God, and saying, 'The time is fulfilled, and the kingdom of God is at hand; repent and believe in the gospel' " (Mark 1:14–15). Jesus came at the exact point in human history when God was ready for his coming. When my son was a small boy, he put a six-foot, hand-drawn timeline of world history on his bedroom wall. Right at the center of it, dividing B.C. from A.D. in the timetable of God's eternal counsel, was the cross of Christ. Jesus came, wrote John Calvin, "when the time which had been ordained by the providence of God was seasonable and fit."[8]

Christ came when the world was ready for his coming, too. The Greeks had provided a common language and culture for sharing the gospel. Through the might of the Romans, there was safe transport for spreading the gospel. But most of all, sinners were ready to be released from their bondage. The Gentiles were tired of serving the old pagan gods. The Jews were weary of being held prisoner by the law they had tried (and failed) to keep for over a thousand years. So it was at just the right time—not a moment too soon, not a moment too late—that Christ came to make us God's sons and daughters.

The second teaching concerns the *origin* of Christ's coming and testifies to his eternal deity. The Bible says, "God sent forth his Son" (Gal. 4:4), and the fact that the Son was *sent* shows that he existed before he was born in Bethlehem. His sending from heaven thus declares his divine nature. Jesus Christ is God the Son, fully equal to the Father in glory and might. His sonship is eternal. He is the only-begotten Son of the Father, the second person of the Trinity, who lived with his Father in glory from eternity past. When the time had fully come, the eternally divine Son of God came down from heaven into the world.

The third teaching concerns the *manner* of Christ's coming. God the Son was "born of woman" (Gal. 4:4). Whereas the word "sent" implies his eter-

---

7. F. F. Bruce, *The Epistle to the Galatians: A Commentary on the Greek Text*, New International Greek Testament Commentary (Grand Rapids: Eerdmans, 1982), 192.

8. John Calvin, *The Epistles of Paul the Apostle to the Galatians, Ephesians, Philippians and Colossians*, Calvin's New Testament Commentaries, trans. T. H. L. Parker, ed. David W. and Thomas F. Torrance (Grand Rapids: Eerdmans, 1996), 73.

nal deity, the word "born" declares his true humanity. Jesus had an ordinary birth. To say that a human mother gave him birth is to say that God the Son became a human being. This is the doctrine of the incarnation: God became man. What better way to emphasize the true humanity of Jesus Christ than to say that he was born of a woman?

When Jesus was delivered by the Virgin Mary and laid in a manger, God the Son took on our flesh and our nature, with all its temptations and aggravations. The Christ who came to save is the God-man; he is one person in two natures, a divine nature and a human nature. In the words of the Westminster Shorter Catechism, "Christ, the Son of God, became man, by taking to himself a true body, and a reasonable soul, being conceived by the power of the Holy Ghost, in the womb of the Virgin Mary, and born of her, yet without sin" (A. 22). And it was just because Jesus is a true man that he can be our Savior. According to Luther, Christianity

> does not begin at the top, as all other religions do; it begins at the bottom. . . . Therefore, whenever you are concerned to think and act about your salvation, you must put away all speculations about the Majesty, all thoughts of works, traditions, and philosophy—indeed, of the Law of God itself. And you must run directly to the manger and the mother's womb, embrace this Infant and Virgin's Child in your arms, and look at Him—born, being nursed, growing up, going about in human society, teaching, dying, rising again, ascending above all the heavens, and having authority over all things. In this way you can shake off all terrors and errors, as the sun dispels the clouds.[9]

The fourth important teaching concerns the *condition* of Christ's coming, which was perfect obedience. Jesus was born a Jew, and therefore he was bound to obey God's law in its entirety. He was "born under the law" (Gal. 4:4). By his birth he was required to keep Torah, which he did with total perfection. Jesus kept the whole law for his people. He was circumcised on the eighth day, as the law required. He never broke even one of the Ten Commandments. He followed the biblical pattern for worship. He went to Jerusalem to keep the feasts. He celebrated Passover. He did everything the law required.

---

9. Martin Luther, *Lectures on Galatians, 1535*, trans. and ed. Jaroslav Pelikan, in *Luther's Works* (St. Louis: Concordia, 1963), 26:30.

Jesus even died under the law. For God's Son, coming under the law included accepting the death penalty his people deserved for breaking it. This is what Paul explained back in chapter 3, when he said, "Christ redeemed us from the curse of the law by becoming a curse for us" (Gal. 3:13). When Christ came under the law, he also came under its curse. He not only kept the whole law for his people, but also suffered the punishment due to their sins.

THE REASON FOR HIS COMING

The fifth teaching concerns the first element of the twofold *purpose* of Christ's coming, which was "to redeem those who were under the law" (Gal. 4:5). Here Paul refers specifically to the atonement that Christ provided on the cross. He first mentioned Christ's death at the very beginning of his letter, when he said that Jesus "gave himself for our sins to deliver us from the present evil age" (Gal. 1:4). But Christ's death was more than a rescue; it was also a redemption. In the ancient world, redemption ordinarily referred to the release of a slave by the payment of a price. Provided that someone was willing to make the payment, a slave's freedom could be purchased. This is precisely what Christ did for his people. Although we were enslaved to the basic principles of the world (Gal. 4:3), Jesus paid the price for our freedom when he died on the cross. He paid the ultimate price. When God sent his Son, he sent him to die.

The death of Christ makes some people uncomfortable, including some people who call themselves Christians. In the spring of 1999, for example, a Lutheran pastor in Germany gained notoriety by arguing that the manger and not the cross should be the symbol of Christianity. The cross, she said, is too threatening; it certainly is not as inviting as baby Jesus asleep on the hay.

Christ had to be born before he could die, of course; there could be no Easter without Christmas. But God the Son was born of the Virgin in order to die on the cross. Christianity is not a religion of stable and straw; it is a religion of thorns and nails, wood and blood. The incarnation cannot save us without the crucifixion. Christ did not redeem us by his life alone; he redeemed us through his death.

What Christ redeemed us from is the law, with its deadly curse. This is why it was necessary for him to be born under the law. What qualified him to redeem us from the law was the fact that he kept it perfectly. Indeed, everything Paul has said so far about Christ's coming—his timely arrival, his eternal deity, his true humanity, and his perfect obedience—qualified him to be our redeemer. John Stott writes, "So the divinity of Christ, the humanity of Christ and the righteousness of Christ uniquely qualified Him to be man's redeemer. If He had not been man, He could not have redeemed men. If He had not been a righteous man, He could not have redeemed unrighteous men. And if He had not been God's Son, He could not have redeemed men for God or made them the sons of God."[10] But Christ did redeem us, and he did it as the perfect God-man who died on the cross to save sinners.

The sixth teaching and second purpose for Christ's coming was "that we might receive adoption as sons" (Gal. 4:5). Christ's coming had an adopting purpose as well as atoning purpose. God sent his Son to make us all his sons and daughters. Christ accomplished our adoption as well as our redemption. It would be enough for God to release us from slavery, to rescue us from our captivity to the law, and so to redeem us from its curse. But God did not stop there. Once Christ had gained our freedom, he gathered us into his family. He went beyond redemption to adoption, turning slaves into sons.

Remember that Paul was not being sexist when he called the Galatians God's sons. In the ancient world, a father's inheritance was only for his sons. By calling his children sons, therefore, God guaranteed that all his sons and daughters would be included in his will and testament: "So you are no longer a slave, but a son; and if a son, then an heir through God" (Gal. 4:7). The promise of eternal life with God in heaven is for everyone who becomes a child of God through faith in Jesus Christ.

When Jesus died and rose again, he not only paid for our freedom, but also provided us with our adoption papers, making us sons and daughters of the Most High God. There is a hint of this in the story of his resurrection. The women ran away from the tomb to tell the disciples that Jesus had risen from the dead. Suddenly, Jesus was standing right in front of them, and they

10. John R. W. Stott, *The Message of Galatians: Only One Way*, The Bible Speaks Today (Downers Grove, IL: InterVarsity, 1968), 106.

fell down to worship him. He greeted them with these words: "go and tell my *brothers* to go to Galilee, and there they will see me" (Matt. 28:10). Jesus called the disciples "brothers" because he had brought them into God's family by his death and resurrection.

Now everyone who believes in the risen Christ is God's own dear child. If we continue to serve God out of fear or duty, however, we show that we do not understand what Christ has done on our behalf. Christianity is not a bondage, but a freedom, for Christ has brought us from slavery into sonship. Our ongoing membership in God's family does not depend on our works, as if somehow we had to earn our keep.

A good example of what this means in practical terms comes from the life of John Wesley. Before Wesley came to Christ, he was a better Christian than most believers, at least as far as his outward behavior was concerned. During his days at Oxford he helped establish a group called "the Holy Club." The students in the club went to church, studied their Bibles, fasted, and prayed. They went into the prisons and workhouses to do evangelism. They provided food, clothing, and education for the poor children of the city. Yet all the while they were spiritual orphans, in bondage to their own religiosity. It was not until years later that Wesley finally came to "trust in Christ only for salvation." As he looked back on everything he had done for God before he came to Christ, he wrote, "I had even then the faith of a *servant*, though not that of a son."[11]

THE SPIRIT OF SONSHIP

A Christian is someone, like John Wesley, who has been brought from slavery into sonship. Yet even after we become God's sons and daughters, we sometimes forget our Father's love. We start thinking of ourselves as slaves rather than as sons, which grieves our Father's heart.

Children have a way of testing their parents' love. Without even realizing what they are doing, sometimes they wound their mothers or their fathers to see if they will still be loved. Adopted children often struggle with their parentage. They wonder if their parents really love them. And of course their

11. Ibid., 109.

parents do love them, so it brings them great anguish when their children refuse simply to rest in their affection.

Like any good parent, God wants his children to receive and to rest in his fatherly love. He wants his adopted children to know for certain that they are beloved. For this reason, he has sent his Spirit into our hearts. "And because you are sons, God has sent the Spirit of his Son into our hearts, crying, 'Abba! Father!' " (Gal. 4:6).

The Galatians had indeed received the Spirit (Gal. 3:2); and when they did, they also received the assurance that they were God's sons. For God sent his Spirit as well as his Son. First, he sent his Son to make us his children (Gal. 4:4); then he sent us his Spirit to let us know that we really are his children (Gal. 4:6). The adoption that was accomplished by the Son is applied by the Spirit.

Here we are drawn into the mystery of the Trinity. The one true God exists in three persons: Father, Son, and Holy Spirit. Adoption is the work of the Triune God. God the Father, just because he is the Father, is the one who adopts us. He did this by first sending his Son to redeem us from bondage, so that we are no longer slaves but sons. Then the Father sent his Spirit to convince us that we are indeed the sons and daughters of God.

The Spirit whom God sends is specifically "the Spirit of his Son" (Gal. 4:6), which shows the intimacy between the Son and the Spirit within the Godhead. The work of the Son is to bring us into relationship with the Father, while the work of the Spirit is to seal that family tie. Thus the Father, the Son, and the Holy Spirit all work together to make us God's true sons and daughters.

The way we know that we really are God's sons and daughters is by calling him "Father." And not just calling him "Father," as if we could be saved by a mere word, but crying out to him as our Father. The biblical word for crying out (*krazon*) is full of the most intense feeling. When in the midst of this lost and dying world a sinner calls out to God for salvation, it is a cry of the heart.

When we cry out to God, we use the very word Jesus used when he called to his Father in the hours before his death: "Abba, Father" (Mark 14:36). "Abba" is a term of respect as well as endearment. It means "Dear Dad," or "Dearest Father."[12] It is the special work of God's Holy Spirit to put this filial word into our hearts and onto our lips. It is the Spirit who assures our

---

12. For a fuller explanation of the meaning of this term, see Philip Graham Ryken, *When You Pray: Making the Lord's Prayer Your Own* (Wheaton, IL: Crossway, 2000), 57–58.

sonship by enabling us to call God "Abba, Father." Elsewhere Paul writes, "For you did not receive the spirit of slavery to fall back into fear, but you have received the Spirit of adoption as sons, by whom we cry, 'Abba! Father!' The Spirit himself bears witness with our spirit that we are children of God" (Rom. 8:15–16). F. F. Bruce thus describes "Abba" as "the voice of the Spirit of Jesus (on the lips of his people)."[13]

For the Galatians this meant that since they had the Spirit of the Son, they already had the full rights of sons. James Dunn explains it like this: "If Paul was correct, the Gentile Galatian believers need do or receive nothing more in order to be sure of belonging to God's family; they were sons already, and so their share in the inheritance of Abraham was secure, even if they were only adopted sons."[14] The inheritance is for sons, not for slaves. It does not come by keeping the law, but by living in the Spirit.

Through Christ we can receive the same inheritance. How do I know that God is my Father, and that I have a share in his eternal estate? Not by trying to work my way into his family. Certainly not by getting circumcised or by keeping God's law. Not by anything I do at all. Luther said, "There is no slavery in Christ, but only sonship."[15] My obedience can prove that I am a servant, but not that I am a son. My sonship is based entirely on the redemption accomplished by the Son of God. God's Spirit confirms this by enabling me to call God "Father." Servants can only say "Lord," but sons are able to say "Abba! Father!"

One implication of this new family relationship is that our prayers help us know that we are God's children. Undoubtedly this is one of the reasons Jesus taught us to begin our prayers by addressing God as Father. John Stott writes, "God's purpose was not only to secure our sonship by His Son, but to assure us of it by His Spirit. He sent His Son that we might have the *status* of sonship, and He sent His Spirit that we might have an *experience* of it. This comes through the affectionate, confidential intimacy of our access to God in prayer, in which we find ourselves assuming the attitude and using the language not of slaves, but of sons."[16]

13. Bruce, *Epistle to the Galatians*, 199.
14. Dunn, *Epistle to the Galatians*, 222.
15. Luther, *Galatians*, 26:390.
16. Stott, *Message of Galatians*, 107.

A simple illustration may help to drive home the point of this passage. Often, when I hold my daughter on my lap, I lean over and whisper in her ear, "You will always be my special girl!" She usually responds to those words by snuggling closer and saying, "You're my special daddy!"

This is a picture of the relationship our Father God has with his children. First God sent his Son to save us from our sins and to make us all his sons and daughters. The Son is the elder brother who picks us up and sets us down on God's lap. Then God sent his Holy Spirit—the Divine Whisper—who tells us that we will always be God's special children. When we hear the Spirit's whisper, our hearts cry out to God, "You will always be my Father."

14

A PLEA FROM A PERPLEXED PASTOR

Galatians 4:8–20

*Formerly, when you did not know God, you were enslaved to those
that by nature are not gods. But now that you have come to know
God, or rather to be known by God, how can you turn back again
to the weak and worthless elementary principles of the world,
whose slaves you want to be once more?. . . My little children, for
whom I am again in the anguish of childbirth until Christ is
formed in you! I wish I could be present with you now and change
my tone, for I am perplexed about you. (Gal. 4:8–9, 19–20)*

Contrary to popular belief, Christianity is not a form of slavery;
it is a kind of sonship. Without Jesus Christ, human beings are
captivated by sin and enslaved by the rules of primitive religion.
But when they come to Christ, they are released from their bondage to
become the sons and daughters of God.

From slavery to sonship—this is the message of Paul's letter to the Galatians. It is also the transition the Tuyuca people made when they first encountered that message. The Tuyucas live in the eastern jungles of Colombia,
along the border with Brazil. As they worked with the missionary Janet
Barnes to translate Galatians, they had trouble understanding salvation by

grace. "If all we have to do to be saved is to believe," one of them asked, "well, then what? How do we live after that?"

The answer, the Tuyucas learned, is that Christians live out their faith by obeying the will of God. They do this not because they are slaves who must satisfy their Master, but because they are children who want to please their Father. "I understand now," said one of the Tuyucas, finally grasping the gospel message of Galatians. "My grandfather said it is better for a son to obey his father out of love than out of fear of being punished. That is how God wants us to obey him—out of love."[1]

FROM SONSHIP TO SLAVERY

By the Spirit of God's Son, the Galatians had learned to call God "Father." Yet they were in imminent danger of going from sonship right back into slavery. They were about to squander their spiritual inheritance by selling their birthright as the sons and daughters of God.

No wonder the apostle Paul was so alarmed! Why would anyone who had been adopted by God want to go back and work for the devil? It made no sense, which is why the apostle tried everything he could think of to stop them. He reminded them of his own conversion by the gospel of Jesus Christ (Gal. 1:11–2:21). He appealed to their experience of the Holy Spirit (Gal. 3:1–5). He argued with them on the basis of biblical history and theology (Gal. 3:6–14). He used examples from everyday life (Gal. 3:15–4:7). Finally, in the middle of chapter 4, Paul pleads with the Galatians on the basis of their personal relationship. Afraid that all his work has been in vain, he pours out his soul to them. His words are full of pathos: "I am afraid I may have labored over you in vain" (Gal. 4:11); "Brothers, I entreat you" (Gal. 4:12). He addresses them not only with the heart of a brother, but also with the affection of a mother: "my little children," he sighs, "for whom I am again in the anguish of childbirth" (Gal. 4:19).

Paul had thought that the Galatians were born again, but now he worries that it may have been a case of false labor. By the end of this section, he is practically at a loss as to what else to say. He is at his wits' end, unsure how

1. This story was recounted in correspondence from Paul Frank of Wycliffe's Summer Institute of Linguistics (March 1999).

to express his emotions in all their complexity: "I wish I could be present with you now and change my tone, for I am perplexed about you" (Gal. 4:20). "We have been listening to Paul the apostle, Paul the theologian, Paul the defender of the faith," writes John Stott, "but now we are hearing Paul the man, Paul the pastor, Paul the passionate lover of souls."[2]

KNOWING GOD'S GRACE

To keep his beloved Galatians from slipping back into slavery, the apostle Paul tried to remind them how they had become the children of God in the first place. From his remarks we learn three things that distinguish a son from a slave. A child of God is someone who knows the freedom of God's grace (Gal. 4:8–11), enjoys the ministry of God's Word (Gal. 4:12–16), and is transformed into the life of God's Son (Gal. 4:17–20).

First, to be a child of God is to know the freedom of God's grace. To put it even more simply, a Christian is someone who knows God: "Formerly, when you did not know God, you were enslaved to those that by nature are not gods. But now that you have come to know God, or rather to be known by God, how can you turn back again to the weak and worthless elementary principles of the world, whose slaves you want to be once more?" (Gal. 4:8–9).

There was a time when the Galatians did not know God at all. Most of them were Gentiles, and thus they were unacquainted with the God of the Bible. They worshiped pagan gods and goddesses. Some of them were into astrology and watched the signs of the zodiac. Others worshiped the deities of ancient Greece. At Lystra there was a temple to Zeus. In Iconium they worshiped the mother goddess Zizimene. All through Galatia people belonged to the Roman imperial cult. None of these deities were really gods at all. They were mere idols. Yet because demonic influences were at work, bowing down to false gods brought real spiritual bondage. Such bondage is the natural condition of humanity. In the famous words of Jean-Jacques Rousseau (1712–1778), who spoke better than he knew, "Man is born free, and everywhere he is in chains."[3] There was a time when the

2. John R. W. Stott, *The Message of Galatians: Only One Way*, The Bible Speaks Today (Downers Grove, IL: InterVarsity, 1968), 111.

3. This is the opening line of Rousseau's *Social Contract* (1762).

Galatians were in chains themselves, and since they did not know God, they did not know any better.

Then the Galatians came to know God through the preaching of the gospel of God's free grace. In other words, they became Christians, for a Christian simply is someone who knows God—not someone who knows about God, as if Christianity were some sort of philosophy, but someone who has a relationship with God. In the Bible, the knowledge of God is always personal. It involves an intimate encounter with God the Father, through the Spirit of his Son. Christianity is not a matter of *what* we know; it is a matter of *whom* we know.

An even better way to say this is that Christianity is a matter of who knows us! We can get to know God only because he already knows us—personally—and has revealed himself to us. So Paul makes this clarification: "now that you have come to know God—or rather to be known by God" (Gal. 4:9). To know God is to be a child of God, but this depends on the even more fundamental truth that we are known by God.

This is the freedom of God's grace, that he knew us long before we ever came to know him. The initiative for membership in God's family comes entirely from God himself. Imagine a tiny baby girl living in an orphanage. A man comes for a visit. As he sees the baby lying in her crib, he loves her so much that he adopts her into his family. She grows up to call the man "Father" because he is the only father she has ever known. But she knows him as her father only because he first knew her as his daughter. This is the love that God has for all his sons and daughters in Christ.

Anyone who receives such grace, such undeserved favor, could never go back to the orphanage. Yet this is exactly what the Galatians were trying to do! Paul could hardly believe it: "But now that you have come to know God, or rather to be known by God, how can you turn back again to the weak and worthless elementary principles of the world, whose slaves you want to be once more?" (Gal. 4:9). The Galatians were converting back to practical paganism. It was like déja vu. They were going back to the first principles of paganism, back to their religious ABCs. Although they had graduated to faith in Jesus Christ, they were re-enrolling for spiritual kindergarten.

Apparently, the Galatians were doing this by following the rituals of Old Testament Judaism: "You observe days and months and seasons and years!" (Gal. 4:10). In other words, the Galatians were starting to follow the Jewish calendar rites as a matter of religious obligation. Like so many Pharisees, they were observing the whole Jewish system of special holidays such as the feast of the new moon and festivals such as Passover and Tabernacles.

As far as Paul was concerned—and this must have shocked the Judaizers—this kind of religion was no better than paganism. If the Galatians wanted to practice the forms of outward religion, they might as well read their horoscopes or practice some other form of paganism. In their legalism, they were reverting to the very kind of religion they had rejected when they were converted to Christ. They had their "lucky days" when they were pagans, too. They followed astronomical signs and celebrated the emperor's birthday. But relapsing into such religion was a sign of profound spiritual ignorance.

Any religion that is based on observing special days is primitive because it reduces a relationship to a ritual. It makes following God a matter of doing one's duty rather than receiving God's grace. This is the potential danger with religiously observing the liturgical calendar the way some churches do. It is also a warning sign that many Americans are really pagans, for our national spirituality focuses on major holidays rather than on living for Christ every day. There are still far too many people who think that all they have to do for God is to go to church at Christmas and Easter.

There is nothing wrong, of course, with taking a day to praise God for the birth or the resurrection of his Son. Elsewhere, Paul says, "The one who observes the day, observes it in honor of the Lord" (Rom. 14:6); "Therefore let no one pass judgment on you in questions of food and drink, or with regard to a festival or a new moon or a Sabbath" (Col. 2:16). But there is an eternity of difference between the optional observance of such a day and making it mandatory as a means of justification. The Galatians needed to be reminded that God's grace comes free. Once we know the freedom of that grace, we become the true children of God, and we can never go back to spiritual slavery.

ENJOYING GOD'S WORD

A second mark that distinguishes God's children is their love for their Father's instruction. To be a son or a daughter of God is to find true enjoyment in the ministry of God's Word. "Enjoyment" is precisely the word that Paul uses when he asks, "What then has become of the blessing you felt?"

(Gal. 4:15). Literally, the Galatians "counted themselves happy" when they first heard the good news about Jesus Christ. They were practically congratulating themselves on their good fortune to hear the gospel that brought them out of slavery and into sonship.

The occasion of their joy was Paul's first missionary visit to Galatia. This visit had come as a surprise, at least to Paul, who was unexpectedly detained by some sort of health problem: "You know it was because of a bodily ailment that I preached the gospel to you at first" (Gal. 4:13). The Galatians knew exactly what Paul was talking about, but unfortunately we don't. Paul's malady is not mentioned in the book of Acts. Some scholars suggest that he picked up malaria on the mosquito coast of the Mediterranean and went up into the highlands of Galatia to recuperate. This illness sounds something like the famous "thorn in the flesh" that tormented Paul for more than a decade, which he mentions in 2 Corinthians 12. The words "in the flesh" and "weakness" (which usually means physical illness) appear in both passages; perhaps there is a connection.

Another possibility is that Paul had chronic difficulty with his eyesight. This would explain his rather alarming comment in verse 15: "For I testify to you that, if possible, you would have gouged out your eyes and given them to me" (Gal. 4:15). If a doctor could have performed an eye transplant for Paul, the Galatians would have been happy to provide a donor!

This statement was obviously hyperbole—an exaggeration to make a point. It does not necessarily mean that Paul was visually impaired. It may have had nothing to do with his eyesight at all. In the ancient world, a man's eye was considered his most valuable possession. When Paul says the Galatians would have given him their eyeballs, he means they would have done anything for him. His statement is reminiscent of a story told by Lucian of Antioch (c. 240–312)—the tale of Dandamis and Amizoces. In an act of heroic friendship, Dandamis sacrificed his eyes in order to ransom Amizoces from captivity. Amizoces did not discover what his friend had done until after he was set free. When he learned of it, he blinded himself because he could not bear to see his friend wander about in darkness.[4]

4. Hans Dieter Betz, *Galatians*, Hermeneia (Philadelphia: Fortress, 1979), 228.

What was the reason for Paul's ill health? It is impossible to make an accurate diagnosis without being able to examine the patient. But whatever his sickness was, there are valuable lessons to be learned from it.

One is that God uses our problems to achieve his purpose. The apostle Paul did not particularly enjoy his illness. If Corinthians is any indication, there were times when he pleaded with God to restore his health and strength. Yet in God's perfect providence, those requests were never granted. Instead, Paul's infirmity became God's opportunity. God used it to demonstrate how his power is made perfect in weakness (2 Cor. 12:9). He made it the occasion for reaching the Galatians with the gospel of free grace. Through their experience, he ultimately used it to teach us the difference between sonship and slavery. Thus there was much to be gained through Paul's illness, however unfortunate it seemed at the time. God is the ultimate economist. He is able to bring the greatest good out of even the smallest setback. Thus there is no profit in complaining about the difficulties of life. It is much better to trust that God knows what he is doing and watch him glorify himself in and through our trials.

The other lesson to be learned from Paul's condition has to do with how we receive God's Word. We are to welcome it with the warmest hospitality. Paul writes, "Though my condition was a trial to you, you did not scorn or despise me" (Gal. 4:14). This suggests that whatever Paul's illness or injury may have been, it was unsightly, perhaps even visually repulsive. As a result, it would have been easy for the Galatians to be turned off by Paul's appearance. His deformity actually posed a temptation for them. Here it helps to know that most ancient Greeks considered disease and disability to be signs of divine displeasure, or even demonic influence. When Paul says that the Galatians did not despise him (Gal. 4:14), he literally says that they did not spit at him, as pagans usually did when they saw someone they thought was disfigured by a demon.

However unattractive Paul may have been, the Galatians did not reject him. Instead, he writes, they "received me as an angel of God, as Christ Jesus" (Gal. 4:14). Rather than treating him as if he had a demon, they greeted him like an angel. Indeed, they gave him the kind of welcome they would have given to Christ himself. The reason for their warm welcome was not so much that they loved Paul as it was that they loved God's Word. They recognized that Paul was an apostle, an official messenger of Jesus Christ. Therefore, they received his ministry the way God's children always receive their Father's Word: with real joy.

The example of the Galatians reminds us that the primary qualification for any Christian minister is that he must preach the Word of God. Too many churches have the wrong expectations of their ministers. Consider this description of the "Perfect Pastor" (which, thankfully, does not come from my own job description):

> He condemns sins, but never upsets anyone. He works from 8:00 A.M. until midnight and is also the janitor. He makes $60.00 a week ... and gives about $50.00 a week to the poor. He is 28 years old and has been preaching for 30 years. . . . The Perfect Pastor smiles all the time with a straight face because he has a sense of humor that keeps him seriously dedicated to his work. . . . He spends all his time evangelizing the unchurched and is always in his office when needed.

Ministers should not be judged by their ability, appearance, personality, popularity, or any of the other standards ordinarily used to judge them. Ministers should be evaluated primarily by their faithfulness to the Word of God. If they are faithful, then to welcome their message is to welcome Christ himself. "Happy is that Christian society," wrote the Scotsman John Brown, "when the minister loves his people, and the people love their minister 'for the truth's sake.'"[5]

Unfortunately, the Galatians were starting to turn against Paul. They may not have wronged Paul before, but they certainly seemed to be wronging him now. Their hospitality was turning into hostility, presumably because the Judaizers had been denigrating the apostle and denying his gospel.

Paul writes to the Galatians, therefore, as a wounded lover. He wonders, "Have I then become your enemy by telling you the truth?" (Gal. 4:16). His gospel has not changed. He is still proclaiming the good news about the cross and the empty tomb. He is still preaching justification by grace alone, through faith alone, in Christ alone. Yet the Galatians were starting to reject the one true gospel. Unwilling to hear the truth, they were treating Paul like an enemy.

5. John Brown, *An Exposition of the Epistle of Paul the Apostle to the Galatians* (Edinburgh, 1853; repr. Evansville, IN: Sovereign Grace, 1957), 218.

The very message that first created the bond of their affection for him was starting to cause a rift between them.

When the Galatians turned against God's message and God's messenger, Paul wondered if they were really God's children after all. Ministers who are faithful to God's Word often tell people things that they don't want to hear. (Truth be told, they sometimes preach things they themselves don't want to hear either.) But if it really is God's message, God's true children rejoice to hear it. They know that if their loving Father is telling them something they would prefer not to hear, it must be for their own good.

FORMED BY GOD'S SON

Something happens to people who enjoy the ministry of God's Word. The more they learn the Bible, the more they start to look like Jesus Christ. They start to think the things he thinks, love the things he loves, do the things he does, even suffer the things he suffers. This brings us to a final characteristic of a child of God: He or she is transformed into the life of God's Son. As Paul puts it, "Christ is formed in you!" (Gal. 4:19).

Paul's opponents wanted to change people, too, but not for the better: "They make much of you, but for no good purpose. They want to shut you out, that you may make much of them" (Gal. 4:17). Paul does not mention his opponents by name, but he is talking about the nefarious Judaizers who came from Jerusalem to contradict his gospel.

The Judaizers were the wrong kind of zealots. In their misguided zeal for the law, they told the Galatians that they had to become Jews in order to be good Christians. This heretical teaching had the result of dividing the Jews from the Gentiles *inside* the church, where we are all supposed to be one in Christ. It also had the result of turning the Galatians away from Paul and the one true gospel of free grace. The Judaizers seem to have envied Paul's missionary success. What they really wanted was their own disciples, as false teachers always do. So they tried to win the Galatians away from Paul by flattering them and courting their affections.

For his own part, the apostle had no interest in having his own disciples. Remember how distressed he became when he discovered that he had groupies in the church at Corinth (1 Cor. 1:10–17). The only disciples he had any interest in were the kind that follow Christ.

This desire is fully in keeping with what the apostle says in verse 12: "Brothers, I entreat you, become as I am, for I also have become as you are" (Gal. 4:12). This is Paul's mission statement, a longer version of which appears in 1 Corinthians 9: "To the Jews I became as a Jew, in order to win Jews. To those under the law I became as one under the law (though not being myself under the law) that I might win those under the law. To those outside the law I became as one outside the law (not being outside the law of God but under the law of Christ) that I might win those outside the law. . . . I have become all things to all people, that by all means I might save some" (1 Cor. 9:20–22). Paul became like others so that others could come to know Christ. To use the popular term for it, he knew how to *contextualize* the gospel. He knew how to become so integrated into the life of a community that he could explain the gospel in words that people could actually understand.

This is the strategy Paul followed when he first visited the Galatians. He entered into their lives so thoroughly that he practically became a Galatian himself. In particular, he was careful not to follow any Jewish cultural practices that might have hindered his evangelism among Gentiles.

This is the model every Christian should follow in doing evangelistic work. Without compromising the gospel, we should become as much like the people we are trying to reach as we possibly can. Our real goal is to make people become like us (insofar as we are like Christ), but first we have to become like them.

Paul knew how to do this. He became like the Galatians in order to help the Galatians become like him. He did not do this because he was trying to clone himself. He simply wanted the Galatians to be like Christ, and he knew that one way for them to learn how to do this was to become like him. He said the same thing to the Corinthians: "Be imitators of me, as I am of Christ" (1 Cor. 11:1). Paul wanted the Galatians to enjoy the kind of freedom he had as a son of God, freedom from the legalism of godless religion.

The apostle's ultimate goal was to see Christ take shape in the lives of his people, to see Christ "formed" in them. Christ was already starting to take shape in Paul's life. Back at the end of chapter 2 he said, "It is no longer I who live, but Christ who lives in me" (Gal. 2:20). Now he wanted the same Christ to live in the Galatians in the same way. This ought to be the goal of every pastor: not the favor of men, but the formation of Christ. As Calvin observed, "If ministers wish to be something, let them labour to form Christ, not themselves," in their hearers.[6]

This kind of spiritual formation does not happen overnight. It takes a while for an embryo to grow into an infant, and then for a child to grow into an adult. Cell must be added to cell, tissue to tissue, sinew to bone. In the same way, the Spirit gradually uses God's Word to make God's children like God's Son.

This process is what Henry Scougal wrote about in his famous book *The Life of God in the Soul of Man*: "True religion is a union of the soul with God, a real participation of the Divine nature, the very image of God drawn upon the soul, or, in the apostle's phrase, 'it is Christ formed within us.'"[7] It is also what the famous English evangelist George Whitefield meant when he spoke of "Christ formed in the heart."[8] It is almost as if Christ becomes incarnate in the life of the Christian.

The more our lives get shaped into the image of Christ, the more consistent we will be in our Christianity. Paul touches on this in verse 18, when he says, "It is always good to be made much of for a good purpose, and not only when I am present with you" (Gal. 4:18). Apparently, the apostle had discovered that some people behave differently when they are in the presence of a minister. Their vocabulary tends to be less colorful. Often, their conversation is more spiritual. Sometimes they make the minister almost as uncomfortable as he makes them! But when Christ is formed in us, we will be like Christ all the time, whether or not the minister is around.

This is what Paul was striving and struggling for. It required such difficult labor that it practically felt like childbirth. Paul thought he had given birth once before, but this time he was determined to carry the Galatians to full term. He wanted to see them safely delivered as sons and daughters of God.

6. John Calvin, *The Epistles of Paul the Apostle to the Galatians, Ephesians, Philippians and Colossians*, Calvin's New Testament Commentaries, trans. T. H. L. Parker, ed. David W. and Thomas F. Torrance (Grand Rapids: Eerdmans, 1996), 83.
7. Henry Scougal, *The Life of God in the Soul of Man* (Fearn, Ross-shire: Christian Focus, 1996), 41–42.
8. See F. F. Bruce, *The Epistle to the Galatians: A Commentary on the Greek Text*, New International Greek Testament Commentary (Grand Rapids: Eerdmans, 1982), 213.

In these verses he has described for us what it means to be a true child of God. It is to know the freedom of God's grace and the joy of God's Word, and so to be formed into the image of Christ. Once this starts to happen—once we have passed from slavery to sonship—it really is unthinkable to go back to being a slave again.

One man who never forgot that God had redeemed him from slavery was John Newton. Newton knew a great deal about slavery because he had been a slave-trader before he committed his life to Christ. Yet from that point on he was no longer a slave to sin; he was a son of God.

To remind himself that he would always be a *former* slave, Newton had these words from the Bible fixed to the wall of his study: "Thou shalt remember that thou wast a bondman [slave] in the land of Egypt, and the Lord thy God redeemed thee" (Deut. 15:15).[9] Like John Newton, anyone who has become God's own dear child needs to remember never to go back into bondage.

---

9. This story is recounted in Stott, *Message of Galatians*, 110.

15

TWO MOTHERS, TWO SONS, TWO COVENANTS

Galatians 4:21–31

Now this may be interpreted allegorically: these women are two
covenants. One is from Mount Sinai, bearing children for slavery;
she is Hagar. Now Hagar is Mount Sinai in Arabia; she corresponds
to the present Jerusalem, for she is in slavery with her children. But
the Jerusalem above is free, and she is our mother. (Gal. 4:24–26)

*I*t is sometimes said that there are two kinds of people in the
world: those who divide the world into two kinds of people,
and those who don't! Apparently, the apostle Paul was in the
former category, for he divided the whole world into two groups: the slaves
and the free. The slaves are under the law and outside of Christ, while the
free are in Christ and no longer under the law because they live by faith.

This contrast between law and faith—between religious bondage and
spiritual freedom—runs throughout Paul's letter to the Galatians. This epistle was written to help the slaves of religion find true freedom in Christ.

JOURNEY TO GALATIA

The contrast between slavery and freedom is drawn most sharply at the
end of chapter 4, which also happens to be one of the most difficult passages
in the New Testament.

To understand this rather complicated biblical argument, it helps first to travel back to Galatia. The apostle Paul himself had traveled to Galatia, in the south of Asia Minor, preaching the good news about Jesus Christ. There he proclaimed the gospel of the cross and the empty tomb. He invited the Galatians to receive eternal life through the crucifixion and resurrection of Jesus Christ.

As a result of Paul's evangelistic efforts, new churches were planted throughout the region. Yet shortly thereafter, a group of Jewish-Christian missionaries arrived in Galatia to "correct" Paul's gospel. These men, who came from Jerusalem, are sometimes known as "the Judaizers." They preached a legalistic form of Christianity. They wanted Gentiles to become Jews in order to be good Christians. Thus they were trying to add the law of Moses on top of the gospel of Jesus Christ.

Under the influence of this teaching, the Galatians began to squander their newfound freedom in Christ. They were keeping Jewish traditions that were unnecessary for Christians. Some of them thought they had to get circumcised. Others were saying that it was mandatory to celebrate Passover and other Jewish festivals. In their effort to prove that they were good Christians, they were becoming enslaved to all kinds of Old Testament rituals.

We often do the same thing. We forget that Christianity is a form of liberty, and not slavery. We reduce faith in Christ to a list of rules or traditions. We evaluate our spiritual standing by what we do for God, rather than by what God has done for us in Jesus Christ. In truth, we are all recovering Pharisees, in constant danger of forgetting to live only by faith and choosing instead to go right back under the law.

In order to persuade the Galatians that they were free from the law, the apostle Paul used a legal argument. In fine rabbinic style, he used the Torah, or Old Testament law, to make his point. "Tell me," he wrote, somewhat sarcastically, "you who desire to be under the law, do you not listen to the law?" (Gal. 4:21). His meaning could be paraphrased like this: "So you want to be under the law, do you? Well, do you have any idea what the law really says? Because if you did, you would realize that the law itself tells you not to be under the law!"

To argue with the legalists on their own terms, Paul took an example from the book of Genesis. His example was Abraham, who is mentioned eight times in this epistle. From this we may infer that the Judaizers claimed the father of the Jews as their hero. Before Paul could help the Galatians understand the

181

gospel of free grace, he had to correct their interpretation of Abraham. He used a Jewish argument to convince the Galatians not to become more Jewish!

The Judaizers had probably told the Galatians something like this about Abraham: "When God first made all his covenant promises, he said they were only for Abraham and his children. We are Abraham's children because we are his direct descendants through Isaac. But you can receive the promise, too. All you have to do is become a child of Abraham in the Jewish way, by getting circumcised."

THE HISTORICAL SITUATION

The apostle Paul met this challenge head-on. His argument in Galatians 4 may be outlined as follows: the historical situation (Gal. 4:22–23); the allegorical interpretation (Gal. 4:24–27); and the practical application (Gal. 4:28–31).

The historical situation was this: "For it is written that Abraham had two sons, one by a slave woman and one by a free woman. But the son of the slave was born according to the flesh, while the son of the free woman was born through promise" (Gal. 4:22–23). The story of these events is told in the book of Genesis. God had promised to make Abraham a great nation, but he still didn't have any children. And what kind of patriarch could he be if he didn't have any patriarchy? His wife was barren, and he wasn't getting any younger. The man was in his eighties! When he gazed at his reflection in the pool, he could see his wrinkled face and his old, white beard.

As hard as this was on Abraham, it must have been even harder on his wife Sarah. Year after year she prayed for a baby, yet she remained childless. Finally, in bitter desperation she said to her husband, "Behold now, the LORD has prevented me from bearing children. Go in to my servant; it may be that I shall obtain children by her" (Gen. 16:2). The maidservant—an Egyptian woman named Hagar—conceived and gave birth to a son named Ishmael (Gen. 16:15).

God had not forgotten his promise, however. He came to Abraham again and said, "As for Sarai your wife, you shall not call her name Sarai, but Sarah shall be her name. I will bless her, and moreover, I will give you a son by her. I will bless her, and she shall become nations" (Gen. 17:15–16). Because of God's promise and against all expectation, Sarah conceived at the age of ninety and gave birth to a son named Isaac (Gen. 21:1–3).

There were many similarities between Ishmael and Isaac. They were both sons of Abraham, and thus they had the same biological father. They were both circumcised. They both grew up in the same home. Yet for all their similarities, there were several crucial differences between them.

One difference was their status in the eyes of the law. Although the boys had the same paternity, they each had a different maternity. From their respective mothers they inherited two different legal standings. Ishmael's mother was a slave, so he was born a slave. Isaac, on the other hand, was born free, the heir of a free woman.

Another crucial difference between the two half-brothers was the manner of their births. Each son was born a different way. Ishmael "was born according to the flesh" (Gal. 4:23). This phrase, which is repeated in verse 29, means that Ishmael was procreated in the ordinary way. However, Isaac was not born "according to the flesh." His birth itself was ordinary enough, but the circumstances surrounding his conception were extraordinary. He was "born through promise" (Gal. 4:23), or "according to the Spirit" (Gal. 4:29). This is what distinguished Isaac from Ishmael: Isaac's birth was the result of God's supernatural intervention.

When God promised her a son, Sarah thought it was just about the funniest thing she had ever heard. After all, the woman had already been through menopause! The Scripture says: "Now Abraham and Sarah were old, advanced in years. The way of women had ceased to be with Sarah. So Sarah laughed to herself, saying, 'After I am worn out, and my lord is old, shall I have pleasure?' " (Gen. 18:11–12).

The answer was "Yes!" Sarah may have been worn out, and her master may have been old, but God was faithful to his promise. Through the supernatural work of his Spirit, Abraham and Sarah produced a child born by God's promise. "By faith Sarah herself received power to conceive, even when she was past the age, since she considered him faithful who had promised" (Heb. 11:11).

This interpretation shows that the story of Isaac and Ishmael is about something more than sibling rivalry. When Abraham got Hagar pregnant, he was operating on the principle that "God helps those who help themselves." He was trying to take the blessing, rather than waiting to receive it. As J. I. Packer so aptly puts it, he was "acting the amateur providence."[1]

---

1. J. I. Packer, *Knowing God* (Downers Grove, IL: InterVarsity, 1973), 228.

Whereas Isaac was a gift, Ishmael is what Abraham got for trying to do things his way instead of God's way.

From the very beginning there was a fundamental spiritual difference between the two sons. One son was born by proxy, the other by promise. One came by works; the other came by faith. One was a slave; the other was free. Thus Ishmael and Isaac represent two entirely different approaches to religion: law against grace, flesh against Spirit, self-reliance against divine dependence.

ALLEGORICAL INTERPRETATION: HAGAR

The spiritual distinction between Isaac and Ishmael was part of Abraham's personal history, but the apostle Paul discovered an even deeper meaning at work. He took the historical situation and gave it an allegorical interpretation. He wrote, "Now this may be interpreted allegorically" (Gal. 4:24).

Allegorical interpretation has fallen out of style, but the method was familiar to the Galatians. For them, when Paul interpreted the story of Hagar and Sarah allegorically as well as literally, he would have clinched his argument. An allegory is a story in which specific people, places, and events stand for deep spiritual truths. Perhaps the most famous allegory is *The Pilgrim's Progress*, written by John Bunyan. The characters in *The Pilgrim's Progress* have names like Christian, Faithful, and Hopeful. They travel to places like Doubting Castle and the Hill of Difficulty. Rather obviously, Bunyan was not writing history or geography; he was telling a story to make a spiritual point.

The story of Abraham's sons is not quite that kind of allegory, because their story is actually history. Isaac and Ishmael were real sons born to real mothers. Thus Paul's allegorical interpretation was based squarely on the facts of their historical situation. He recognized that the history of Abraham's sons had something significant to say about the way God always deals with his people. Isaac and Ishmael stand for something. There is an analogy between what God did for them and what he offers to us. In the eyes of God, everyone is either an Ishmael or an Isaac. Ultimately, their story is about the gospel of God's free grace.

To understand what Isaac and Ishmael represent, it helps to start with their mothers: "these women are two covenants. One is from Mount Sinai, bearing children for slavery; she is Hagar. Now Hagar is Mount Sinai in Arabia; she corresponds to the present Jerusalem, for she is in slavery with her children. But the Jerusalem above is free, and she is our mother" (Gal. 4:24–26). The analogy is complex. To take it step by step, the two mothers (Hagar and Sarah), with their two sons (Ishmael and Isaac), stand for two covenants (a covenant of works and a covenant of grace), which correspond to two cities (the present Jerusalem and the Jerusalem above).

Hagar stands for the old covenant, which God gave through Moses on Mount Sinai. The reason she is associated with Sinai probably has to do with geography. Hagar's children, the Ishmaelites, were the Arabs who lived in and around the Sinai Peninsula. So it was natural to associate her with the covenant God gave there. The old covenant came from Hagar's territory.

A covenant is a binding agreement God makes with his people. The old covenant contained all the rituals and regulations that God's people had to keep in order to receive God's blessing. It stated "Thou shalt" and "Thou shalt not." Therefore, it was based on a principle of works and keeping it was a kind of bondage, as Paul had already explained: "we were held captive under the law, imprisoned until the coming faith would be revealed" (Gal. 3:23).

Hagar was the perfect woman to represent the old covenant. The old covenant meant slavery to the law, and she herself was a slave. Furthermore, all of her children were slaves like Ishmael. So anyone who is still in bondage to legalism is one of Hagar's spiritual children. Anyone who reduces Christianity to a list of "dos and don'ts" is a slave like Ishmael.

This is how the allegory lines up so far: Hagar, the slave woman—Ishmael, her son born the ordinary way—Mount Sinai, where the old covenant was given. The punch line comes next: "Now Hagar is Mount Sinai in Arabia; she corresponds to the present Jerusalem, for she is in slavery with her children" (Gal. 4:25). When Paul mentioned Jerusalem, he was speaking not only geographically, but also spiritually. Jerusalem stands for God's people. In this case, it refers especially to the Jews and to the Judaism of Paul's day— the institution of Jewish religion. Paul may also have mentioned Jerusalem because this is where the Judaizers came from. The Jewish legalists who wanted the Galatians to add the law to the gospel came from the mother church in Jerusalem. And when Paul said that Jerusalem corresponded to Hagar, he was saying that although the Judaizers were Jews, they were really Ishmaelites, spiritually speaking! This was the shocker, like calling a Jew a Gentile, or an Israeli an Arab.

The Judaizers prided themselves on being the true sons of Abraham. Paul admitted that they were children of Abraham, but he said that they were spiritually illegitimate. He reasoned that since they were giving up the gospel to go back under the law, they must be sons of Hagar rather than children of Sarah. This meant that they were still in spiritual bondage. The same is true of anyone who seeks to be justified by keeping the law. Charles Spurgeon explained it like this:

> Hagar never was a free woman, and Sarah never was a slave. So, beloved, the covenant of works never was free, and none of her children ever were. All those who trust in works never are free, and never can be, even could they be perfect in good works. Even if they have no sin, still they are bond-slaves; for when we have done all that we ought to have done, God is not our debtor; we are debtors still to him, and still remain as bond-slaves. If I could keep all God's law, I should have no right to favor; for I should have done no more than was my duty, and be a bond-slave still. This law is the most rigorous master in the world; no wise man would love its service; for after all you have done, the law never gives you a "thank you" for it, but says, "Go on, sir, go on!" The poor sinner trying to be saved by law is like a blind horse going round and round a mill, and never getting a step further, but only being whipped continually; yea, the faster he goes, the more work he does; the more he is tired, so much the worse for him. The better legalist a man is, the more sure he is of being damned; the more holy a man is, if he trust to his works, the more he may rest assured of his own final rejection and eternal portion with Pharisees. Hagar was a slave; Ishmael, moral and good as he was, was nothing but a slave, and never could be more. Not all the works he ever rendered to his father could make him a free-born son.[2]

Allegorical Interpretation: Sarah

By contrast, Sarah never was a slave. This brings us to the other side of the allegory. Abraham's wife was the free woman Sarah. The son born to her by promise was Isaac, who was also free. Sarah represents the new covenant, which is not a covenant of law, but of promise. In the new covenant, God does not say "Thou shalt" and "Thou shalt not." Instead he says, "I will":

2. Charles Haddon Spurgeon, *The New Park Street Pulpit* (1857; repr. Pasadena, TX: Pilgrim, 1975), 2:126.

"I will be your God"; "I will redeem you from your sins"; "I will give you the free gift of eternal life." The new covenant is the gospel, which gives salvation through the death and resurrection of Jesus Christ.

The new covenant does not match up with the present city of Jerusalem, "but the Jerusalem above is free, and she is our mother" (Gal. 4:26). If Jerusalem represents the people of God, then the "Jerusalem above" is the church of Jesus Christ. Notice that Paul does not speak chronologically, saying, "the Jerusalem to come." Instead, he speaks spatially, saying, "the Jerusalem above."

This is because the New Jerusalem is not just for the future. God has already started to build his eternal city. The "new" Jerusalem has replaced the "now" Jerusalem. The spiritual Jerusalem has superseded the earthly Jerusalem in the plan of God. The promises of the Old Testament were not for the Jews only, but they are fulfilled in the church of Jesus Christ. Anyone who receives Jesus as Savior and Lord is a son or daughter of Sarah, a true child of Abraham. If we belong to God's family in this way, we are free in Christ. We are citizens of the New Jerusalem and enjoy the freedom of that eternal city.

To review, there are two mothers, two sons, two covenants, two cities, and two families. Ronald Fung has prepared a helpful chart to illustrate the allegory:

Slavery	**Freedom**
Hagar—a slave woman	Sarah—a free woman
Ishmael—born according to the flesh	Isaac—born through God's promise
The Sinaitic covenant of law (included a works principle)	The covenant of promise (based on faith)
The present Jerusalem (= Judaism)	The Jerusalem above (= the Church)
The children of the present Jerusalem (= legalists)	The children of the Jerusalem above (= Christians)
Righteousness by Law	**Righteousness by Faith**[3]

The allegory shows the difference between spiritual slavery and spiritual freedom. Those who try to justify themselves by keeping the law are the slave

3. Ronald Y. K. Fung, *The Epistle to the Galatians*, New International Commentary on the New Testament (Grand Rapids: Eerdmans, 1988), 213.

187

children of Hagar, but those who are justified by faith in Christ are God's free sons and daughters.

Whenever Paul thought about the joy of freedom in Christ, he burst into song, as he does here:

> Rejoice, O barren one who does not bear;
>> break forth and cry aloud, you who are not in labor!
> For the children of the desolate one will be more
>> than those of the one who has a husband. (Gal. 4:27; cf. Isa. 54:1)

This quotation from Isaiah is doubly appropriate because it relates to both Sarah and Jerusalem. The connection with Sarah is obvious. She was a barren woman whom God blessed with a joyous multitude of sons and daughters. When Isaiah prophesied about the barren woman, however, he was not thinking primarily of Sarah, but of the city of Jerusalem. The "now" Jerusalem of his day was barren because her children had been carried away into exile. But Isaiah promised that one day God would establish a "new" Jerusalem, which would be filled with far more children than the old Jerusalem could ever contain.

Isaiah's happy promise is being fulfilled at this very moment, not in an earthly city, but in a spiritual one that spreads across the globe. As men, women, and children come to faith in Jesus Christ, they become citizens of the New Jerusalem, to the praise and glory of God.

PRACTICAL APPLICATION

This brings Paul's allegorical interpretation to the point of practical application. There are two mothers (Hagar and Sarah), two sons (Ishmael and Isaac), two covenants (old and new), and two cities (the "now" and "new" Jerusalems). The question is, To which of these two do you belong?

The reason this matters is that to be a true child of Abraham is to be a son or daughter of God, which is the greatest privilege in the world. But it is not enough to claim Abraham as our father, as the Judaizers did, because Abraham had two sons, and only one of them was free. F. F. Bruce says: "If you insist on the priority in the inheritance of Abraham's descendants *according to the flesh* . . . remember this: Abraham indeed had a son *according to the flesh*, of whom it is expressly stated that he was *not* to share the inheritance."[4] Therefore, the crucial question becomes, "Who is your mother?"

Paul wanted the Galatians to see that by the promise of God, they were free sons and daughters of Sarah: "Now you, brothers, like Isaac, are children of promise" (Gal. 4:28). Remember what this promise was. It was the promise God first gave to Abraham, that all the nations of the world would be blessed through him (Gal. 3:8). In other words, it was the promise of the gospel, the promise of the coming Christ, the promise of justification by grace alone through faith alone. According to that promise, all it takes to be a child of God is to believe that Jesus died on the cross for our sins and rose again from the dead.

Paul called the Galatians "brothers" because they were the children of that promise. God's promise to Abraham is not simply for the Jews as Jews. Rather, it is for every believer, whether Jew or Gentile: "in Christ Jesus you are all sons of God, through faith," Paul wrote at the end of the previous chapter (Gal. 3:26). "And if you are Christ's, then you are Abraham's offspring, heirs according to promise" (Gal. 3:29). The ones who truly belong to Abraham are the ones who belong to Christ. Anyone who has faith in Jesus is God's true child in the line of Isaac, born again free by the promise of God.

One implication of belonging to God's family is that we are likely to get persecuted. Here again, Paul's argument is based on history: "But just as at that time he who was born according to the flesh persecuted him who was born according to the Spirit, so also it is now" (Gal. 4:29). The son born the ordinary way was Ishmael, while the one born by the Spirit was Isaac. Although they were born fourteen years apart, the two siblings were rivals. In Genesis we read, "And Abraham made a great feast on the day that Isaac was weaned. But Sarah saw the son of Hagar the Egyptian, whom she had borne to Abraham, laughing" (Gen. 21:8–9). Ishmael, who was seventeen at the time, was not just teasing his little half-brother; he was treating him with contempt.

Paul's point was that Christians should expect exactly the same kind of treatment that Isaac received from his big brother. "So also it is now," he said (Gal. 4:29). In fact, it was happening in Galatia. The sons of Hagar were per-

---

4. F. F. Bruce, *The Epistle to the Galatians: A Commentary on the Greek Text*, New International Greek Testament Commentary (Grand Rapids: Eerdmans, 1982), 215.

secuting the sons of Sarah. Jews were persecuting Christians, and the Gentiles who came to faith in Jesus Christ were being oppressed by the Judaizers, who would not let them live by God's free grace.

Persecution is one way to tell the difference between true and false religion. Persecution is the opposition Christians face for speaking or doing God's will. It can include ridicule, loss, violence, and even martyrdom. One of the distinguishing marks of real Christians is that they are willing to suffer persecution for their faith, and even to die for it. By contrast, it is false religion that always does the persecuting. So whenever people who claim to be religious start to oppress minorities, hate Jews, or attack homosexuals, we can be sure that they do not represent true Christianity, even if they do it in the name of Jesus. Sooner or later, they will start persecuting the real Christians as well. Often, the most serious persecution comes from people who claim to be religious.

Christians should be prepared for this. If what we really want is to be liked, then we will never make very good Christians. Indeed, one wonders if we can really be Christians at all. Martin Luther said, "If someone does not want to endure persecution from Ishmael, let him not claim that he is Christian."[5]

One reason Christians are willing to be disliked, or even persecuted, for their faith is that they know what God has in store for them. We are God's children, and our heavenly Father has promised us an eternal inheritance of infinite delight.

Those who are not God's children have no such promise: "But what does the Scripture say? 'Cast out the slave woman and her son, for the son of the slave woman shall not inherit with the son of the free woman'" (Gal. 4:30). Ishmael never received his father's inheritance, even though Abraham asked God to give it to him (Gen. 17:18). God blessed Ishmael in many ways, but he never gave him the promise of salvation, which was only for Isaac. Therefore, the day finally came when Sarah "said to Abraham, 'Cast out this slave woman with her son, for the son of this slave woman shall not be heir with my son Isaac'" (Gen. 21:10). Sarah was not just being selfish about this. It was right for the slave to be cast out because God's promise of saving grace

---

5. Martin Luther, *Lectures on Galatians, 1535*, trans. and ed. Jaroslav Pelikan, in *Luther's Works* (St. Louis: Concordia, 1963), 26:451.

was only for Isaac. So God said to Abraham, "Whatever Sarah says to you, do as she tells you, for through Isaac shall your offspring be named" (Gen. 21:12).

When Paul quoted Sarah's words, it was a not-too-subtle way of saying that the Galatians needed to drive the Judaizers and their legalism right out of the church. By trying to place Gentiles under the law, they proved that they themselves were actually slaves, spiritually speaking, and therefore had no part in God's inheritance. If salvation comes by grace, then the church cannot tolerate salvation by works. Freedom in Christ can be preserved only by abolishing bondage to the law.

We can apply this by standing firm against legalism in the church, and against any other false doctrine of salvation. We can also ask God to cast every last trace of legalism out of our hearts. God still works today the way he worked with Hagar and Sarah. Salvation comes by grace and not by works. Righteousness comes through faith and not through the law. Christianity is not a list of "dos and don'ts." It is the good news about salvation for sinners through Jesus Christ.

This is why we cannot be saved through any other religion except Christianity. The other religions—such as Judaism, Hinduism, Islam, and Mormonism—are all slave religions. The same may even be said of versions of Christianity—such as Roman Catholicism and liberal Protestantism—that add works to faith as the basis for our righteousness before God. They bring bondage to human regulations because ultimately they are about what we do for God, not about what God has done for us in Jesus Christ.

What God has done in Jesus Christ is offer his free salvation to everyone who trusts in him. Martin Luther explained it like this: "Those who try to achieve the status of sons and heirs by the righteousness of the Law or by their own righteousness are slaves, who will never receive the inheritance even though they work themselves to death with their great effort; for they are trying, contrary to the will of God, to achieve by their own works what God wants to grant to believers by sheer grace for Christ's sake."[6]

If we are working to gain God's acceptance, we need to realize that we are still in spiritual slavery. If we want to be free, we need to ask God for the gift of his grace. Then we will be able to join with all his sons and daughters in saying, "We are not children of the slave but of the free woman" (Gal. 4:31).

---

6. Ibid., 26:449.

16

THE ONLY THING
THAT MATTERS

Galatians 5:1–6

You are severed from Christ, you who would be justified by the law; you have fallen away from grace. For through the Spirit, by faith, we ourselves eagerly wait for the hope of righteousness. For in Christ Jesus neither circumcision nor uncircumcision counts for anything, but only faith working through love. (Gal. 5:4–6)

Galatians can be divided into three parts—biography, theology, and ethics. In chapters 1 and 2 Paul recounted his spiritual autobiography to show that he was a genuine apostle of the one true gospel. In chapters 3 and 4 he explained the theology of that gospel in terms of justification by grace alone through faith alone in Christ alone. However, the only kind of theology that interested Paul was practical theology, so his epistle ends with ethics. Beginning with chapter 5, the apostle takes the good news of the cross and the empty tomb and applies it to daily life.

The theme of these chapters is announced in the very first verse: "For freedom Christ has set us free" (Gal. 5:1). To put it another way, "Christ has freed you to be free; so be free!" Paul had just finished explaining that the Galatians were not children of Hagar, the slave woman, but sons and daughters of Sarah, born again free by the promise of God. Now what they needed to do was to live free in Christ by the power of the Holy Spirit.

When Freedom Is Really Slavery

Americans prize nothing more highly than freedom. The trouble is that they generally want the wrong kind of freedom. Some speak of freedom in political terms: freedom of speech, freedom of assembly, freedom to vote. Others work for freedom from oppressive social structures. However, what most Americans mainly want is personal freedom. Sociologist Robert Bellah has concluded that "freedom is perhaps the most resonant, deeply held American value. . . . Yet freedom turns out to mean being left alone by others, not having other people's values, ideas, or styles of life forced upon one, being free of arbitrary authority in work, family, and political life."[1] In other words, what Americans really want is the freedom to be left alone.

The reason we want to be left alone is that we are naturally selfish. We want to do what we want to do, whenever, wherever, however, and with whomever we please. If this is what freedom means to us, then believing in God becomes extremely inconvenient. If there is a God, he undoubtedly has opinions about what we ought to do, where we ought to do it, and with whom.

What many Americans want these days, therefore, is not freedom *of* religion, but freedom *from* religion. Consider these words from *Free Inquiry*, a leading magazine for secular humanists: "Some ideas can enslave you; some can set you free. . . . If you crave freedom from baseless dogma . . . if you want to think for yourself instead of submitting to tradition, authority, or blind faith. . . . Put aside religion, despair, guilt, and sin . . . and find *new meaning and joy in life*."[2] In other words, you have to be free from God before you can be free at all.

Freedom *from* religion is not freedom at all, of course; it is another form of bondage. Freedom is not necessarily a virtue. We always need to ask what is meant by "freedom." Whether freedom is worth having or not depends on what kind of freedom it is. The best and truest freedom is the kind described by John Stott: "freedom from my silly little self, in order to live responsibly in love for God and others."[3]

1. Robert Bellah et al., *Habits of the Heart: Individualism and Commitment in American Life* (New York: Harper & Row, 1985), 23.
2. From a direct mailing by *Free Inquiry*, 1999.
3. John R. W. Stott, *The Contemporary Christian* (Downers Grove, IL: InterVarsity, 1992), 55

FREE IN CHRIST

When the Bible talks about freedom, it always means freedom in Jesus Christ: "For freedom Christ has set us free!" (Gal. 5:1). To quote from Stott again, "Our former state is portrayed as a slavery, Jesus Christ as a liberator, conversion as an act of emancipation and the Christian life as a life of freedom."[4]

The freedom Jesus has to offer is emancipation from the old slaveholders of humanity: sin, death, and the devil. Every human being is born into this triple slavery. We are born in sin, and thus we are evil by nature. We are destined to die, having been made mortal by God's curse against Adam's sin. Finally, we are tormented by the devil, who tempts us to sin and seeks to drag us down to the very pit of hell.

True freedom, therefore, is not self-fulfillment. It is not merely political independence or social equality. It is not the kind of liberty that leads to license, the freedom to do whatever we want or believe whatever we choose. True freedom means liberation from sin, death, and the devil. And by the grace of God, this is exactly the kind of liberation Christ has come to provide.

First, Jesus set us *free from sin*, and especially from its guilt. He did this by his crucifixion. In the words of an old hymn: "Mercy there was great, and grace was free. / Pardon there was multiplied to me. / There my burdened soul found liberty . . . at Calvary." When he was crucified on that hill outside Jerusalem, Jesus was cursed for our sins. He died on the cross to atone for our guilt. He offered his life as the just price for our sins, so that we would never have to face the wrath of God for ourselves.

Second, Christ has set us *free from death*. He did this by his resurrection. On the third day Jesus was raised from the dead with a real, live, glorious, immortal body. If we are in Christ, then death is not the end for us. We, too, will be raised again to eternal life.

Third, Christ has set us *free from the devil*. Through his crucifixion and resurrection, Jesus has broken Satan's stranglehold on humanity. As the writer to the Hebrews explained it, God gave us Jesus "that through death he might destroy the one who has the power of death, that is, the devil, and

---

4. John R. W. Stott, *The Message of Galatians: Only One Way*, The Bible Speaks Today (Downers Grove, IL: InterVarsity, 1968), 132.

deliver all those who through fear of death were subject to lifelong slavery" (Heb. 2:14–15).

Sin, death, and the devil—the only way to be free from the tyrants of humanity is by trusting in Jesus Christ. The only way to be free from the guilt of sin is to hold on to the cross where he died for sins. The only way to be free from death is to believe in the empty tomb where he was raised to give eternal life. And the only way to be free from the devil is to trust in God's final victory through Jesus Christ.

Another way to say all this is that Christ has freed us from *the law*, which is one of Paul's primary concerns throughout Galatians. Christ has not set us free from the moral law, which is God's eternal will for his people, but from the law that leads to sin and death. This is the law that we break when we sin, that Satan uses to accuse us of our guilt, and that sentences us to death. But the gospel of free grace says that the law no longer has that kind of power over me. Jesus Christ has conquered sin, death, and the devil. He has freed me from the law's deadly curse against my sin. He has kept the law I could not keep, paid the penalty I could not pay, and won the victory I could not win. Therefore, "the law of the Spirit of life" has set me "free in Christ Jesus from the law of sin and death" (Rom. 8:2).

Now I am free to be who God wants me to be and to do what God wants me to do. There is nothing I have to do to win God's acceptance. Now that God has accepted me through Jesus Christ, I am free in him. And this freedom is the key to gospel holiness. The old Princeton theologian Archibald Alexander (1772–1851) asked a question that continues to trouble thoughtful Christians today. He wanted to know why "Christians commonly are of so diminutive a stature and such feeble strength in their religion." There are many answers to this question, but here is the one that Alexander emphasized:

> There is a defect in our belief in the freeness of divine grace. To exercise unshaken confidence in the doctrine of gratuitous pardon is one of the most difficult things in the world; and to preach this doctrine fully without verging towards antinomianism is no easy task, and is therefore seldom done. But Christians cannot but be lean and feeble when deprived of their proper nutriment. It is by faith that the spiritual life is made to grow; and the doctrine of free grace, without any mixture of human merit, is the only true object of faith. . . . Here, I am persuaded, is the root of the evil; and until religious teachers inculcate clearly,

195

fully, and practically, the grace of God, as manifest in the Gospel, we shall have no vigorous growth of piety among professing Christians.[5]

ENSLAVED TO WORKS

The Galatians were free in Christ, but they were in danger of going back into slavery. Hence the need for Paul's warning: "For freedom Christ has set us free; stand firm therefore, and do not submit again to a yoke of slavery" (Gal. 5:1). The apostle's concern was that the Galatians were about to revoke his declaration of their emancipation. J. B. Phillips offers this helpful paraphrase: "Plant your feet firmly therefore within the freedom that Christ has won for us, and do not let yourselves be caught again in the shackles of slavery."

What Paul meant by "a yoke of slavery" was the Old Testament law, considered as a means of justification. Advocates of the New Perspective on Paul and the law argue that the Jews of this period did not treat the law as a legalistic means of justification. However, this perspective is contradicted by the critique of Jewish religion that Jesus and Paul make in the New Testament, as well as by a more careful reading of first-century Judaism.[6] By and large, first-century Judaism did not believe in grace alone, but in grace plus the keeping of the law. Thus the Jews of Paul's day often referred to the law of Moses as a yoke, calling it "the yoke of the commandments," or even "the yoke of the kingdom of heaven."[7]

The irony is that even though the Jews called the law a yoke, they did not recognize that they were enslaved by it. Peter saw it, though. At the Jerusalem Council he referred to the law as "a yoke . . . that neither our fathers nor we have been able to bear" (Acts 15:10). Paul saw it, too. He recognized that his people had become beasts of burden. They were so loaded down with the law that they couldn't even stand up straight. How could the Galatians take a firm stand for freedom when they, too, were doubled over by the yoke of the law?

5. Archibald Alexander, *Thoughts on Religious Experience* (1844; repr. London: Banner of Truth, 1967), 165–66.
6. See especially A. Andrew Das, *Paul, the Law, and the Covenant* (Peabody, MA: Hendrickson, 2001), and D. A. Carson, Peter T. O'Brien, and Mark A. Siefrid, eds., *Justification and Variegated Nomism*, 2 vols. (Grand Rapids: Baker, 2001, 2004).
7. F. F. Bruce, *The Epistle to the Galatians: A Commentary on the Greek Text*, New International Greek Testament Commentary (Grand Rapids: Eerdmans, 1982), 226.

The ones who were hitching the Galatians up to this yoke were the Judaizers—Jewish-Christian legalists who wanted to add the law of Moses to the gospel of Jesus Christ.[8] In particular, the Judaizers were insisting that Gentile Christians had to be circumcised. There have been hints of this issue throughout the letter, but here the apostle brings it right out into the open: "if you accept circumcision" (Gal. 5:2); "every man who accepts circumcision" (Gal. 5:3).

Since the time of Abraham, circumcision had signified belonging to God's covenant. Even after they became Christians, some Jews wanted to hold on to that sign. In fact, some went so far as to say that it was absolutely necessary for salvation. In the book of Acts we read what some of them taught: "Unless you are circumcised according to the custom of Moses, you cannot be saved" (Acts 15:1). According to the Judaizers, the only good Christian was a circumcised Christian.

If circumcision was only minor surgery, why did it become such a major issue? Because Paul understood that what was really at stake was the justification of sinners: What makes a person right with God? Getting circumcised was a way of saying that sinners have to *do* something to get right with God. This is what Paul meant when he spoke of those "who would be justified by the law" (Gal. 5:4). He was talking about circumcision as something that stood for the whole law of God (and not simply as a sign of belonging to God's people, which is the view taken by the New Perspective on Paul and the law). The Jews were circumcised already, of course, and there was nothing wrong with this. The problem was Gentiles' using circumcision as a means of justification. If circumcision became mandatory for all Christians, whether Jews or Gentiles, then salvation would be based on a work rather than on God's free grace.

Either people are justified before God partly by what they do for themselves or they are justified exclusively by what Jesus Christ has done for them. When the Galatians were thinking about getting circumcised, they were really thinking about getting justified. According to F. F. Bruce, "They could seek justification through faith in Christ (and obtain it) or they could seek

---

8. The Judaizers were legalists in the sense that they wanted to make the law part of the basis for salvation. For a helpful breakdown of various forms of legalism, see Daniel Doriani, *Putting the Truth to Work* (Phillipsburg, NJ: P&R, 2001).

it through legal works (and miss it). To seek it through faith in Christ was to seek it on the ground of God's grace; to seek it through legal works was to seek it on the ground of their own merit."[9] Circumcision was a way of saying that Jesus Christ was not enough for the Galatians, that they needed something more. The great English Bible scholar J. B. Lightfoot explained it like this: "Circumcision is the seal of the law. He who willingly and deliberately undergoes circumcision, enters upon a compact to fulfil the law. To fulfil it therefore he is bound, and he cannot plead the grace of Christ; for he has entered on another mode of justification."[10]

What is your mode of justification? Getting circumcised is one alternative to faith in Christ, but there are many others. Some people base their standing before God on the work they do in the church, or on the quality or frequency of their personal devotions. Others depend on the decision they made for Christ when they walked down the aisle or raised their hand at an evangelistic rally, as if they were saved by that gesture. Still others seek to justify themselves by the fact that they are baptized and confirmed members of a Christian church.

If we try to be justified before God by anything we do, no matter how small it is, we are not free. This is why justification must come by faith *alone*. What Jesus did on the cross and through the empty tomb justifies sinners all by itself. Therefore, if I am a Christian, my standing before God depends entirely on what Christ has done, not on anything that I have done. Otherwise, I am enslaved by my own works.

WHY WORKS ARE FATAL

The apostle Paul was worried that the Galatians were going to slip back into slavery. Before they did, he wanted them to know that anyone who goes back under the yoke of the law, whether by getting circumcised or by performing some other work, faces three fatal consequences.

The first is that *Jesus Christ can no longer do us any good.* We no longer have anything to gain from his benefits. The apostle could hardly be more emphatic: "Look: I, Paul, say to you that if you accept circumcision, Christ will be of no advantage to you" (Gal. 5:2). The apostle said something sim-

9. Bruce, *Epistle to the Galatians*, 231.
10. J. B. Lightfoot, *St. Paul's Epistle to the Galatians* (1865; repr. Lynn, MA: Hendrickson, 1981), 203.

ilar back in chapter 2: "if justification were through the law, then Christ died for no purpose" (Gal. 2:21). Trying to get right with God by getting circumcised—or by doing anything else—makes Christ utterly useless.

Why is this? Because we do not need him any more! If we accept circumcision, we are saying that we can keep the law for ourselves. But in that case, what do we need a Savior for? He becomes completely unnecessary. Why would we need him to do for us what we can do for ourselves, namely, keep the law?

We cannot have it both ways. Justification is either by law or by grace, either by works or by faith. Either we can rely on observing the law, or we can trust Christ alone to bear its curse on our behalf. But we cannot do both. With Christ, it is all or nothing. To receive him by faith is to admit that we cannot save ourselves at all. As the Puritan William Perkins said, "He must be a perfect Savior, or no Savior."[11] If we will not let Christ do everything for us, he can do nothing for us, at least as far as our justification is concerned. If we try to help ourselves, Christ will be no help at all.

When the Judaizers told the Galatians that they had to get circumcised to become good Christians, they were adding the law to the gospel. They were saying that Moses had to finish what Christ could only begin.

To illustrate the problem with this kind of theology, consider the man who had an old baseball autographed by Babe Ruth. The man had heard that the ball might be valuable, so one day he decided to sell it. He was worried, however, because he could see that the signature was badly faded. In order to make it clearer, he took out his baseball and carefully traced over the letters with a marking pen: "B-A-B-E R-U-T-H." The effect was to obliterate the real autograph, so that by the time he was finished, he had turned something priceless into something worthless.

It is the same with Jesus Christ. His finished work cannot be refinished; it can only be destroyed. What Christ did on the cross and through the empty tomb must be received by faith alone. If we try to add our works to his work, then his work no longer does us any good.

A second fatal consequence of basing salvation on our own work is that *we become debtors to God's law*. Paul wrote, "I testify again to every man who

---

11. William Perkins, *A Commentary on Galatians*, Pilgrim Classic Commentaries, ed. Gerald T. Sheppard (London, 1617; repr. New York: Pilgrim, 1989), 329.

accepts circumcision that he is obligated to keep the whole law" (Gal. 5:3). Another way to say this is that if we try to justify ourselves, we may be in for more than we bargained for! Not only are we unable to profit from Christ, but God's law holds us in its debt.

Getting circumcised was a way of belonging to the old covenant. But the old covenant required perfect obedience to the whole law of God. There-fore, if the Galatians wanted to get circumcised, they would have to keep the entire covenant from beginning to end. This is how Martin Luther described their dilemma: "The same principle by which you are obliged to receive cir-cumcision obliges you to accept the whole Law. . . . You must give up either Christ or the righteousness of the Law. If you keep Christ, you are righteous in the sight of God. If you keep the Law, Christ is of no avail to you; then you are obligated to keep the whole Law."[12]

The problem, of course, is that no one (except Jesus Christ) can keep God's whole law. So if getting circumcised demands perfect obedience, then anyone who gets circumcised is doomed. As Paul said earlier, "All who rely on works of the law are under a curse; for it is written, 'Cursed be everyone who does not abide by all things written in the Book of the Law, and do them'" (Gal. 3:10). The yoke of the law is unbearable. Since it cannot be kept, it holds sinners in its infinite debt.

This principle can be illustrated from an old Jewish rabbi, Gamaliel II. The rabbi had been reading Ezekiel, which describes the life of a man who is "righteous and does what is just and right" (Ezek. 18:5). When Gamaliel finished reading, he began to weep, saying, "Only he who keeps all these requirements will live, not he who keeps only one of them."[13] The rabbi was weeping because he knew that he could never meet the perfect standard of God's law. The Galatians couldn't meet it either, which is why Paul warned them not to get circumcised.

The third fatal consequence of working for our salvation is that *we are cut off from the grace of Jesus Christ.* Paul said, "You are severed from Christ,

---

12. Martin Luther, *Lectures on Galatians, 1535*, trans. and ed. Jaroslav Pelikan, in *Luther's Works* (St. Louis: Concordia, 1963), 27:15, 17.

13. Gamaliel II, *Babylonian Talmud, Sanhedrin* 81a, quoted in Bruce, *Epistle to the Galatians*, 230. This quotation is a further example of the kind of legalism that prevailed in Second Temple Judaism. Gamaliel II clearly regarded law-keeping as a means of justification, and not simply as a marker of his identity as a Jew.

you who would be justified by the law; you have fallen away from grace" (Gal. 5:4). Literally, those who try to be justified by works are cut off from Christ. Here again Paul shows that his concern is not simply the relationship between Jews and Gentiles in the church (as the New Perspective on Paul and the law maintains), but the sinner's relationship with God. His choice of words is significant. Circumcision involved cutting off the male foreskin. In the old covenant, this was a way of saying that a Jew was separated from the world. But it was also a way of saying that if he ever rejected God, he himself would be cut off from God's people. Here Paul was telling the Galatians just the opposite. They belonged to the new covenant, not to the old, and if they got circumcised now, they would be cutting themselves off from Christ! Rather than separating themselves from sin, they would be severing their relationship with the Savior. The underlying principle is that if we try to justify ourselves before God on the basis of our own works, Jesus Christ becomes a stranger to us; we lose access to his grace.

When Paul told the Galatians that they had "fallen away from grace" (Gal. 5:4), he was not making a comment about eternal security. No one who is truly united to Christ can ever lose his or her salvation, as the Bible clearly teaches elsewhere (John 10:28; Rom. 8:28–30). What Paul means here is that it is possible for someone to leave the community of God's grace. Anyone who rejects the only salvation that Christ has to offer has no business belonging to the church any longer. Those who go back under the yoke of the law—presumably because they never fully trusted Christ alone for their salvation—are outside the realm of grace.

This is a serious matter. Martin Luther applied Paul's warning as follows:

> For just as someone on a ship is drowned regardless of the part of the ship from which he falls into the sea, so someone who falls away from grace cannot help perishing. The desire to be justified by the law, therefore, is shipwreck; it is exposure to the surest peril of eternal death. What can be more insane and wicked than to want to lose the grace and favor of God and to retain the law of Moses, whose retention makes it necessary for you to accumulate wrath and every other evil for yourself? Now if those who seek to be justified on the basis of the moral law fall away from grace, where, I ask, will

those fall who, in their self-righteousness, seek to be justified on the basis of their traditions and vows? To the lowest depths of hell![14]

Those who try to justify themselves are bound for hell. Enslaved by a law they cannot keep, they are in God's infinite debt. Since they are trusting in themselves, Christ can no longer do them any good. They have fallen from grace.

FAITH THAT WORKS

If we cannot be saved by our own works, how can we be saved? The answer is simple: "For through the Spirit, by faith, we ourselves eagerly wait for the hope of righteousness" (Gal. 5:5). Faith comes up again in the following verse, where it is described as the only thing that really counts (Gal. 5:6). The way that we become righteous in God's sight (that is to say, the way that we are justified) is by faith alone.

Notice that justification is not something we work for; it is something we *wait* for. God gives his righteousness to those who wait for it in faith. When Paul speaks of waiting for righteousness, he is looking forward to the day of judgment, when God finally will render his verdict on every person who has ever lived. The Christian waits for that day with eager expectation, almost the way a little girl looks forward to her birthday party. The Christian hopes for a favorable verdict, trusting to be declared "Not guilty!" on the day of God's justice.

Are you waiting with confidence for the day of judgment? A good example of what it means to hope for God's righteousness comes from the life of a holy man named Arsenius:

Although Arsenius had lived for a long time in the greatest sanctity and self-denial, he still began to fear and grieve deeply when he sensed that death was not far off. When he was asked why he feared death although he had spent his entire life in saintliness and had served God continually, he replied that he had indeed lived blamelessly according to the judgment of men, but that the judgments of God were different from those of men. With his saintliness and asceticism this man attained nothing except a fear and a horror of death.

14. Luther, *Galatians*, 27:18.

By the grace of God, eventually Arsenius was delivered from all his sin and fear. He realized that if he was to be saved, "it was necessary that he lose all his own righteousness and trust only in the mercy of God, saying: 'I believe in Jesus Christ, the Son of God, our Lord, who suffered, was crucified, and died for my sins.'"[15]

This kind of faith comes only from the Holy Spirit, which is why Paul speaks of waiting "through the Spirit" (Gal. 5:5). From this point on, life in the Spirit becomes one of the main themes of Paul's letter. The Holy Spirit is mentioned here because he is the one who gives the gift of faith. The faith he gives is the kind that expresses itself through love: "For in Christ Jesus neither circumcision nor uncircumcision counts for anything, but only faith working through love" (Gal. 5:6).

This was a shocking thing to say, even for someone as radical as Paul. The apostle must have meant it, however, because he makes a similar statement near the end of his letter: "For neither circumcision counts for anything, nor uncircumcision, but a new creation" (Gal. 6:15). How could Paul say that circumcision doesn't matter?!? His whole reason for writing to the Galatians in the first place was precisely their thinking of getting circumcised. But notice the context. It is "in Christ" (Gal. 5:6) that circumcision becomes irrelevant. Both the circumcised (Jews) and the uncircumcised (Gentiles) are one in Christ. Once we are in Christ, we have everything we need. Nothing can improve our standing before God. As far as salvation is concerned, the only thing that matters is whether we are trusting in Christ.

Circumcision matters only when it is being used as a way to get right with God. This explains why Paul handled the cases of Timothy and Titus so differently. Both men were missionaries, and both were Greeks, but only one of them got circumcised. Paul allowed Timothy to be circumcised to help him in his work among the Jews (Acts 16:3), but he refused to allow Titus to do the same. This was because some Jewish Christians were insisting that Titus *had* to be circumcised to be saved (Gal. 2:1–5). But this was completely unnecessary, Paul insisted, because Titus was already justified by his faith. For him to be circumcised as a prerequisite for salvation would overturn God's doctrine of justification.

15. Ibid., 27:14–15.

The last thing Paul says about justifying faith is that it actually works. The only kind of faith that is worth anything is the kind of faith that expresses itself through love. This does not mean that we are justified by love. The Scripture never says that we are justified by faith plus love. It does not even say, as Roman Catholics maintain, that faith is formed by love, so that love becomes part of faith. Faith is faith, and love is love. When the Bible speaks of justification, it always says that we are justified by faith, which is another way of saying that justification comes by faith alone.

The faith that alone justifies is never alone, however. True faith is always a working faith, a faith that works. It is an expressive faith, a faith that expresses itself in love to God and to others. As Luther said, "He who wants to be a true Christian or to belong to the kingdom of Christ must be truly a believer. But he does not truly believe if works of love do not follow his faith."[16] Love is the outworking of genuine faith.

The relationship between faith and love is the theme of a wonderful book by the Puritan John Preston called *The Breast-plate of Faith and Love*. The first half of the book is about justification by faith alone. However, Preston did not want to leave the impression that faith could ever be unloving. Thus he wrote, "Now lest we should be mistaken in this, as if [God] should require nothing . . . but an empty idle faith, he [Paul] addeth further, it must be such a faith as is effectual, as is working: And that is not enough, but it must be such a faith as works by love."[17]

This is what the apostle James was concerned about. It is sometimes suggested that Paul and James disagreed about the doctrine of justification. While it is true that they used the term "justification" in different ways, they both believed the same gospel of free grace. Where Paul spoke of faith expressing itself through love, James said, "Show me your faith apart from your works, and I will show you my faith by my works" (James 2:18). Both apostles understood that real faith is faith that works. And only a working faith can bring real freedom. We are most free when we so trust in God that we are filled with his love, and thus enabled to love others with selfless sacrifice. And as far as justification is concerned, the faith that can produce such love is the only thing that really matters.

16. Ibid., 27:30.
17. John Preston, "Of Love," in *The Breast-plate of Faith and Love*, 5th ed. (London, 1634; repr. Edinburgh: Banner of Truth, 1979), 2.

17

WHY CHRISTIANITY IS SO OFFENSIVE

Galatians 5:7—12

I have confidence in the Lord that you will take no other view
than mine, and the one who is troubling you will bear the
penalty, whoever he is. But if I, brothers, still preach circumcision,
why am I still being persecuted? In that case the offense
of the cross has been removed. (Gal. 5:10–11)

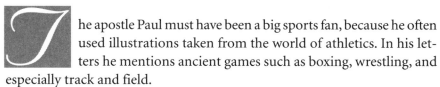he apostle Paul must have been a big sports fan, because he often used illustrations taken from the world of athletics. In his letters he mentions ancient games such as boxing, wrestling, and especially track and field.

Paul often thought of the Christian life as a footrace, a race he himself was determined to finish: "I do not account my life of any value nor as precious to myself," he once said, "if only I may finish my course" (Acts 20:24). Later, with great satisfaction, he was able to claim, "I have finished the race" (2 Tim. 4:7).

KEEP RUNNING!

The Christian life may be a race, but it is not a sprint. It is more like a marathon than a hundred-yard dash, and the longer the race, the more things can go wrong. Some of the runners pull up with injuries. Others stumble and get knocked off their stride. Still others get dehydrated and collapse before they ever reach the finish line.

Paul had experienced similar difficulties himself. Earlier he mentioned a time when he feared that his race was over. Some Christians started adding the law to the gospel, and that made him worry that he had been running in vain (Gal. 2:2). Now the apostle had the same fear for the Galatians. They had started well. As soon as they received the good news of the cross and the empty tomb, they were off and running in the Christian life. One thinks of the famous scene in the film *Chariots of Fire* when Eric Liddell, the great Scottish athlete and missionary, says, "When I run, I feel His pleasure." The Galatians, too, knew the pleasure of running free in Christ. From the moment the gun sounded, they had been running hard.

But then, just as suddenly, they were in danger of being disqualified: "You were running well. Who hindered you from obeying the truth?" (Gal. 5:7). As the Galatians were jockeying for position, someone cut them off. They got knocked off course and fell out of the running.

The term Paul uses for "cutting in" (*enekopsen*) was often used at the ancient Greek games. Races were not held on oval tracks in those days, but "to the post and back." There were rules against tripping, of course, but sometimes it was possible to get away with a fair amount of interference, especially near the post, where runners had to change directions.[1] One unsporting strategy for winning was to impede the progress of opponents by "cutting in on them."

This happened at a modern Olympics in one of the women's distance races. The favorite was the American track star Mary Decker Slaney. The contender was the young South African Zola Budd. Early in the race, Miss Budd inadvertently tripped Mrs. Slaney while they were running in the pack. Slaney fell awkwardly on the infield, she was unable to finish the race, and her dreams of winning the gold medal ended in tears.

The Galatians were not just going for the gold; they were running for eternal life. The Scripture says that they were being hindered from "obeying the truth" (Gal. 5:7). What Paul meant by "the truth" was *the* truth—what he

---

1. Scot McKnight, *Galatians*, The NIV Application Commentary (Grand Rapids: Zondervan, 1995), 251.

had called "the truth of the gospel" (Gal. 2:5, 14). The truth is the good news of salvation from sin and death through the crucifixion and resurrection of Jesus Christ.

Notice that this truth is to be obeyed. Running a good race in the Christian life means something more than just knowing the truth; it means actually practicing it. As far as our standing before God is concerned, all we need to do is believe in Jesus Christ. We are justified by faith alone. However, once we have been justified, we need to be sanctified. When it comes to living for Christ, we must obey the gospel truth. What we believe and how we behave cannot be separated. There is an unbreakable bond between theological integrity and spiritual vitality.[2] As John Stott says, our creed is expressed in our conduct, and our conduct is derived from our creed.[3] Christianity is not simply something we know; it is something we do. It is not merely a belief system or a moral code; it is a theology that comes to life.

THE TROUBLE WITH TROUBLEMAKERS

When Paul asked who had cut in on the Galatians, he already knew the answer. The teachers who were guilty of such poor sportsmanship were the Judaizers who wanted to add the law of Moses to the gospel of Jesus Christ. In the verses that follow, Paul tries to help the Galatians see where this legalism came from (Gal. 5:8), what it was doing to their church (Gal. 5:9), and where it would lead in the end (Gal. 5:10, 12).

Where did this legalism come from? What was its origin? One thing is for sure: Paul knew where it did *not* come from. However persuasive the Judaizers may have been, their words did not come from God. "This persuasion," he wrote, "is not from him who calls you" (Gal. 5:8).

The one who called the Galatians was God himself, and it is worth remembering how he did it. Back at the beginning of this letter, Paul referred to God as "him who called you in the grace of Christ" (Gal. 1:6). The Galatians were called by God's grace. Grace is something we do not deserve. It is unmerited favor. In particular, it is the gift of God's forgiveness for those who trust

2. Timothy George, *Galatians*, New American Commentary 30 (Nashville: Broadman & Holman, 1994), 364.
3. John R. W. Stott, *The Message of Galatians: Only One Way*, The Bible Speaks Today (Downers Grove, IL: InterVarsity, 1968), 135.

in Jesus Christ. Since it involves forgiveness, the free gift of divine grace is only for sinners. Think of the words of the old hymn by Will Thompson: "Softly and tenderly Jesus is calling, / calling for you and for me . . . / earnestly, tenderly, Jesus is calling, / calling, O *sinner*, come home!" The one who calls is God; the ones he calls are sinners; and the way he calls them is by his grace.

If the salvation God offers comes by grace, then what the Galatians were hearing from those who were trying to cut them off obviously did not come from God. The message of the Judaizers was about keeping the law rather than believing and obeying the gospel. They claimed that people had to be circumcised to be saved, in which case salvation came by human works, and not by divine grace.

Obviously, such a message could not possibly come from the God who calls sinners by his grace. Therefore, the message of legalism must come instead from the father of lies, the devil himself. For if anyone wants us to trust in ourselves, it is Satan. He knows that no matter how hard we work, we will never be able to work our way to heaven. Thus whenever we are persuaded to trust ourselves rather than to trust in Jesus, the persuasion is not divine, but demonic.

What was this persuasion doing to the church? What effect was it having? Paul quoted a well-known proverb to show that legalism is always lethal: "A little leaven leavens the whole lump" (Gal. 5:9). This proverb came from the bakery. Bread does not rise unless the dough contains an active culture of yeast. But a pinch is all it takes: "A little yeast works through the whole batch of dough" (Gal. 5:9 NIV). In the same way, a pinch of law thoroughly contaminates the whole gospel.

Here Paul was drawing on the Old Testament. When the people of God prepared for Passover, they always made unleavened bread. God said, "Seven days you shall eat unleavened bread. On the first day you shall remove leaven out of your houses, for if anyone eats what is leavened, from the first day until the seventh day, that person shall be cut off from Israel" (Ex. 12:15; cf. Deut. 16:2–4). In this case, the leaven represented the spread of sin, and sweeping it out of the house reminded God's people to sweep the sin right out of their lives.

When Paul mentioned yeast to the Galatians, he was thinking specifically of the teaching of the Judaizers. Their "yeast" was to add works to faith as the basis for justification. In particular, they wanted the Galatians to get circumcised. Paul recognized that all the trouble the church was having came from this single error. If the Judaizers could persuade the Galatians to get circumcised, then they would have to keep the rest of the law as well, in which case the whole gospel would be overturned.

This tells us something about theological error. Like yeast in a loaf of sour-dough bread, heresy has a way of spreading until it works its way through the whole church. Each fundamental doctrine of the Christian faith is related to all the others. To get even one of them wrong is to threaten the whole system of doctrine. This connection led Martin Luther to observe that "in theology a tiny error overthrows the whole teaching."[4]

From this we learn the necessity of resisting any and every error that strikes at the fundamentals of the gospel. False doctrine usually does not sound all that false at the beginning. " 'Justified by faith' or 'justified by faith *alone*,' " people say, "Who cares?" Or they say, "What difference does it make whether Jesus is *the* way or simply *a* way to God?"

It makes all the difference in the world. It certainly made all the difference in Galatia. Circumcision may not seem like a big deal, but if the Galatians allowed themselves to be circumcised, they would end up denying two central doctrines of the Christian faith: the doctrine of the atonement and the doctrine of justification. They would be saying that Christ's death on the cross was not enough, that they needed something more to atone for their sins. In this way they would deny the sufficiency of Christ's atonement. And they would be saying that they could not be justified by faith alone, but only by faith plus works, and thus they would deny the biblical doctrine of justification.

Where would it all lead in the end? Paul was confident that the Galatians would eventually come around to see things his way. He felt sure that they would come to their senses and reject the legalism of the Judaizers. So he said, "I have confidence in the Lord that you will take no other view than mine" (Gal. 5:10). The apostle's confidence was not so much in the Galatians themselves, but in their Lord, who would bring them back to the one true gospel of free grace.

Paul was equally confident that whoever was preaching a false gospel would come to an unhappy end: "and the one who is troubling you will bear

4. Martin Luther, *Lectures on Galatians, 1535*, trans. and ed. Jaroslav Pelikan, in *Luther's Works* (St. Louis: Concordia, 1963), 27:37.

the penalty, whoever he is" (Gal. 5:10). This statement gives the impression that the Judaizers had a ringleader. Paul did not name any names, so he may or may not have known who the man was. But the one thing Paul knew for sure was that—whoever he was—one day the man would have to answer to God for causing trouble in the church.

The word "penalty" (*krima*) is really the word "judgment," meaning divine judgment. Paul calls it "*the* judgment" because he has the final judgment in mind. The day will come when every error will be exposed and God's truth will reign supreme. Do not be dismayed by the unbelief of liberal theology, discouraged by the spread of new cults, or disheartened by the slow decline of evangelical orthodoxy. The day will come when every false teacher will be judged for every false word.

In the meantime, if the Judaizers wanted people to get circumcised, Paul almost wished that the knife would slip and they would end up castrating themselves. His sarcastic words sound savage to the postmodern ear: "I wish those who unsettle you would emasculate themselves!" (Gal. 5:12). Talk about a cutting remark! The word for "unsettle" (*anastatountes*) is used elsewhere to describe political subversives, the kind of troublemakers who foment rebellion by causing urban uprisings (Acts 17:6; 21:38). Obviously, Paul was getting a little agitated himself. In the words of one commentator, this is the "crudest and rudest" expression in all of his writings.[5]

The apostle was not actually threatening the Judaizers with violence. Although he mentioned physical mutilation, he was speaking spiritually, of course. Here it helps to know that some pagan religions required ritual castration. The priests of Cybele, for example, who lived in Northern Galatia, were made eunuchs at an annual festival. So perhaps Paul was saying something like this: "Look, if you insist on getting circumcised, you are trying to be saved by a ritual. But that is just another form of paganism, so you might as well go the whole way and become one of their priests!"

There is another possible interpretation, however, which comes from the Old Testament. According to biblical law, eunuchs were not allowed to enter the temple: "No one whose testicles are crushed or whose male organ is cut off shall enter the assembly of the LORD" (Deut. 23:1). When Paul told those

---

5. Richard N. Longenecker, *Galatians*, Word Biblical Commentary (Dallas: Word, 1990), 234.

troublemaking Judaizers to emasculate themselves, therefore, he was saying that they should be cut off from the church.

PREACHING THAT LEADS TO PERSECUTION

Galatians 5:12 is the kind of verse that some people find offensive. But what is really offensive about this passage is not so much Paul's vocabulary, which admittedly is somewhat vulgar, as it is his theology, which teaches that God does *not* help those who help themselves.

Christians are offensive for lots of reasons. We are sinners, after all, and sinners tend to be selfish, insensitive, rude, and even violent. Christians are all of that, and worse, but even if we were not so offensive, our theology still would be. Christianity is offensive because it insists that salvation comes only by the grace of God in Jesus Christ.

The apostle Paul could illustrate this from his own experience as a preacher, which seemed to result in more than its share of persecution. At various times and in various places—including Galatia—Paul had been beaten, arrested, imprisoned, stoned, and left for dead. Why did this keep happening to him? Was it his looks? His personality? His ethnic background? No, Paul was persecuted for preaching salvation in Christ alone.

The Judaizers seem to have started a rumor to the contrary. They told the Galatians that Paul was still preaching circumcision. This was somewhat plausible. After all, Paul was the man who "became as a Jew, in order to win Jews" (1 Cor. 9:20). When he took the gospel to the synagogue, he was always careful to conform to Jewish traditions as much as he could. To give just one example, when Timothy joined Paul's missionary team in Galatia, the apostle had him circumcised (Acts 16:3).

The reason Paul had Timothy circumcised was to help him do evangelistic work in the Jewish community. This may have seemed inconsistent to some people. How could Paul be opposed to circumcision if he had the young man circumcised? But remember that Timothy's mother was Jewish, so he was not a Gentile. And remember, too, that Paul was not opposed to circumcision in and of itself. He didn't place any value on circumcision at all (Gal. 5:6; cf. 1 Cor. 7:18–19). What he was opposed to was thinking of circumcision as a means of justification, as a way of gaining God's approval.

The one thing Paul most certainly did not do, therefore, was *preach* circumcision. To preach circumcision was to make it a matter of salvation. Paul may have done so when he was still a Pharisee, but certainly not since he had received the law-free gospel on the Damascus road.

In order to prove that he no longer preached circumcision, he raised this question: "But if I, brothers, still preach circumcision, why am I still being persecuted?" (Gal. 5:11). It was a good question. As long as Paul preached circumcision, he was safe. As long as he maintained the ethnic and religious barrier between Jew and Gentile, the Jews would have no reason to persecute him. Yet he was persecuted up and down Asia Minor because the Jews hated his law-free gospel. Persecution was Paul's proof that he did not preach circumcision.

CIRCUMCISION OR THE CROSS?

If Paul did not preach circumcision, then what *did* he preach? He preached the cross where Christ was crucified for sinners.

As we have seen, to preach circumcision is to preach salvation by human merit. Circumcision says that I can be saved by some ritual I undergo or some work that I do. Whether that work involves removing a foreskin, keeping a commandment, undergoing a penance, or performing an act of devotion, the underlying theology is the same. To preach circumcision is to say that my contribution is essential to my salvation.

Over against preaching circumcision stands the preaching of the cross. This is what Paul had preached to the Galatians from the beginning. He clearly portrayed to them "Jesus Christ . . . as crucified" (Gal. 3:1). In the words of the great Scottish theologian James Denney (1856–1917), "The aim of the Epistle to the Galatians is to show that all Christianity is contained in the Cross."[6]

To preach the cross is to preach salvation in Christ *alone.* It is to preach that only his sacrificial death is sufficient to atone for sin. It is to preach salvation by his infinite worth rather than by our own unworthy merits. There is nothing we can do to make things right with God, but God has made things right with us through the bloody death of his Son.

6. James Denney, *The Death of Christ* (New York: Armstrong, 1903), 152.

One can preach either circumcision or the cross, but not both. As Paul said earlier, "if you accept circumcision, Christ will be of no advantage to you" (Gal. 5:2). Those who preach circumcision end up with a cross-less Christianity. John Stott explains it like this:

> "Circumcision" stands for a religion of *human* achievement, of what man can do by his own good works; "Christ" stands for a religion of *divine* achievement, of what God has done through the finished work of Christ. "Circumcision" means law, works and bondage; "Christ" means grace, faith and freedom. Every man must choose. The one impossibility is what the Galatians were attempting, namely to add circumcision to Christ and have both. No. "Circumcision" and "Christ" are mutually exclusive.[7]

Every preacher must choose, and so must every Christian. Which will it be, circumcision or the cross? Law or grace? Works or faith? Often, the choice comes down to this: Do you want to be popular or do you want to be faithful?

The problem with preaching the cross is that it has a way of offending people. As a woman who was wrestling with the claims of Christ once said to me, "If I started telling people *that*, I wouldn't have any friends any more!" In a way, she was right. To preach Christ crucified is to invite ridicule, opposition, hardship, persecution, and even death. Paul called this phenomenon "the offense of the cross" (Gal. 5:11). It was something he experienced almost every time he went out to preach the gospel. People were scandalized by what he said about the crucifixion.

When Paul called the cross an "offense," he was using the Greek word for "scandal," which literally meant a "stumbling block." He used the same word when he wrote to the Corinthians: "we preach Christ crucified, a stumbling block to Jews and folly to Gentiles, but to those who are called, both Jews and Greeks, Christ the power of God and the wisdom of God" (1 Cor. 1:23–24). To return to the image of the race for a moment, the cross was an obstacle, something that kept tripping people up. For people throughout the ancient world, the cross was *the* major stumbling block to accepting Christianity.

The cross offended the Romans. To them it was an abomination, the most gruesome means of execution imaginable, what Cicero called "a most cruel

---

7. Stott, *Message of Galatians*, 138.

213

and disgusting punishment."[8] Indeed, the Romans would not allow their own citizens to be crucified, and in time the Latin word *crux* became a swearword.[9]

The cross scandalized the Jews as well. To them it was accursed. They knew the Old Testament law that Paul had quoted back in chapter 3, the one that said, "Cursed is everyone who is hanged on a tree" (Gal. 3:13; cf. Deut. 21:23). The Christian gospel offended the Jews, therefore, because its most basic fact seemed like the ultimate contradiction: "Crucified Messiah."

The Jewish attitude toward the cross is illustrated by an ancient dialogue between Justin the Christian and Trypho the Jew. Trypho refused to believe that God's Christ could have been crucified. He said, "But whether Christ should be so shamefully crucified, this we are in doubt about. For whosoever is crucified is said in the law to be accursed, so that I am exceedingly incredulous on this point."[10] The cross scandalized the Jews as much as it offended the Romans.

To this day, the cross remains a stumbling block to every moral individual. It is offensive because it is so unflattering. People hate to be told they need to go to the cross. What they see when they get there is Jesus of Nazareth hanging as a naked and bloody sacrifice. What that says about them is that they are sinners who need a Savior.

The cross offends people because they do not want to admit that they need someone else to save them. "What do you mean, I'm a sinner?" they protest. "Why would I need someone to die for my sins?" One thinks of the proper English lady who, when the preacher tried to convince her that she needed to be saved, said, "I am a lady; how dare you call me a sinner!" Whether she was a lady or not, she certainly was a sinner, and she needed to go to the cross to have her sins forgiven.

What makes Christianity so offensive is the cross. Most people would rather think that they can do something to save themselves than to admit that they need Christ to save them. But the cross, writes F. F. Bruce, "cuts the ground from under every thought of personal achievement or merit where

---

8. Cicero, *In Verrem*, in John Stott, *The Cross of Christ* (Downers Grove, IL: InterVarsity, 1986), 24.

9. James Montgomery Boice and Philip Graham Ryken, *The Heart of the Cross* (Wheaton, IL: Crossway, 1999), 137–38.

10. Justin Martyr, *Dialogue with Trypho, a Jew*, ed. Alexander Roberts and James Donaldson, in *Ante-Nicene Fathers* (New York, 1885; repr. Peabody, MA: Hendrickson, 1994), 1:244.

God's salvation is in view. To be shut up to receiving salvation from the crucified one, if it is to be received at all, is an affront to all notions of proper self-pride and self-help—and for many people this remains a major stumbling-block in the gospel of Christ crucified."[11]

Christ crucified—more than anything else, this is why Christianity is so offensive to a postmodern culture. Most people think well of Jesus Christ, at least as a moral teacher. Nor do people mind Christians very much, provided that we mind our own business. No, what people dislike about Christianity is the exclusive claim of the crucified Christ. The only Christianity they will accept is based on a Christ without a cross.

Realizing this helps us understand our mission to the world. The problem with most Christians is that we don't know when to be offensive. We want to fit in with our culture. We want people to like us. At the very least, we don't want to offend anyone. And as a result, we end up getting rid of the very thing that is supposed to offend people: Jesus Christ crucified. Not that we ourselves should be any more offensive than we have to be, of course. We should never add our own personal offense to the offense of the cross, which is offensive enough! But if Christianity must offend people, then let it be the cross that offends them. For where else can people see that they are sinners, and where else can they meet the Savior?

11. F. F. Bruce, *The Epistle to the Galatians: A Commentary on the Greek Text*, New International Greek Testament Commentary (Grand Rapids: Eerdmans, 1982), 238.

18

LIBERTY WITHOUT LICENSE

Galatians 5:13—18

For you were called to freedom, brothers. Only do not use your freedom as an opportunity for the flesh, but through love serve one another. . . . I say, walk by the Spirit, and you will not gratify the desires of the flesh. (Gal. 5:13, 16)

he Epistle to the Galatians is the Magna Carta of Christian liberty. Liberty must always be defended from its two great enemies—legalism and license. To this point, the apostle Paul has been fighting against legalism. This was his concern at the beginning of chapter 5: "For freedom Christ has set us free; stand firm therefore, and do not submit again to a yoke of slavery" (Gal. 5:1).

Paul feared that the Galatians might fall back into bondage to the law. Some teachers were trying to persuade them to keep the law instead of believing the gospel. So Paul challenged the Galatians to remain free in Christ: free from sin, guilt, and the curse of the law. He warned them to watch out for anyone who tried to take away their freedom.

LICENSE TO KILL

There is another threat to liberty, however, and that is license. License is loose living. It is freedom taken to its immoral extreme. The *Oxford English Dictio-*

nary defines it as "a liberty of action, especially when excessive; disregard of law or propriety; abuse of freedom." Whereas legalism demands responsibility without freedom, license grants freedom without responsibility.

Everyone wants to be free. "It's a free country!" Americans like to say. In our free-market economy we enjoy free trade and free enterprise. People want to have a free hand, a free rein, and a free lunch. Then there are the four famous freedoms enunciated by Franklin Delano Roosevelt: freedom of speech, freedom of worship, freedom from want, and freedom from fear.

The trouble comes whenever and wherever there is freedom without responsibility. Unfortunately, this is precisely what most people want. Consider the ancient Greek proverb that "the free man is one who lives as he chooses."[1] Or consider a more recent example: "free love." During the 1960s, this phrase meant the freedom to have indiscriminate sexual relations. It had little to do with love, of course, because true love requires commitment. Nor did it offer real freedom, because sexual sin always brings intense spiritual bondage. "Free love" meant freedom without responsibility, which is not liberty at all, but merely license.

The apostle Paul understood that license poses as great a threat to liberty as legalism does. Hence his brotherly warning: "For you were called to freedom, brothers. Only do not use your freedom as an opportunity for the flesh" (Gal. 5:13). The Galatians had been liberated from legalism, but they were not to use their liberty as an opportunity for license.

When Paul speaks of the "flesh," the Greek term he uses is *sarx*. Spiritually speaking, "the flesh" means something more than simply the body. It is the part of me that does not want what God wants, my corrupt human nature in all its weakness and depravity. The body is part of that fallen condition, but only a part. "The flesh" refers to the unspiritual life of the whole person, which is inclined to sin.

But the Christian must resist this inclination: "do not use your freedom as an opportunity for the flesh," or as the New International Version has it, "do not use your freedom to indulge the sinful nature" (Gal. 5:13). The Greek word for "indulge" (*aphormēn*) comes from the military term for a base of operations. The idea is that we must not allow sin to use our freedom in

1. James D. G. Dunn, *The Epistle to the Galatians*, Black's New Testament Commentary (Peabody, MA: Hendrickson, 1993), 287.

Christ as a beachhead to launch a spiritual attack against us. The fact that we are liberated from legalism must not become an excuse for satisfying our sinful desires.

When some people hear about God's free grace, they hope it means that they can sin as much as they please. Even some people who consider themselves Christians have this attitude. If God has already accepted me in Jesus Christ, they wonder, then who cares how much I sin?

John Calvin encountered this licentious attitude during the Reformation in Geneva. He warned about the kind of man who wants to "extend Christian liberty to include everything . . . without any exceptions . . . so that nothing may hinder him or prevent him from having a good time. . . . These frantic people without any distinction abolish all the law, saying that it is no longer necessary to keep it, since we have been set free from it."[2]

The truth is that anyone who uses freedom to indulge the flesh is not really free at all. Jesus said, "Truly, truly, I say to you, everyone who commits sin is a slave to sin" (John 8:34). In other words, license is the very opposite of liberty. It is really a form of slavery. Real liberty comes when Christ frees me *from* sin, not *to* sin.

Not only is license self-enslaving, it is also self-destroying, as Paul goes on to say: "But if you bite and devour one another, watch out that you are not consumed by one another" (Gal. 5:15). This verse gives some idea what kinds of sins the Galatians were indulging. They were waging civil war against one another, only it was not so civil. There were quarrels and arguments, disputes and dissensions. Some of their differences may have been doctrinal. Scot McKnight imagines the Judaizers boasting, by virtue of their circumcision, that they were "just a cut above the rest!"[3] Undoubtedly some of their differences were also social, as the legalistic teaching of the Judaizers exacerbated ethnic tensions within the Christian community. But whatever the Galatians were arguing about, Paul was worried that all the bickering would end up splitting the church.

Paul was also worried that the Galatians were eating one another alive. The words "bite" and "devour" suggest that they were acting like a pack of wild animals. Their behavior was beastly. Ben Witherington comments that

2. John Calvin, *Treatises against the Anabaptists and against the Libertines*, ed. B. W. Farley (Grand Rapids: Baker, 1982), 271.
3. Scot McKnight, *Galatians*, NIV Application Commentary (Grand Rapids: Zondervan, 1995), 267.

here Paul "describes a clear progression—first the animal bites the prey, then it tears at the flesh of the victim, then finally it consumes its prey."[4] When the Galatians traded liberty for license, it turned out to be a license to kill. Conflict in the church is a kind of spiritual suicide. Sin is always self-destructive, and the sin of divisiveness inevitably leads to the destruction of the church. It means the death of Christian witness and fellowship.

Sadly, the history of Christianity includes many tragic stories of factions and divisions, splits and schisms. In his commentary on these verses, John Calvin pleads with us to remember, "when the devil tempts us to disputes, that the disagreement of members within the Church can lead to nothing but the ruin and consumption of the whole body. How unhappy, how mad it is, that we who are members of the same body should voluntarily conspire together for mutual destruction."[5]

A FREE SPIRIT

The only way to be free from fleshly desire is to be sanctified by God's Spirit. His influence alone can prevent liberty from degenerating into license, for "where the Spirit of the Lord is, there is freedom" (2 Cor. 3:17). The third member of the Trinity, one might say, is a "free" Spirit. He helps us hold on to our liberty without becoming either legalistic or licentious.

Paul uses several different expressions to describe this liberating work of the Holy Spirit. In verse 16 he says, "Walk by the Spirit." One English word that comes from this Greek verb for walking (*peripateō*) is "peripatetic," which means "going from place to place." Aristotle's philosophy students were called the Peripatetic School because their teacher typically taught them while he was on the move. Similarly, the way to learn the Christian life is to walk with the Holy Spirit every day, "to order our lives according to the direction, and motion of the Spirit."[6]

---

4. Ben Witherington III, *Grace in Galatia: A Commentary on Paul's Letter to the Galatians* (Edinburgh: T & T Clark, 1998), 384.

5. John Calvin, *The Epistles of Paul the Apostle to the Galatians, Ephesians, Philippians and Colossians*, Calvin's New Testament Commentaries, trans. T. H. L. Parker, ed. David W. and Thomas F. Torrance (Grand Rapids: Eerdmans, 1996), 102.

6. William Perkins, *A Commentary on Galatians*, Pilgrim Classic Commentaries, ed. Gerald T. Sheppard (London, 1617; repr. New York: Pilgrim, 1989), 365.

Then in verse 18 this lifestyle is described as being "led by the Spirit." The verb for being led is related to the word "pedagogue," which we first encountered back in chapter 3, where the law was the pedagogue. It was like a parole officer—"our guardian until Christ came" (Gal. 3:24). Now that we have come to Christ, however, we need a different kind of pedagogue. Christ has set us free from sin, guilt, death, and eternal judgment. Now we need the inward work of the Holy Spirit to teach us how to handle our newfound freedom. He becomes our pedagogue and guide, leading us to live free in Christ.

The Holy Spirit brings at least three kinds of freedom. The first is *freedom from sin*. Paul has already warned us not to indulge the flesh. The way to do this—the way to use our freedom without abusing it—is to walk with the Holy Spirit: "But I say, walk by the Spirit, and you will not gratify the desires of the flesh" (Gal. 5:16). This verse contains both a command and a promise. The command is to walk with the Holy Spirit; that is, to live within the atmosphere of his grace. The promise is that when we live a Spirit-controlled life, we will no longer follow through on our sinful desires. The promise is emphatic: You will *not* sin.

This explains how we get sanctified. Sanctification has to do with holiness. It is the process by which the Christian becomes like Christ: holy in thought, word, and deed. Often, when people want to become more holy, they try to do it in a legalistic way, by keeping a list of rules. But notice that God is the one who sanctifies us. And notice how he does it: not by the law, but by his Spirit. This is why God is able to guarantee our sanctification, saying, "You will not gratify the desires of the flesh" (Gal. 5:16). As we live under the control of God's Spirit, he gradually frees us from our bondage to sin.

In the second place, the Holy Spirit brings *freedom to serve*: "do not use your freedom as an opportunity for the flesh, but through love serve one another" (Gal. 5:13). The kind of love Paul has in mind is the selfless love that comes from falling in love with Jesus Christ. It is the kind of love that enables me to love my neighbor as spontaneously and as instinctively as I love myself. To love in this way is to enjoy real liberty. As long as I serve myself, I am a slave to self; but when the Spirit enables me to offer loving service to others, then I am free. The person who is most free is the one empowered by the Holy Spirit to love and to serve others.

What does it mean—in practical terms—to serve one another in love? It means, wrote Martin Luther,

> performing unimportant works such as the following: teaching the erring; comforting the afflicted; encouraging the weak; helping the neighbor in whatever way one can; bearing with his rude manners and impoliteness; putting up with annoyances, labors, and the ingratitude and contempt of men in both church and state; obeying the magistrates; treating one's parents with respect; being patient in the home with a cranky wife and an unmanageable family, and the like.

In other words, serving others in love requires costly service in the ordinary duties of daily life. "But believe me," Luther went on to say, "these works are so outstanding and brilliant that the whole world cannot comprehend their usefulness and worth."[7]

The curious thing about having the freedom to serve others in all these ways is that such service is actually a new form of slavery. The word "serve" (*douleuete*; Gal. 5:13) is the Greek word for "be a slave"—the kind of person who washes the dishes and takes out the trash. So here is the paradox: By setting us free to serve, the Holy Spirit enslaves us to one another in love.

This should not surprise us because it is the very paradox of the life and death of our Lord Jesus Christ. Though he is Lord of all, he became the servant of sinners. As Paul explained to the Philippians, although Christ was in very nature God, he "did not count equality with God a thing to be grasped, but made himself nothing, taking the form of a servant" (Phil. 2:6–7). The word "servant" is the same word that we find in Galatians; it means "slave." Jesus made himself our slave by suffering and dying for our sins on the cross.

Now we are called to the same kind of voluntary enslavement. Martin Luther captured the paradox: "A Christian is a perfectly free lord of all, subject to none. A Christian is a perfectly dutiful servant of all, subject to all."[8] Luther meant that the freedom we have in Christ obligates us to serve one another in love. "In this liberty," Luther went on to say, the Christian must "empty himself, take upon himself the form of a servant, . . . serve, help, and

7. Martin Luther, *Lectures on Galatians, 1535*, trans. and ed. Jaroslav Pelikan, in *Luther's Works* (St. Louis: Concordia, 1963), 27:56.
8. Martin Luther, *Christian Liberty*, rev. ed., ed. Harold J. Grimm (Philadelphia: Fortress, 1957), 7.

in every way deal with his neighbor as . . . God through Christ has dealt . . . with him."[9] Our freedom is not self-seeking, but self-sacrificing.

The amazing thing is that this kind of "slavery" really *is* freedom! Now that Christ has freed me from sin and death, I am no longer enslaved by selfish desire. Instead, I am liberated to serve others with his love. This truth is beautifully expressed in the last verse of an 1850 hymn by Anna Waring:

> In service which thy will appoints
> there are no bonds for me;
> my secret heart is taught the truth
> that makes thy children free;
> a life of self-renouncing love
> is one of liberty.

THE LAW OF LOVE

The Holy Spirit gives us real liberty in Christ. True Christian freedom is not to sin but to serve. It is not license to indulge our sinful nature, but liberty to serve one another in self-renouncing love.

When we love one another in the Spirit, we also enjoy a third kind of freedom: *freedom to fulfill the law.* Here we come to one of the most surprising verses in Galatians. After we are commanded to "serve one another" through love (Gal. 5:13), we are told that "the whole law is fulfilled in one word: 'You shall love your neighbor as yourself' " (Gal. 5:14; cf. Rom. 13:9–10). The Spirit makes us free to keep the law of love.

This law of love is familiar. It comes from the law of Moses: "you shall love your neighbor as yourself: I am the LORD" (Lev. 19:18). Jesus taught the same thing. When someone asked him to name the greatest commandment, he said, "You shall love the Lord your God with all your heart and with all your soul and with all your mind. This is the great and first commandment. And the second is like it: You shall love your neighbor as yourself" (Matt. 22:37–39).

Some have wondered why Paul mentions only the second greatest commandment, and not the first, but what better way to prove that we love God

9. Ibid.

222

than to love our neighbor? Indeed, loving our neighbor is the very heart of God's commandment; love fulfills his law. But how can Paul say this? Isn't fulfilling the law just another form of legalism? Wasn't it Paul who said all those disparaging things about the law, such as "All who rely on works of the law are under a curse" (Gal. 3:10), and "You are severed from Christ, you who would be justified by the law; you have fallen away from grace" (Gal. 5:4)? How can Paul command us to fulfill the very law he condemns?

The answer is that the law has to be kept in its place. As we have noted before, the Protestant Reformers spoke of several different uses of the law. The first is to drive us to Christ. The law does this by showing that we cannot justify ourselves before God. The law is not the means of our salvation. It cannot make us right with God. The most it can do for us, before we come to Christ, is to show us our sin.

Once the law has driven us to Christ, however, it does something else for us. It shows us how to live for God by telling us to love our neighbor, among other things. It does not tell us this as a way of getting right with God—as far as justification is concerned, we are "not under the law" (Gal. 5:18; cf. 4:21)—but as a way of living free in the Spirit. Our liberty is not lawless. We are not *under* the law; nevertheless, we *fulfill* the law. Charles Spurgeon (1834–1892) explained this in a picturesque way:

> What is God's law now? It is not *above* a Christian—it is *under* a Christian. Some men hold God's law like a rod, in terror, over Christians, and say, "If you sin you will be punished with it." It is not so. The law is under a Christian; it is for him to walk on, to be his guide, his rule, his pattern: "we are not under the law, but under grace." Law is the road which guides us, not the rod which drives us, nor the spirit which actuates us. The law is good and excellent, if it keep its place.[10]

It is vital to understand that God has never done away with his law. His basic commands have not changed. His will for our lives, as expressed in his moral law, is eternal. Jesus said, "If you love me, you will keep my commandments" (John 14:15). God still wants us to love our neighbor as ourselves, and by doing so to fulfill his law.

---

10. Charles Haddon Spurgeon, *The New Park Street Pulpit* (1857; repr. Pasadena, TX: Pilgrim, 1975), 2:124.

The way to keep the law in its place is always to think in the proper theological categories. Although the law cannot justify, it can help to sanctify. Justification has to do with God declaring us righteous; sanctification has to do with God making us holy. The law cannot justify us because it declares that we are *not* righteous. But once God has declared us righteous in Christ, the law helps to sanctify us by showing us how to be holy. John Stott writes, "Although we cannot gain acceptance by keeping the law, yet once we have been accepted we shall keep the law out of love for Him who has accepted us and has given us His Spirit to enable us to keep it."[11]

One way to illustrate the different uses of the law is to compare God's law to a pair of ice skates. The value of ice skates as a mode of transportation depends entirely on where they are being used. They are rather awkward, for example, on hot asphalt or in a grassy meadow. The only place ice skates are much use is at the skating rink, or perhaps on an icy pond. In the same way, before we come to Christ, the law cannot help us to please God. In fact, the more we try to use it to become good enough for God, the more we stumble and fall. But coming to faith in Christ is like going to the ice rink. Once we receive his Spirit, the ice skates of God's law help us to glide through the Christian life.

We are free from the law; now the Spirit uses the law to help us exercise our freedom. What enables us to live a holy life is not simply the outward constraint of the law, but the inward compulsion of the Spirit. This is what the prophets meant when they promised that God's law would be written on our hearts (Jer. 31:33), or what the apostle James meant when he spoke of "the law of liberty" (James 1:25). It is also what Paul explained to the Romans: "For the law of the Spirit of life has set you free in Christ Jesus from the law of sin and death. For God has done what the law, weakened by the flesh, could not do. By sending his own Son in the likeness of sinful flesh and for sin, he condemned sin in the flesh, in order that the righteous requirement of the law might be fulfilled in us, who walk not according to the flesh, but according to the Spirit" (Rom. 8:2–4).

11. John R. W. Stott, *The Message of Galatians: Only One Way*, The Bible Speaks Today (Downers Grove, IL: InterVarsity, 1968), 143.

We could never be saved by the law because we are lawbreakers. Instead, we are saved by Jesus, who kept the law on our behalf. And now the law is fulfilled in us as we live by the Spirit. Donald Hagner writes:

> Here is the paradox again in its fullness: We are set free from the law *in order to produce a righteousness that corresponds to the righteousness that the law demanded.* This is because the teaching that serves as our guide to righteousness—the teaching of Christ and his apostles—is in effect an exposition of the ultimate meaning of the Mosaic law. . . . The content of the law, then, has not fundamentally changed. It is only the dynamic—the means by which we can arrive at righteousness—that differs dramatically. Living out the righteousness of the law does not result in a right relationship with God; rather, being in a right relationship with God through faith in Christ results in living out the righteousness of the law. The Christian—through the power of the indwelling Holy Spirit, and not through the dynamic of his or her own efforts to be righteous by keeping the law—manifests a life of increasing growth in righteousness.[12]

THE WAR WITHIN

With all this talk of freedom, it would be easy to think that the Christian life is one spiritual triumph after another. After all, we are free from sin: If we live by the Spirit, we will not gratify the desires of the sinful nature. And we are free to serve: As we are led by the Spirit, we fulfill the law of love. Yet the reality is that Christians often suffer bitter spiritual defeats. We still sin. We do not always want to serve. Thus we fail to fulfill the law of God's love. How can we explain the apparent contradiction between our freedom and our failings?

Martin Luther faced the same dilemma. Despite all his attempts to live a godly life, there were times when he was tempted to sin. And not just tempted. There were times when he committed very fleshly sins. This made him worry that he was not really a Christian. Perhaps you have had some doubts of your own. Do your sins ever cause you to question your salvation?

One of the verses that helped Luther most in his spiritual struggle came from Galatians 5: "For the desires of the flesh are against the Spirit, and the desires of the Spirit are against the flesh, for these are opposed to each other,

---

12. Donald Hagner, "The Law in Paul's Letter to the Galatians," *Modern Reformation* 12.5 (Sept./Oct. 2003): 36.

to keep you from doing the things you want to do" (Gal. 5:17). Luther used this verse to preach to himself, "Martin, you will never be completely without sin, because you still have the flesh. Therefore you will always be aware of its conflict, according to the statement of Paul: 'The desires of the flesh are against the Spirit.' Do not despair, therefore, but fight back, and do not gratify the desires of the flesh."[13]

This verse describes the war within, the constant conflict raging inside the human heart. One desire grapples with the other, like two giant sumo wrestlers trying to push each other out of the ring—flesh against spirit, sinful nature against regenerate nature. The result of this conflict is that we do not always do what we want to do. Often, we do exactly the opposite, for the flesh wars against the Spirit. Paul expanded on this idea in his letter to the Romans: "I do not understand my own actions. For I do not do what I want, but I do the very thing I hate. . . . I know that nothing good dwells in me, that is, in my flesh. For I have the desire to do what is right, but not the ability to carry it out. For I do not do the good I want, but the evil I do not want is what I keep on doing" (Rom. 7:15, 18–19).

At the same time, the Spirit fights to prevent the flesh from indulging its sinful desires. Here is how one commentator describes the ensuing battle: "The flesh opposes the Spirit that men may not do what they will in accordance with the mind of the Spirit, and the Spirit opposes the flesh that they may not do what they will after the flesh. Does the man choose evil, the Spirit opposes him; does he choose good, the flesh hinders him."[14]

Notice that this is the spiritual condition of the *believer*. When Paul says, "You do not do what you want," he is talking to Galatian Christians who had already received the Holy Spirit (Gal. 3:3) and who were members of the church of Jesus Christ. The spiritual battle between flesh and Spirit takes place within the Christian.

This is what Martin Luther meant when he said that the Christian is "partly righteous and partly sinner" (*simul justus et peccator*). He or she is practically a self-contradiction, pulled by flesh and Spirit in two different directions at once. What takes place within the heart, mind, soul, and body of the

13. Luther, *Galatians*, 27:73.
14. E. De Witt Burton, *A Critical and Exegetical Commentary on the Epistle to the Galatians* (Edinburgh: T & T Clark, 1921), 302.

believer is nothing less than civil war, a violent confrontation between opposing forces, an "irreconcilable antagonism."[15]

This helps us to recognize that the spiritual life will always be a struggle. How can it be otherwise, when our flesh desires what is contrary to God's Spirit? We should not be surprised by sin, as if we expected God to make us perfect in this life. Nor should sin cause us to doubt our salvation. On the contrary, we are most aware of our sin when the Spirit is most active in fighting against our old adversary: sinful desire.

Realize, too, that the war will not last forever. We are not fighting a losing battle. Nor will the struggle between the flesh and the Spirit end in a stalemate. One day the Spirit will gain total victory, and the flesh will torment us no longer. Then we will be free in all the ways that the Spirit wants to make us free: free from sin, free to serve, and free to fulfill God's law. We will be free to do what we most want to do, which is what God wants us to do.

Even now, we can begin to experience that victory by following God's marching orders: "Live by the Spirit. Walk in the Spirit. Be led by the Spirit." The great eighteenth-century Scottish preacher Ralph Erskine (1685–1752) wrote about this in one of his "Gospel Canticles":

When once the fiery law of God
Has chas'd me to the gospel-road;
Then back unto the holy law
Most kindly gospel-grace will draw.

The law most perfect still remains,
And ev'ry duty full contains:
The Gospel its perfection speaks,
And therefore give whate'er it seeks.

A rigid master was the law,
Demanding brick, denying straw;
But when with gospel-tongue it sings,
It bids me fly, and gives me wings.[16]

15. Stott, *Message of Galatians*, 146.
16. Ralph Erskine, quoted in Timothy George, *Galatians*, New American Commentary 30 (Nashville: Broadman & Holman, 1994), 384.

19

How to Grow Good Spiritual Fruit

Galatians 5:19–26

And those who belong to Christ Jesus have crucified the flesh with its passions and desires. If we live by the Spirit, let us also walk by the Spirit. (Gal. 5:24–25)

One fine summer evening I walked down a quiet residential street in Center City Philadelphia. As I looked up, I saw a maple tree illuminated by a streetlight. The leaves on the tree were dancing and shimmering in the breeze. As I paused for a moment to admire its beauty, I noticed that the tree next to it was dead—barren of any leaves, blossoms, or fruit. Galatians 5 closes with a similar contrast. Verses 19 to 21 describe the fruitless existence of the flesh, or the sinful nature. The verses that follow describe the fruitful and productive work of the Holy Spirit in the life of the Christian.

The contrast is as absolute as the difference between life and death. The apostle Paul has already explained that the flesh and the Spirit are mortal enemies, locked in deadly combat. The passions of the sinful nature are at war with the desires of the regenerate nature (Gal. 5:17). This warfare takes place within the heart, mind, soul, and body of the believer. In this conflict the Christian is ordered to live by the Spirit rather than to indulge the flesh.

THE WORKS OF THE FLESH

To follow these orders, the Christian needs to know the difference between flesh and Spirit, between the sinful nature and the regenerate nature. Fortunately, the difference is not hard to tell: "Now the works of the flesh are evident: sexual immorality, impurity, sensuality, idolatry, sorcery, enmity, strife, jealousy, fits of anger, rivalries, dissensions, divisions, envy, drunkenness, orgies, and things like these" (Gal. 5:19–21).

Catalogues of vices were common in the ancient world, and the Galatians would have encountered lists like this before. There are other examples in the New Testament (e.g., Rom. 1:29–31; 2 Tim. 3:2–5), and also in the writings of many classical authors. No two lists are the same, either in the Bible or in pagan literature.

The sins in this list are so familiar that they require little by way of explanation. The catalogue begins with "sexual immorality," which is sometimes called "fornication." This general term was used to refer to any kind of sexual sin, but especially to sexual intercourse between persons who are not married to one another. Sexual sin was common in the pagan world, as was "impurity," which refers not only to sexual sin, but also to any kind of uncleanness. "Sensuality" is indecency, a lack of respect for what is right and good. It involves not only engaging in wanton behavior, but flaunting it in public.

"Idolatry," of course, means the worship of other gods. It is the quest to find our identity and security in anything or anyone besides the one true God. "Witchcraft," or sorcery, is the worship of what is evil. This would obviously include contemporary forms of the occult, such as black magic and Satan worship. However, the Greek word that is used here for "witchcraft" (*pharmakeia*) provides the origin for the English word "pharmacy." This is a reminder that in the ancient world witches often prepared and administered lethal poisons. Thus the postmodern parallels to ancient witchcraft would include abortion and euthanasia—forms of killing that in our culture are usually performed by doctors. According to the Bible, these activities are among the self-evidently wicked deeds of the flesh.

Many of the other vices on Paul's list relate to the breakdown of Christian community. Thus they confirm what we have already grown to suspect, namely, that divisiveness was a major problem for the Galatian church. The

Greek word for "enmity" (*echthra*) is closely related to the Greek word for "enemy" (*echthros*). This form of hatred includes any kind of political, racial, or religious hostility, whether public or private. "Strife" is rivalry or discord, which comes from a quarrelsome spirit. "Jealousy" is the wrong kind of zeal, such as Paul had before he became a Christian (cf. Phil. 3:6). It often leads to "fits of anger," the rage-filled outbursts that come from having a bad temper. Aristotle compared this term to dogs that "bark if there is but a knock at the door, before looking to see if it is a friend."[1]

The list goes on, for the sinful nature produces a seemingly endless variety of sins. Some people want to get ahead at the expense of others, so they are guilty of "rivalries." Others take sides, causing "dissensions" and "divisions." The English word for "heresy" comes from the Greek term for "divisions" (*haireseis*), and indeed, theological error always divides the church, as a clear separation must be made between true and false doctrine.

What are some other works of the flesh? People tend to be unhappy when others succeed, and the proper term for such a grudging spirit is "envy." "The envious," said Socrates, "are pained by their friends' successes."[2] To give a more contemporary example, envy is the vice depicted in the cartoon that features a dog sitting at a bar and saying, "It's not just that dogs have to win, but cats have to lose." Whenever we rejoice at the misfortunes of others, including our friends, we are guilty of envy.

Finally, there are two more sins of the body, drinking to excess and eating to excess: "drunkenness" and "orgies." The Bible does not prohibit alcohol, any more than it prohibits food, but it always condemns getting drunk. The term used here refers to drinking bouts—what people today would call "getting wasted." The orgies to which Paul refers were not simply sexual, but involved wild partying of all kinds, including revels held at pagan temples.

Later in the chapter the apostle adds several more sins to his list: "Let us not become conceited, provoking one another, envying one another" (Gal. 5:26). This verse is about spiritual pride, the work of the flesh that destroys fellowship. If the proud think they are superior, they provoke others by putting them down. Those who feel inferior, on the other hand, envy others and resent their success. Either way, they destroy relationships.

---

1. Aristotle, *Nicomachean Ethics*, in *The Basic Works of Aristotle*, ed. Richard McKeon, trans. W. D. Ross (New York: Random House, 1941), 1046 (7.6.1).
2. Xenophon, *Memoirs of Socrates* 3.9.8.

All in all, it is quite a list. It includes social sins and sexual sins, sins of both the body and the soul, sins common among Christians as well as pagans. Paul ends his catalogue with "things like these" to show that he could keep going. But his point has less to do with any particular sin than it does with the entire lifestyle that these acts of the flesh represent. The only thing the sinful nature can produce is an unchaste, unholy, uncharitable, and undisciplined life. This is plain for all to see. The sinfulness of the sinful nature is so obvious as to be self-evident, partly because we have committed so many of these deadly deeds ourselves. The Puritan William Perkins said this list of vices is a mirror to reveal the corruption of our own hearts.[3]

What Paul says next is most alarming. Having listed the deeds of the flesh, he goes on to warn where they naturally lead (or rather, where they do *not* lead): "I warn you, as I warned you before, that those who do such things will not inherit the kingdom of God" (Gal. 5:21). This sounds like an echo from the teaching of Jesus, who had a great deal to say about the coming of God's kingdom. What Paul means by "kingdom" is God's final kingdom—the place of his eternal rule, namely, heaven. To inherit God's kingdom is to come into its rightful possession by receiving the free gift of eternal life.

Apparently, Paul had warned the Galatians about this before. He had told them that while good works cannot get someone into heaven, evil deeds can certainly keep someone out of it! People who perform the acts of the sinful nature will *not* inherit eternal life. It is perhaps significant that he refers to the deeds of the sinful nature as "*works* of the flesh." This is a reminder that works cannot save. Whether they are works of the law, works of the flesh, or any other kind of works, they do not lead to heaven.

Does this mean that anyone who is guilty of any of the vices that Paul describes in Galatians 5:19–21 is going to hell? Certainly anyone who commits these sins deserves to go there, and for this reason we should not think lightly of these or any other sins. But remember that the Christian, even the "Spirit-filled Christian," still has a sinful nature. From time to time, therefore, even believers commit these very sins. With this in mind, it is important to know that when Paul refers to "those who do such things" (Gal. 5:21), the Greek verb (*prassontes*) indicates habitual action, not an occasional lapse.

---

3. William Perkins, *A Commentary on Galatians*, Pilgrim Classic Commentaries, ed. Gerald T. Sheppard (London, 1617; repr. New York: Pilgrim, 1989), 373.

Paul is not talking about Christians who from time to time commit one of these sins against their better judgment, all the while knowing that they are grieving the Holy Spirit and wishing that they could stop. Rather, he is talking about people whose lives are dominated by sin, who are committed heart and soul to immorality, idolatry, sorcery, and envy.

This is not the kind of life that leads to heaven. Quite the opposite. Why would someone who loves to break God's rules even want to go to the place where God's rules are always kept? People who make a regular practice of vice need to repent of their sins and leave their old lifestyle behind, lest they fall into eternal judgment.

But what about Christians who feel—perhaps with some justification—that they are dominated by an addictive sin such as pornography or anorexia? They should heed Paul's warning that people who live this way will not inherit the kingdom of God. But they should not despair. The very fact that they are concerned about their spiritual condition shows that the Spirit is at work, and that he will enable them to live a life that is more and more pleasing to God.

THE FRUIT OF THE SPIRIT

There is a reason why the flesh produces such bad behavior. It is simply "doing what comes naturally." Jesus said, "Either make the tree good and its fruit good, or make the tree bad and its fruit bad, for the tree is known by its fruit" (Matt. 12:33). The sinful nature produces sin because it was a bad tree to start with. The Spirit, by contrast, is a good tree producing lush and abundant virtue: "But the fruit of the Spirit is love, joy, peace, patience, kindness, goodness, faithfulness, gentleness, self-control" (Gal. 5:22–23).

The greatest of these is "love" (cf. 1 Cor. 13:13), which is the highest of all virtues and the foundation for all godliness: "Love is not one virtue among a list of virtues, but the sum and substance of what it means to be a Christian."[4] The Greek word used here for "love"—*agapē*—seems to have been patented by the writers of the New Testament. It is the kind of selfless, sacrificial affection that enables us to serve one another in love (Gal. 5:22). Love is also what we return to God, who first loved us through the sufferings and

---

4. C. B. Cousar, *Galatians*, Interpretation (Atlanta: John Knox, 1982), 131.

death of his Son, and then poured his love "into our hearts through the Holy Spirit" (Rom. 5:5).

Then comes "joy," which is not so much happiness as contentment. Joy is the ability to take good cheer from the gospel. It is not, therefore, a spontaneous response to some temporary pleasure. It does not depend on circumstance at all. It is based rather on rejoicing in one's eternal identity in Jesus Christ. With joy comes "peace," a sense of wholeness and well-being. John MacArthur writes, "If joy speaks of the exhilaration of the heart that comes from being right with God, then *peace* refers to the tranquility of mind that comes from saving relationships."[5] Such tranquility may be enjoyed both with God and with others. "We have peace with God through our Lord Jesus Christ" (Rom. 5:1), and since we have peace with God, we are able to make peace with others.

Like peace, the next several virtues bring harmony to human relationships. "Patience" is long-suffering in the face of hardship—the ability to endure through adversity. A patient person has a slow fuse. He or she is steadfast and persistent, willing to suffer aggravation or even persecution without complaint. "Kindness" is more than a random act of consideration. It is a constant readiness to help, the extension of God's grace to the people around us through practical actions of caring. Closely related to it is "goodness," which was a common general term for virtue among the pagans. It connotes complete moral excellence. Here it is sanctified by the Holy Spirit, and indicates a willingness to be generous.

Next comes "faithfulness," the trustworthiness that comes from trusting in the God of the Bible. The faithful person is reliable for important tasks, loyal to friends, and dependable in emergencies. With faithfulness goes "gentleness," an inward grace that is sometimes called "meekness" and is often described as "power under control." The gentle person has a sweet temper of spirit toward God, others, and the daily frustrations of life. He or she is not prone to anger, but humble, sweet, and mild.

Finally, there is "self-control," which means temperance or moderation, especially in sensual matters like eating, drinking, and sex. This sober virtue prevents liberty from becoming license in the Christian life. A person with

5. John MacArthur, *Galatians*, The MacArthur New Testament Commentary (Chicago: Moody, 1987), 166.

self-control has the restraint and self-discipline not to be ruled by passion, and therefore is able to resist temptation.

This catalogue of spiritual virtues is not exhaustive. Paul hints at this when he refers to the fruit of the Spirit as "such things" (Gal. 5:23). Some graces that are not on this list—such as hope, for example, or godliness—appear elsewhere in the New Testament. Once again, the point is not so much the specific character traits as it is the entire lifestyle they represent.

All the graces of the Spirit belong together, which perhaps explains why the word "fruit" occurs in the singular. The fruit of the Spirit is one whole spiritual life that is rooted in the one Spirit of God. To change the image for a moment, these virtues are not nine different gems, but nine different facets of the same dazzling jewel. Spiritual fruit is different from spiritual gifts in this respect, since most Christians have only a handful of gifts. But one does not pick and choose among spiritual fruit the way one sorts through fruits and vegetables at the supermarket. There is only one fruit, which every Christian produces, albeit in varying quantities and with different degrees of sweetness.

The contrast between the special produce of the Spirit and the bitter fruit of the sinful nature could hardly be sharper. The fruit of the Spirit is the very opposite of the works of the flesh. When it comes to godliness, the Spirit really produces! He brings forth good fruit from a good tree, the product of a whole new spiritual nature in Christ.

One helpful way to study this passage is to contrast the fruit of the Spirit with what might be called "the weeds of the devil." Each fruit has its opposite, a weed that tries to choke it out. In fact, many of these weeds grow in Paul's list of vices (Gal. 5:19–21). The weed that tries to choke out love is enmity. Dissension stunts the growth of peace. Patience is crowded out by anger. The weed that grows around self-control is sensuality; and so forth.[6]

Another way to study the fruit of the Spirit is to compare it to the character of God. Love, peace, goodness, faithfulness—these are all divine attributes. We see them displayed in the work of God the Son, who was patient in suffering, faithful to his disciples, gentle with children, and loving in his kindness to sinners. James Dunn rightly calls Galatians 5:22–23 a "charac-

---

6. This idea is fully developed by John W. Sanderson in *The Fruit of the Spirit* (Phillipsburg, NJ: Presbyterian and Reformed, 1985); see especially the chart on page 43.

ter-sketch" of Christ.[7] Since the Spirit is the Spirit of Christ, it is only natural for him to reproduce the virtues of Christ in the life of the Christian. Jesus is the vine; we are the branches (John 15:5). The Holy Spirit connects us to the vine, and thereby produces in us the fruit of Christ himself.

We do not grow this fruit on our own. This is why it is called the *fruit* of the Spirit rather than the *works* of the Spirit. S. H. Hooke comments: "A vine does not produce grapes by Act of Parliament; they are the fruit of the vine's own life; so the conduct which conforms to the standard of the Kingdom is not produced by any demand, not even God's, but it is the fruit of that divine nature which God gives as the result of what he has done in and by Christ."[8] The fruit of the Spirit is the natural produce of his gracious inward influence, the spontaneous and inevitable result of his uniting us to Jesus Christ. It will take time to grow, but grow it must, for God will make it grow. What we are to do in the meantime is cultivate this spiritual fruit.

Notice that this is a catalogue of virtues rather than a list of rules. Perhaps this is why Paul ends by saying, "Against such things there is no law" (Gal. 5:23). This is a deliberate understatement. The reason there is no law against these virtues is that they are positively lawful, and thus people who practice them fulfill the law.

This does not mean that the Spirit issues a command for every situation. Indeed, if we think of this list as a how-to guide for the Christian life, we are in danger of slipping back into works-righteousness. Remember, we are not under the law. Nevertheless, the Spirit is not lawless. His liberty does not lead to license. Instead, he works into us those dispositions that lead to godliness. His fruit is habits of the heart that produce a rich harvest of loving obedience. And paradoxically, the life that the Spirit produces in us conforms to the very law that cannot justify us. To repeat a quote from Donald Hagner:

> We are set free from the law *in order to produce a righteousness that corresponds to the righteousness that the law demanded.* . . . The content of the law has not fundamentally changed. It is only the dynamic—the means by which we can arrive at righteousness—that differs dramatically. Living out the righteous-

7. James D. G. Dunn, *The Epistle to the Galatians* (London: A & C Black, 1993), 310.
8. S. H. Hooke, *The Siege Perilous* (London: SCM Press, 1956), 264.

ness of the law does not result in a right relationship with God; rather, being in a right relationship with God through faith in Christ results in living out the righteousness of the law.[9]

In time, it becomes almost natural to live in the Spirit, except that it is really *super*-natural. J. I. Packer writes, "Holiness is the *naturalness* of the spiritually risen man, just as sin is the naturalness of the spiritually dead man, and in pursuing holiness by obeying God the Christian actually follows the deepest urge of his own renewed being."[10] We do not have to live like legalists to fulfill the law. What we need is the Holy Spirit.

MORTIFY THE FLESH

The Holy Spirit does not produce fruit in the Christian life without our cooperation. There are two things every Christian must do to remain fruitful. The first is to mortify the flesh: "And those who belong to Christ Jesus have crucified the flesh with its passions and desires" (Gal. 5:24). Mortification is one of the most neglected doctrines of the Christian faith, but also one of the most important. Indeed, spiritual growth is hardly possible without it. Mortification is what Paul was talking about when he told the Romans, "Consider yourselves dead to sin" (Rom. 6:11). It simply means putting sin to death, what the Puritan William Ames (1576–1633) called "the wasting away of sin."[11]

As we have seen, the Spirit is engaged in mortal combat with the flesh. The desires of the regenerate nature wage war against the passions of the sinful nature. In this war there will be no truce. The spiritual nature cannot enter into peace negotiations with the sinful nature. Nor can it surrender. The Spirit must battle sin to the death. Therefore, when the Spirit captures the flesh, he does not simply hold it as a prisoner; he commits the ultimate act of war. The Spirit puts the sinful nature to death. And not just any death. The means of execution is crucifixion. This is how John Stott explains it: "To

9. Donald A. Hagner, "The Law in Paul's Letter to the Galatians," *Modern Reformation* 12.5 (Sept./Oct. 2003): 36.

10. J. I. Packer, *Keep in Step with the Spirit* (Tarrytown, NY: Revell, 1984), 107.

11. William Ames, *The Marrow of Theology*, trans. and ed. John Dykstra Eusden (Durham, NC: Labyrinth, 1983), 170.

'take up the cross' was our Lord's vivid figure of speech for self-denial. Every follower of Christ is to behave like a condemned criminal and carry his cross to the place of execution. Now Paul takes the metaphor to its logical conclusion. We must not only take up our cross and walk with it, but actually see that the execution takes place. We are actually to take the flesh, our wilful and wayward self, and nail it to the cross."[12]

Consider how appropriate it is for the sinful nature to be crucified. Crucifixion was a *shameful* way to die. It was reserved for hardened criminals, for traitors and murderers, the scum of society. But what is more shameful than the sinful nature, which rebels against God and murders the human soul?

Crucifixion was a *painful* way to die, as painful a means of execution as human beings have ever devised. It was excruciating, in the full and proper sense of the word. Likewise, the mortification of sin is painful. It is not painful to the body (as if we had to abuse ourselves in order to please God), but to the soul. The reason sanctification is such a painful process is that there is always something excruciating about putting our sins to death. Our sinful nature loves them so much that we secretly hope that they will live.

Crucifixion was a *gradual* way to die, with its victims often lingering on the cross for days before they drew their last breath. John Brown wrote, "Crucifixion was a punishment appropriated to the worst crimes of the basest sort of criminals, and produced death, not suddenly, but gradually." Similarly, "True Christians . . . do not succeed in completely destroying [the flesh] while here below; but they have fixed it to the Cross, and they are determined to keep it there till it expire."[13] When it comes to eliminating sin, there are no shortcuts, only a long, slow, painful death.

The last thing to be said about crucifixion is that it was always *final*. Those who were crucified may have died slowly, but they always died eventually, because soldiers ensured that the victims were not taken down from their crosses until they were really and truly dead. The same is true in the Spirit's war against the flesh. God is not fighting a losing battle. The sin-

12. John R. W. Stott, *The Message of Galatians: Only One Way*, The Bible Speaks Today (Downers Grove, IL: InterVarsity, 1968), 150.

13. John Brown, *An Exposition of the Epistle of Paul the Apostle to the Galatians* (Edinburgh, 1853; repr. Evansville, IN: Sovereign Grace, 1957), 309.

ful nature has already received its mortal blow, and the Spirit will see to it that it remains on the cross until it expires. The question is not if it will die, but only when.

Sin received this death blow on the cross of Christ. We find the death of our own sinful nature in the death of Christ, through what J. I. Packer calls "cocrucifixion with Jesus Christ."[14] There is a connection between Galatians 5:24 and Galatians 2:20 ("I have been crucified with Christ. It is no longer I who live, but Christ who lives in me"). But notice one very important difference. In chapter 2, we are crucified; in chapter 5, we do the crucifying: "And those who belong to Christ Jesus have crucified the flesh" (Gal. 5:24). This verse describes a crucifixion carried out by those who are literally "of Christ." In other words, God's own people are the executioners. Since the verb is expressed in the past tense, we know that this event has already taken place. But when? We first crucified the sinful nature at our conversion, when we came to faith in Jesus Christ. At that time we went to Calvary, where Christ was crucified. There we were united to him in his death. When we put our trust in him, it was not only to die for our sins, but also to put our sins to death. The cross of Christ means death to our flesh.

The trouble is that our sinful nature has a way of trying to climb back down from that cross. When it does, it is able to make a remarkably speedy recovery, partly because we have a way of helping it. We are sometimes tempted to remove the nails, help our old sinful nature down from the cross, and nurse it back to health. This is why we struggle with so-called besetting sins—sins that we commit so often that they become bad habits.

This has to stop. Do not administer first aid to your flesh. Instead, treat it the way Jesus was treated at Calvary. Mortify your sinful nature. Put it to death! From time to time, whenever it shows signs of life, say, "Oh no you don't! Don't try to climb down from there. Get back up on that cross where you belong!" Then pound the nails in a little deeper. If you belong to Christ, you have crucified your sinful nature, with all its selfish desire. Do not resuscitate it. Do not give it CPR. Do not keep it on life support. Just leave it on the cross and let it die.

14. Packer, *Keep in Step with the Spirit*, 106.

KEEP IN STEP WITH THE SPIRIT

There are two sides to sanctification in the Christian life. One is mortification, the putting to death of the sinful nature. The other is vivification, the coming to life of the regenerate nature. At the same time that we are putting our flesh to death, we are being revived by the Holy Spirit. These two aspects of sanctification—mortification and vivification—go together. As Calvin put it, "The death of the flesh is the life of the Spirit."[15]

This brings us to the second thing that the Christian must do to remain fruitful, which is to walk with the Spirit: "If we live by the Spirit, let us also walk by the Spirit" (Gal. 5:25). The New English Bible offers a helpful paraphrase: "If the Spirit is the source of our life, let the Spirit also direct our course."

In this verse, as he so often does, the apostle Paul follows an indicative with an imperative; he tells us to become what we are. It is a fact: Those who belong to Jesus live in the Spirit. At regeneration, the Holy Spirit enters the heart of every Christian. Yet we must keep on living in the Spirit, which is precisely what the Galatians were failing to do. Paul had already asked them, "Having begun by the Spirit, are you now being perfected by the flesh?" (Gal. 3:3).

By starting and then stopping in this way, the Galatians had fallen out of step with God's Spirit. The way the New International Version translates this verse accurately captures the metaphor: "let us keep in step with the Spirit" (Gal. 5:25). When the apostle speaks of "keeping in step," he is really talking about following orders. The Greek term for "keeping in step" (*stoichōmen*) comes from the military. It means to stay in formation. First, soldiers would line up in ranks and files. Then, in order to maintain good military discipline, they would stay in line as they marched.

Soldiers not only march in formation, but also run in formation. When they do, there is only one thing they have to worry about, which is keeping in step. They do not need to worry about where they are going, or how they will get there. They do not need to guess how much farther they have to go. Their commanding officer will give them their orders as necessary. The only

15. John Calvin, *The Epistles of Paul the Apostle to the Galatians, Ephesians, Philippians and Colossians*, Calvin's New Testament Commentaries, trans. T. H. L. Parker, ed. David W. and Thomas F. Torrance (Grand Rapids: Eerdmans, 1996), 106.

thing soldiers need to know how to do is step in time.[16] It is the same way in the Christian life. The Holy Spirit is God's drill sergeant. It is his job to keep us in line. As he barks out the cadence, all we have to do is keep our place in the formation, running in step with his commands.

This analogy shows us where we ought to be in relation to other Christians. We do not run alone. Our brothers and sisters are right beside us. Ideally, we are matching them stride for stride. As long as we maintain good discipline, there will not be any pushing and shoving in the ranks, the kind of "provoking" and "envying" that Paul warns about in Galatians 5:26. Instead, by staying in formation, we will maintain our unity in the Spirit. A good unit never lets one of its men fall behind. If a soldier stops running because of injury, discouragement, or fatigue, his buddies will circle around and gather him back into his unit. So also in the church we are called to maintain unity by going back to help those who have fallen.

Keeping in step takes discipline, and so does spiritual growth. The Holy Spirit rarely works in extraordinary ways. Instead, he uses the ordinary means of grace to bring spiritual growth: the reading and preaching of God's Word, the sacraments of baptism and communion, and the life of prayer. Contrary to what so many Christians seem to believe, true spiritual growth does not come from some special experience of the Holy Spirit. Instead, it comes from walking with the Spirit every day until, finally, keeping in step with him becomes a holy habit.

J. I. Packer's explanation of how the Spirit works is worth quoting at length:

> The Spirit works through *means*—through the objective means of grace, namely, biblical truth, prayer, fellowship, worship, and the Lord's Supper, and with them through the subjective means of grace whereby we open ourselves to change, namely, thinking, listening, questioning oneself, examining oneself, admonishing oneself, sharing what is in one's heart with others, and weighing any response they make. The Spirit shows his power in us, not by constantly interrupting our use of these means with visions, impressions, or prophecies . . . (such communications come only rarely, and to some believ-

---

16. I am indebted for this observation to the Reverend Richard D. Phillips of First Presbyterian Church in Margate, Florida, and formerly a tank commander in the United States Army and a faculty member at the United States Military Academy (West Point).

ers not at all), but rather by making these regular means effective to change us for the better and for the wiser as we go along. . . . . Habit forming is the Spirit's ordinary way of leading us on in holiness. . . . Love, joy, peace, patience, kindness, goodness, faithfulness, gentleness, self-control are all of them habitual . . . ways of thinking, feeling, and behaving.[17]

Packer goes on to stress that "Holiness by habit forming is not self-sanctification by self-effort, but is simply a matter of understanding the Spirit's method and then keeping in step with him."[18] This is how God grows good spiritual fruit. The more we keep in step with the Holy Spirit through the Word, sacraments, and prayer, the more fruitful we become.

17. Packer, *Keep in Step with the Spirit*, 109.
18. Ibid., 110.

20

THE SPIRITUAL LIFE

Galatians 6:1—6

> *Brothers, if anyone is caught in any transgression, you who are*
> *spiritual should restore him in a spirit of gentleness. Keep watch*
> *on yourself, lest you too be tempted. Bear one another's burdens,*
> *and so fulfill the law of Christ.* (Gal. 6:1–2)

One of the most unusual figures in church history was a man named Simeon the Stylite. He was the first of the so-called Desert Fathers. Around the year 423, he constructed a short pillar on the edge of the Syrian desert, climbed to the top, and lived on it for the next six years. Simeon received many visitors to his desert perch. No doubt many of them came to see if he was out of his mind. But the hermit explained that he was simply a Christian who wanted to commune with God in solitude, free from worldly distractions. Living on top of a pole in the desert was his way of separating himself from sin and consecrating himself to God.

As strange as it may seem, the life of Simeon the Stylite raises an important question: What does it mean to be spiritual? As far as Simeon was concerned, one could be more spiritual in the desert than in the city, and more spiritual off the ground than on it (the higher, the better). But was he right about what it means to be spiritual? As he reflected on Simeon's spirituality, one recent writer asked: "Is there child-care in the desert?"[1] The writer

---

1. See Ernest Boyer Jr., *Finding God at Home: Family Life as a Spiritual Discipline* (San Francisco: Harper & Row, 1984).

was married, with children, and his point was that not everyone is able to go and live alone in the desert. Isn't there some other way to be spiritual?

TRUE SPIRITUALITY

Everyone seems to be interested in spirituality these days, but no one seems to agree on what it means. In the contemporary marketplace of ideas, spirituality sells. The bookstores are loaded with titles about angels, near-death experiences, and ancient pagan religions. The Internet is full of Web sites set up by New Age gurus and operated by strange cults. Covens and spirit shops proliferate.

One of the strange things about this new fascination with the spiritual life is that many people want to become spiritual without getting religious. For them, spirituality is something private and spontaneous, whereas religion is public and rigid. The reason spirituality sells is that people can make it whatever they want it to be. According to sociologist Robert Wuthnow, "Growing numbers of Americans piece together their faith like a patchwork quilt. Spirituality has become a vastly complex quest in which each person seeks in his or her own way."[2]

Unfortunately, the same may be said of the church, where there is widespread confusion about the meaning of true spirituality. Some Christians find their spirituality in acts of private devotion. Having one's quiet time, fasting, and going to a retreat center are the basic acts of spiritual life. The way to become more spiritual is to find a spiritual director and begin to practice the spiritual disciplines.

For others, the spiritual life begins at church, in the context of public worship. True spirituality comes from reciting an ancient liturgy, lighting candles, and waving incense. Or it comes from playing the right music on the right instrument, or from not using instruments at all.

Still other Christians crave an exciting spiritual experience. They want to be miraculously healed or delivered through a "power encounter" with the Holy Spirit. They divide the church between those who have had a particu-

2. Robert Wuthnow, "Spirituality in America since the 1950s," *Theology, News and Notes* (March 1999), 4; see also Wuthnow's *After Heaven: Spirituality in America since the 1950s* (Berkeley: University of California Press, 1998).

lar experience and those who haven't, or between those who exercise a special gift and those who don't.

Galatians offers an entirely different way of thinking about the spiritual life. Over against the pluralism of this age, Christian spirituality is based on a relationship with a personal God who has spoken an eternal word. The spiritual life is not, therefore, something that one defines for oneself. Rather, it is a life defined by the existence and character of the one true God.

Contrary to what some Christians seem to think, this spiritual life is not something that we produce within us through some ritual or method. To put it very simply, spiritual life flows from the third person of the Trinity. The life of the Holy Spirit can be nurtured by using the means of grace—reading Scripture, attending public worship, and so on—but the life itself comes from God. Only his Spirit can produce the fruit of love, joy, peace, patience, kindness, goodness, faithfulness, gentleness, and self-control.

The Holy Spirit does not produce this fruit for our private enjoyment. True spirituality is not an individualistic quest for self-fulfillment—the kind of thing one has to climb to the top of a pillar to discover. The life of the Spirit flourishes for the sake of others. It is not experienced in private, primarily, but exercised in public. Therefore, it does not grow in isolation, but within the community of faith. Spiritual life is meant to be shared. It is less like a fruit tree hidden away somewhere in a secret garden, and more like one that grows in a public park.

RESTORE ONE ANOTHER FROM SIN

At the beginning of Galatians 6, the apostle Paul plucks some of this spiritual fruit and begins to share it. In these verses he teaches that the way to be truly spiritual is to "one another" each other. Spiritual people restore one another from sin (Gal. 6:1), bear one another's burdens (Gal. 6:2), consider others more important (Gal. 6:3–5), and share with one another (Gal. 6:6).

Being spiritual means, first of all, restoring one another from sin: "Brothers, if anyone is caught in any transgression, you who are spiritual should restore him in a spirit of gentleness. Keep watch on yourself, lest you too be tempted" (Gal. 6:1). Each word in this verse is significant. The word "brothers" is a reminder that the church is God's family. We are sons and daughters of the Most High God, adopted through faith in his Son.

The fact that we are brothers and sisters in Christ does not keep us out of sin, however. As we have seen, the flesh wars against the Spirit. Thus there are times when the sinful nature knocks us off our stride, when a false step keeps us from walking with the Spirit. There are times when, through weakness, a Christian gets "caught in transgression." This phrase may refer to a person who gets caught in the act, like the woman who was "caught in the act of adultery" (John 8:4). Or perhaps the sinner catches himself in the act. Temptation has a way of sneaking up on us unawares, catching us off guard. The sad reality is that sometimes Christians are surprised by sin; indeed, there are as many sinners in the church as anywhere else.

The phrase "caught in any transgression" does not refer to deliberate, habitual sin. It refers rather to an unexpected sin, something a Christian does almost against his or her better judgment. It may even involve one of the very sins that Paul has already condemned as "works of the flesh" (Gal. 5:19–21). A Christian who falls into this kind of sin needs proper spiritual care. Thus Paul explains what to do, who should do it, and how.

What should be done? It is very simple: "restore him" (Gal. 6:1). The verb that Paul uses here (*katartizete*) is a term for healing that means "to return to its former condition." It was used in medicine, for example, to describe the setting of a broken bone or dislocated joint. In much the same way, a sinner needs to be put back in order.

Unfortunately, Christians do not always offer sinners very good treatment. Sometimes we ignore sin. Lacking the courage to confront it, we simply pretend it isn't there. We act like timid medical students who see a patient with a bone fragment sticking out of his arm, but are afraid to touch it. The bone is never set and the wound never heals. Sometimes Christians notice the broken bone of sin, but never get past making a diagnosis. They simply stand around talking about what bad shape the sinner is in. "Wow," people say, "would you look at that broken bone! I mean, just look at the way it's sticking out! Boy, am I glad I don't have a fracture like that!" Meanwhile, the brother or sister continues in the pains of sin. This kind of treatment is better known as gossip. Sadly, there are even times when Christians condemn sinners, blaming them (or even punishing them) for needing to go to the spiritual emergency room in the first place. They treat them like outcasts, harshly scolding them for being spiritually out of joint and apparently forgetting that they themselves are sinners in need of grace.

When Christians are caught in sin, they do not need isolation or amputation; they need restoration. The proper thing to do is to help them confess their sins and find forgiveness in Christ, and then to welcome them back into the fellowship of the church.

Who should do this? "You who are spiritual" (Gal. 6:1). The rehabilitation of sinners is a job for spiritual people, which in one sense would include all Christians. The moment that anyone receives Jesus Christ as Savior and Lord, the Holy Spirit enters that person's heart (see Gal. 3:2). From that point on, he or she is a spiritual person.

There is another sense, however, in which some Christians are more spiritual than others. They are more mature in the Christian life. They do such a good job of what Paul was talking about in chapter 5—walking in the Spirit, being led by the Spirit, keeping in step with the Spirit—that the fruit of the Spirit's work within them is obvious. Setting sinners back to rights is a job for Christians who have the fruit of the Spirit in abundant supply.

The reason only spiritual people should restore sinners is that only spiritual people can. How should sinners be restored? "In a spirit of gentleness" (Gal. 6:1). But remember that gentleness (or meekness) is part of the fruit of the Spirit (see Gal. 5:23). Therefore, if sinners are to be restored gently, it will take a spiritual person to do it, because only a spiritual person has true spiritual gentleness.

This proves that being harsh or judgmental is a sign of spiritual immaturity. Some Christians think that angry words are necessary to defend God's righteous cause. But the only way to restore a believer who has fallen into sin is with gentle sensitivity. "One test of true spirituality," writes F. F. Bruce, "is a readiness to set those who stumble by the wayside on the right road again in a sympathetic . . . spirit."[3] If we cannot do this gently, we had better not do it at all. We should let someone else do it, someone spiritual enough to perform such a delicate task.

Elsewhere, the Bible gives a step-by-step process for restoring fallen sinners. Perhaps Paul was familiar with the teaching of Jesus: "If your brother sins against you, go and tell him his fault, between you and him alone. If he listens to you, you have gained your brother. But if he does not listen, take

---

3. F. F. Bruce, *The Epistle to the Galatians: A Commentary on the Greek Text*, New International Greek Testament Commentary (Grand Rapids: Eerdmans, 1982), 260.

one or two others along with you, that every charge may be established by the evidence of two or three witnesses. If he refuses to listen to them, tell it to the church. And if he refuses to listen even to the church, let him be to you as a Gentile and a tax collector" (Matt. 18:15–17). This careful process, which gradually moves from private confrontation to public condemnation, is sometimes called church discipline. The Reformers considered it so important that they identified it as one of the marks of the true Christian church.

The apostle Paul recognized that the whole process demands gentleness. The goal at each step of church discipline is to heal the church by restoring the sinner back into the fellowship of his spiritual family. This is likely to happen only if the sinner is embraced with a gentle spirit. Consider the way Martin Luther instructed a pastor to help a fallen brother: "Run unto him, and reaching out your hand, raise him up again, comfort him with sweet words, and embrace him with motherly arms."[4]

In some ways, restoring a sinner is not all that different from setting a broken bone. The process is bound to be painful, no matter who does it. But the more deftly the bone is set, the sooner healing can begin. In the same way, someone who tends a sinner's wounds must do so with gentle kindness.

Such restoration requires humility. The Scripture gives this warning to those who practice spiritual surgery: "Keep watch on yourself, lest you too be tempted" (Gal. 6:1). Even spiritual people may stumble. The particular temptation that Paul seems to have in mind is spiritual pride. It is hard not to feel at least a little self-righteous when we are correcting someone else's sin. The more we learn about someone else's depravity, the easier it is to look down on him or her. This temptation must be resisted, and the way to resist it is by examining our own hearts. We are as prone to fall into sin as anyone else, maybe more so. As Paul warned on another occasion: "Therefore let anyone who thinks that he stands take heed lest he fall" (1 Cor. 10:12).

BEAR ONE ANOTHER'S BURDENS

There is a second kind of spiritual work that demands less gentleness than restoring a sinner, but also takes more effort. Martin Luther said that this

4. Martin Luther, *Lectures on Galatians, 1535*, trans. and ed. Jaroslav Pelikan, in *Luther's Works* (St. Louis: Concordia, 1963), 27:111.

work requires "strong shoulders and mighty bones."[5] It is less like setting a broken bone and more like carrying the stretcher. It is the work of bearing someone else's burden: "Bear one another's burdens, and so fulfill the law of Christ" (Gal. 6:2).

This verse implies that Christians will have burdens, and heavy ones at that. Being caught in sin from time to time is one burden, but there are many others as well: sorrow, worry, doubt, failure, poverty, loneliness, illness, divorce, disability, and depression. Not only do we face such hardships, but we are incapable of handling them by ourselves. Sometimes our burdens are so heavy that they must be shared if they are to be carried at all.

There is a sense, of course, in which God carries our burdens for us. Our biggest burden of all—the infinite burden of our sin and guilt—is a burden that only God *could* bear. He did this when Jesus carried his cross to Calvary and died on it for our sins. If God has already carried our greatest burden on the cross, then surely he can handle our lighter loads as well: "Cast your burden on the LORD," wrote David, "and he will sustain you; he will never permit the righteous to be moved" (Ps. 55:22). Perhaps the apostle Peter had this very psalm in mind when he spoke of "casting all your anxieties on him, because he cares for you" (1 Peter 5:7). God's shoulders are broad enough to carry all our burdens.

The fact that God carries our burdens, however, does not mean that he is the only one with whom we should share them. Often the way God lightens our load is by getting other Christians to do some of the carrying. If we are discouraged in the Christian life, it may be because we are trying to carry too much weight all by ourselves. God has given us one another. Every believer is called to be one of God's bellhops, always ready to pick up someone else's baggage. This means that we do not need to keep all our troubles to ourselves; indeed, it means that we must not.

Many times people in the church suffer heavy losses, losses too heavy to bear alone. When they do, they usually share their burden with one of their pastors and a few close friends. Together, everyone helps to carry the load. Some do it through prayer. Others offer warm hugs and speak kind words of comfort and sympathy. Still others help in practical ways, by cleaning the house, bringing a meal to share, or sharing an appropriate Christian book.

---

5. Martin Luther, *A Commentary on St. Paul's Epistle to the Galatians* (London: James Clark, 1972), 540.

This ought to happen every time a member of the church is in difficulty, whether physical, emotional, or spiritual. If we have a heavy load, we need to let someone else help us to carry it. And if we see someone else struggling under the weight of trouble, we need to put our own shoulder to the task. Christians always rally around to help.

Whenever Christians bear one another's burdens, they are fulfilling the law. Paul wrote, "Bear one another's burdens, and so fulfill the law of Christ" (Gal. 6:2). This would be a surprising verse if Paul had not surprised us already. After spending two-thirds of his letter explaining that justification comes by faith in Christ, and not by works of the law, he amazed us by telling us to keep the law: "For the whole law is fulfilled in one word: 'You shall love your neighbor as yourself'" (Gal. 5:14). We are called to keep the law of love, even though our salvation does not depend on it. Though we are not under the law, nevertheless we fulfill the law.

What the apostle means by "the law of Christ" is the moral law. It is called "the law of Christ" because Christ himself taught it throughout his ministry, interpreting, clarifying, and applying the moral requirements of God's eternal law. And of all the ethical instructions Jesus gave—and he repeated all the main points of the Old Testament law, including the Ten Commandments—his most basic instruction was to love our neighbors as ourselves. Jesus said, "A new commandment I give to you, that you love one another: just as I have loved you, you also are to love one another" (John 13:34). Or again, "This is my commandment, that you love one another as I have loved you" (John 15:12). The law of Christ is the law of loving one another.

One way to fulfill the law of love is to bear one another's burdens. By caring for one another, we become law-abiding Christians. Of course, we are not saved by keeping the law. However, God's will for our lives, as expressed in his moral law, has not changed. Now that we have been saved, we must keep the law of Christ. We must continue to love our neighbors as ourselves, bearing one another's burdens, just as Christ showed his love for us when he bore the burden of our sin on the cross.

CONSIDER OTHERS MORE IMPORTANT

The only way to love our neighbors as ourselves is to recognize that our neighbor is at least as valuable in the sight of God as we are. This brings us to a third thing that spiritual people do: They consider others more important than themselves.

The way we treat others depends in large measure on what we think about ourselves. People who have a rather high opinion of themselves are generally unwilling to carry anyone else's baggage. They are too self-centered to be self-giving. They think serving others is beneath their dignity. Why should *they* stoop to shoulder someone else's burden? This attitude was especially common in the ancient world, where it was considered demeaning to help others.

Often the only way to manage someone else's burden is by putting down our own burdens for a while. Needy people have a way of demanding our time, changing our plans, and rearranging our schedules. Helping them requires the kinds of sacrifices that we will make only if we consider them more important than ourselves. In fact, helping others is possible only for those who have the mind of Christ, "who, though he was in the form of God, did not count equality with God a thing to be grasped, but made himself nothing, taking the form of a servant" (Phil. 2:6–7).

I once knew a woman who had learned to honor Christ by valuing others more highly than herself. I caught a glimpse of her attitude one day when she was waiting in line to use the photocopying machine. She noticed that the man in front of her had a pile of papers to copy. Taking them from his hand, she said, "Let me take care of those; your time is more important than mine."

What the Scripture says to people who think that they are something special is that actually they are nothing: "For if anyone thinks he is something, when he is nothing, he deceives himself" (Gal. 6:3). People who are fascinated by their own abilities and attributes are only fooling themselves. A stewardess once told the heavyweight boxing champion Muhammad Ali to prepare for takeoff. "Superman don't need no seatbelt!" he objected. She replied, "Superman don't need no airplane." Sooner or later, people who think they are something they are not end up crashing back to earth.

Was the apostle Paul right to call people "nothing"? Some commentators suggest that he was exaggerating to make a point, and he may have been. However, we really *are* nothing, in and of ourselves. Calvin said, "We have nothing of our own to boast about, but are destitute of every good thing."[6]

---

6. John Calvin, *The Epistles of Paul the Apostle to the Galatians, Ephesians, Philippians and Colossians,* Calvin's New Testament Commentaries, trans. T. H. L. Parker, ed. David W. and Thomas F. Torrance (Grand Rapids: Eerdmans, 1996), 110.

Everything we have comes from God. If we are anything at all, it is only because we are created and redeemed in Christ.

The way to avoid thinking that we are something we are not is to see ourselves the way that God sees us. This is what the Scripture means when it says, "But let each one test his own work, and then his reason to boast will be in himself alone and not in his neighbor" (Gal. 6:4). The New International Version renders the verse like this: "Each one should test his own actions. Then he can take pride in himself, without comparing himself to somebody else." There is a way to be concerned for others without comparing ourselves to them. Such comparisons are usually odious. Either we get discouraged because we are less spiritual than someone else, or we become proud because we are more spiritual (especially compared to someone caught in a sin). But either way, we are making the wrong comparison.

Instead of comparing ourselves to others, we should test ourselves against God's standard, which is the only one that counts. This kind of testing—or self-examination, as the Puritans called it—is a necessary part of the spiritual life. There is a danger in being overly introspective, of course. Some people spend so much time examining and reexamining their lives that they hardly know how to live. But we need to prove our thoughts, words, and actions the way that precious metal is proved in the fire.

It is not easy to make an accurate assessment of our gifts and shortcomings. Often it requires the help of Christian friends. Usually we do not want to know what they really think of us, but sometimes it would help us if we did. Self-examination also requires good judgment. As Paul wrote to the Romans, "I say to everyone among you not to think of himself more highly than he ought to think, but to think with sober judgment, each according to the measure of faith that God has assigned" (Rom. 12:3).

Knowing how we measure up to God's standard will help us to bear one another's burdens. The people who "one another" most effectively are those who know their own strengths and weaknesses. Testing ourselves also enables us to take pride in what we do, in the right sense of the word. When Paul speaks of boasting, he obviously does not mean that God wants us to go around bragging that we are better than someone else. What he means is that we should be confident of who we are in Christ. When our actions meet God's test—as they do whenever they truly are done according to his Word, in service to Christ, for the advancement of his glory—then we can properly take pleasure in his praise.

The apostle then adds a rather curious comment: "For each will have to bear his own load" (Gal. 6:5). At first this seems like a contradiction. Verse 2 told us to bear one another's burdens, whereas verse 5 commands us to carry our own load. So which is it? Should we share our burdens or keep them to ourselves?

These two verses are not contradictory, but complementary. What they mean is that mutual accountability must be balanced by a sense of personal responsibility. To see this, it helps to know the difference between two different Greek terms: *baros* and *phortion*. The word *baros* refers to a heavy load, like cargo being loaded onto a freighter. Not surprisingly, *baros* is the word used in verse 2 to describe a weight that must be shared because it is too heavy for one person to carry. The word *phortion*, on the other hand, refers to a man's traveling pack, almost like a backpack. When the Scripture says that everyone must carry his own weight, it has this lighter burden in mind. There is a weight that every person must carry—the weight of our own personal responsibility before God.

God has given you a unique set of gifts for your situation in life. You will not have to answer for what you might have done with someone else's gifts. But you, and you alone, will have to answer for the way you carry the responsibilities that God has given you. Martin Luther wrote, "A faithful sexton is no less pleasing to God with his gift than is a preacher of the Word, for he serves God in the same faith and spirit."[7] This is true because God will not judge sextons on the basis of their ability to preach (or preachers on the basis of their ability to repair the church). God will judge us all on the basis of our calling, gifts, and obedience. So do your own work. Do it without comparing yourself to anyone else. And do it well, for one day you will have to answer to God, both for what you have done and for what you have left undone.

SHARE WITH ONE ANOTHER

There is one more thing that spiritual people do, and that is to share with one another. The kind of sharing that Paul mentions is primarily the kind

7. Luther, *Galatians*, 27:103.

that takes place between a pastor and his congregation: "One who is taught the word must share all good things with the one who teaches" (Gal. 6:6). Both the minister and the church have something to share. The minister shares good, solid teaching from the Bible. The word Paul uses for "teaching" is *katēcheō*, from which we get the English word "catechism." It refers to any kind of oral instruction in biblical truth.

Teaching the Word—this is as simple and as clear a job description of the gospel ministry as there is. These days ministers are tempted to perform many other jobs. They have become salesmen, businessmen, musicians, entertainers, comedians, janitors . . . anything and everything except preachers. But a true minister is nothing more and nothing less than a minister of the Word. The center of any gospel ministry must be the exposition of Holy Scripture.

This is a full-time job, which brings us to what the church has to share with its minister: "all good things" (Gal. 6:6). This refers to all kinds of goods, but especially the material support that someone needs to survive and thrive. Teaching the Bible is the minister's livelihood, so he should be paid generously for what he does. God insists on this. As the Scripture says, "The Lord commanded that those who proclaim the gospel should get their living by the gospel" (1 Cor. 9:14; cf. Luke 10:7).

One is almost tempted to say that pastors are professionals, but this would leave the wrong impression. The Scripture does not speak of contracts and salary packages, but about *sharing*. Unlike pagan religions, in which priests charged fees for their services, pastors were to be supported by the voluntary gifts of God's people.

The reason this kind of sharing is necessary is very simple. As Martin Luther explained, "It is impossible that one man should be devoted to household duties day and night for his support and at the same time pay attention to the study of Sacred Scripture, as the teaching ministry requires."[8] Preparing to preach—if it is to be done well—is costly labor. Therefore, a minister must be free to spend his time preparing to teach God's Word. It is much easier for him to throw himself into this work when he is not distracted by financial concerns. The Presbyterian Church in America puts it

8. Ibid., 27:126.

253

well when it instructs congregations to leave their ministers "free from worldly care."

It must be easy for ministers to abuse this privilege, because they often do. Some men abuse the privilege of the pastorate by seeking to become wealthy. They are in the ministry for the money (and so are their wives, in some cases), and so they "fleece" their flocks. Others abuse the pastorate by becoming lazy, and thus fail to give their congregations a good return on their investment. Greed and sloth are two of the deadliest vices for ministers.

When it comes to finances, it is also easy for churches to abuse their ministers. Some people use the purse strings to control the minister and the church. Others try to sanctify their minister by keeping him in a state of relative poverty. Still others fail to recognize the importance of a minister's preparation. Perhaps this was true in Galatia. Paul had just finished explaining that everyone should carry his own load (Gal. 6:5). "All right, then!" someone might have said. "Let's see the minister get a real job for a change, instead of freeloading all the time!"

This is not the way that a spiritual person thinks, however. A spiritual person knows how to share, including with his minister. John Calvin struck the proper balance:

> He [God] does not want them [ministers] to have an immoderate and super-fluous abundance, but merely that they should not lack any of the necessary supports of life. Ministers should be satisfied with frugal fare, and the danger of luxury and pomp must be avoided. Therefore, so far as their needs demand, let believers regard all their property as at the disposal of godly and holy teachers. What return will they make for the inestimable treasure of eternal life which they receive by their preaching?[9]

Sharing with one another is part of what it means to be spiritual. But it is hard to share from the top of a pole in the desert. Remember Simeon the Stylite? Eventually, Simeon decided he wanted to become more spiritual. After all, his pillar was only six feet high. So with the help of friends he built a column sixty feet high and three feet in diameter, with a crossbar to keep him from falling off in his sleep. There he remained until his death thirty years later! God blessed Simeon in many ways. Still, one suspects that he

---

9. Calvin, *Galatians, Ephesians, Philippians and Colossians*, 112.

would have been even more fruitful if he had climbed back down from his pole and lived the spiritual life in the biblical way: restoring sinners, bearing burdens, and sharing all good things. It is not easy to do very much "one anothering" from a pole sixty feet off the ground!

A better example to follow comes from a little Baptist church in Buckinghamshire in England. In 1790, the church meeting at Stony Stratford signed a covenant to treat one another according to the principles of Galatians 6. They promised

> to walk in love toward those with whom we stand connected in the bonds of Christian fellowship. As the effect of this, we will pray much for one another. As we have opportunity, we will associate together for religious purposes. Those of us who are in more comfortable situations in life than some of our brethren, with regard to the good things of Providence, will administer as we have ability and see occasion, to their necessities. We will bear one another's burdens, sympathize with the afflicted in body and mind, so far as we know their case, under their trials; and as we see occasion, advise, caution, and encourage one another. We will watch over one another for good. We will studiously avoid giving or taking offenses. Thus we will make it our study to fulfill the law of Christ.[10]

This was a good covenant to make, and an even better one to keep. Anyone who is able to make and keep such commitments knows what it means to live the spiritual life.

---

10. "The Church Covenant of the Particular Baptist Church, meeting in Horse Fair, Stony Stratford, Buck," cited in Timothy George, *Galatians*, New American Commentary 30 (Nashville: Broadman & Holman, 1994), 415.

21

You Reap What You Sow

Galatians 6:7—10

Do not be deceived: God is not mocked, for whatever one sows,
that will he also reap. For the one who sows to his own flesh will
from the flesh reap corruption, but the one who sows to the Spirit
will from the Spirit reap eternal life. (Gal. 6:7–8)

Every year the Rykens plant tulips, though not always successfully. The first year, we planted them in our city window box. When springtime came, so did our tulips, except that they were small and scraggly. Eventually we discovered why: we had planted dwarf tulip bulbs! Not wanting to make the mistake twice, the next year we planted full-sized tulips. Most of them never came up at all, and the ones that did never flowered. The problem this time was that the window box was not deep enough for large tulips to grow properly. Finally we discovered that the best place to plant our tulip bulbs is under the tree in front of the house. In the springtime the tulips grow bright and tall, and our little flower bed is streaked with brilliant colors: red, white, yellow, orange, and pink.

This shows that a man reaps what he sows. It is one of the fixed laws of nature. If someone plants dwarf tulip bulbs, then dwarf tulips it will be, no matter how much they get watered. And if bulbs are planted in the wrong kind of soil, nothing will grow at all. But when the right bulbs get planted in the right place, springtime is full of joy. This is the way it has always been.

When God made the world, he decreed that reaping should follow sowing. And so it will always be, for God promised Noah: "While the earth remains, seedtime and harvest, cold and heat, summer and winter, day and night, shall not cease" (Gen. 8:22).

THE SEEDS OF DESTRUCTION

You reap what you sow. This principle is true spiritually as well as agriculturally. Job observed that "those who plow iniquity and sow trouble reap the same" (Job 4:8). The apostle Paul applied this rule to the Galatians: "Do not be deceived: God is not mocked, for whatever one sows, that will he also reap. For the one who sows to his own flesh will from the flesh reap corruption, but the one who sows to the Spirit will from the Spirit reap eternal life" (Gal. 6:7–8).

The contrast in these verses is between sowing to the flesh and sowing to the Spirit. Paul first introduced the contrast between flesh and Spirit back in chapter 5. The flesh is the sinful nature we inherit from Adam; the Spirit is our regenerate nature in Christ. These two natures are constantly at war. The works of the flesh are opposed to the fruit of the Spirit, so that impurity, hatred, and discord battle against peace, love, and self-control.

In chapter 6 Paul changes the image from fighting to farming: A man reaps what he sows. William Perkins explained it like this: "There are two sorts of seeds which men sow in this life, good and evil. Two kinds of sowers, spiritual men, and carnal men. Two sorts of ground, in which this seed is sown; the flesh and the spirit. Two sorts of harvests, which men are to reap according to the seed; corruption, and life."[1]

Actions have consequences. Our present conduct determines our future condition. Ultimately, we have to bear the responsibility for our own behavior. If we pander to the flesh we will reap judgment, but if we pursue the Spirit we will gain eternal life. Thus the old saying is true: "Sow a thought, reap an act; sow an act, reap a habit; sow a habit, reap a character; sow a character, reap a destiny."

1. William Perkins, *A Commentary on Galatians*, Pilgrim Classic Commentaries, ed. Gerald T. Sheppard (London, 1617; repr. New York: Pilgrim, 1989), 496.

Some people sow the seeds of their own destruction by sowing to their flesh (Gal. 6:8). The flesh, or the sinful nature, has not yet been brought under the control of God's Spirit. The unbeliever—who does not have the Spirit—is dominated by the flesh, with all its sinful desires. Yet even the Christian struggles with the flesh, fighting against his fallen nature.

What the Christian needs to do with the flesh is to mortify it; that is, to put it to death. Yet instead of crucifying the sinful nature (Gal. 5:24), the Galatians were coddling it. Some of them were having themselves circumcised, and thus trying to be saved by their own works. When Paul warned the Galatians that they would reap whatever they sowed, it was mainly the Judaizers that he had in mind. Other members of the church were giving in to the passions of the flesh, committing the very sins that the apostle had warned against: sexual immorality, impurity, idolatry, jealousy, envy, drunkenness, and so forth (Gal. 5:19–21).

Trying to satisfy the flesh is very selfish, which perhaps is why Paul refers to someone who "sows to his own flesh" (Gal. 6:8). It is also extremely self-destructive. The trouble with "sowing wild oats," as people call it, is that we always reap what we sow: "For the one who sows to his own flesh will from the flesh reap corruption" (Gal. 6:8). The word "corruption" suggests a gradual decay, almost like the decomposition of a corpse. Since sin is as harmful to the body as it is to the soul, this decay is both physical and spiritual. In the end, living for selfish pleasure yields the miserable harvest of eternal death. Yet even in this life, sin proves to be self-destructive. Consider some common examples:

> A young couple in love gets caught up in the passions of the moment. They engage in sexual activity outside of marriage. They experience some pleasure, of course, but they are also sowing the seeds of destruction. After they break up, they discover that they have damaged their capacity for true intimacy.

> A man fantasizes about taking control of his organization. He comes to think of his colleagues as rivals, and he schemes his way past them. But his selfish ambition is sowing the seeds of destruction, not only for others, but also within his own soul.

> A woman secretly despises another woman in her church. From time to time they have their petty disagreements, but it is really a matter of personality as

much as anything else. With every contemptuous thought, she is sowing seeds destructive to her own spiritual health and the fellowship of the church.

A husband and wife allow resentment to build in their marriage without ever resolving their differences. They, too, are sowing the seeds of destruction. Year by year, as they drift further and further apart, they reap loneliness, bitterness, and unbelief.

We always, always reap what we sow. This is true in every area of life. John Stott writes:

> Every time we allow our mind to harbor a grudge, nurse a grievance, entertain an impure fantasy, or wallow in self-pity, we are sowing to the flesh. Every time we linger in bad company whose insidious influence we know we cannot resist, every time we lie in bed when we ought to be up and praying, every time we read pornographic literature, every time we take a risk which strains our self-control, we are sowing, sowing, sowing to the flesh. Some Christians sow to the flesh every day and wonder why they do not reap holiness. Holiness is a *harvest*; whether we reap it or not depends almost entirely on what and where we sow.[2]

GOD CANNOT BE MOCKED

When it comes to sowing and reaping, the Scripture warns, "Do not be deceived" (Gal. 6:7). The deception it has in mind is one of the most popular falsehoods of our times. It is the lie that I can do whatever I want without ever being held accountable for what I have done. It is the lie that I can sin with impunity; no matter what I do now, I can always become a spiritual person later. It is the lie, wrote the Scotsman John Brown, "that a man may attain ultimate happiness without living a spiritual life."[3]

Make no mistake, "God is not mocked" (Gal. 6:7). To put it more literally, we cannot "turn our noses up at God." We cannot despise him by pleasing our sinful nature and then sneering at him whenever we get the chance.

2. John R. W. Stott, *The Message of Galatians: Only One Way,* The Bible Speaks Today (Downers Grove, IL: InterVarsity, 1968), 170.

3. John Brown, *An Exposition of the Epistle of Paul the Apostle to the Galatians* (Edinburgh, 1853; repr. Evansville, IN: Sovereign Grace, 1957), 336.

259

At least, we cannot do these things and get away with them. People who think that they can fool with God are only fooling themselves. No one can flout his authority forever. The Scripture says, "He will render to each one according to his works: to those who by patience in well-doing seek for glory and honor and immortality, he will give eternal life; but for those who are self-seeking and do not obey the truth, but obey unrighteousness, there will be wrath and fury" (Rom. 2:6–8). One day we will reap what we sow, and if we sow to please the sinful nature, we will reap destruction.

Many people have tried to mock God, but no one has ever gotten away with it. Goliath mocked God's kingdom when the Philistines fought the Jews in the Valley of Elah (1 Sam. 17). He shook his fist at the armies of the living God. But God cannot be mocked, so Goliath ended up with a stone in his forehead and a sword through his neck. King Herod mocked God's glory when the people proclaimed that he was a god (Acts 12:21–23). Herod sat on his throne in shimmering silver robes, basking in the glow of his people's worship. But God cannot be mocked. Because he refused to give God the glory, Herod was eaten by worms and died.

People will go on mocking God and his judgment until the very day that Christ returns. But there will be a harvest. Jesus spoke about this often, saying, "The harvest is the close of the age, and the reapers are angels. Just as the weeds are gathered and burned with fire, so will it be at the close of the age. The Son of Man will send his angels, and they will gather out of his kingdom all causes of sin and all law-breakers, and throw them into the fiery furnace. In that place there will be weeping and gnashing of teeth" (Matt. 13:39–42).

Are you sowing the seeds of destruction? If you think you can get away with what you are doing, you are badly mistaken. God cannot be mocked.

Sowing to the Spirit

There is more than one way to sow, and thankfully, the seeds of destruction are not the only seeds that we can sow. Good seed is available, and when it is sown in a fertile field, it yields a rich harvest: "the one who sows to the Spirit will from the Spirit reap eternal life" (Gal. 6:8). What does it mean to sow to the Spirit?

The idea of sowing and reaping may refer back to verse 6, which was about sharing good things with the minister. One way to sow to the Spirit is to support the ministry of God's Word. Up through the time of the Reformers, that is how this passage was usually interpreted. But sowing to the Spirit means much more than providing for one's pastor. It is really another way of describing what Paul was talking about earlier, when he mentioned walking with the Spirit (Gal. 5:16), being led by the Spirit (Gal. 5:18), and keeping in step with the Spirit (Gal. 5:25). Sowing to the Spirit means following the Spirit's lead, obeying his instructions for holy living.

To be more specific, sowing to the Spirit means sowing the kind of seed that comes from the fruit of the Spirit: love, joy, kindness, faithfulness, and the like. It means cultivating good spiritual fruit by using the means of grace: Bible study, prayer, worship, and the sacraments.

Sowing to the Spirit means living for God's pleasure instead of our own pleasure. So, for example, a young couple sows to the Spirit when they preserve the purity of their marriage bed. A man sows to the Spirit when he denies his own ambition in order to serve others. A woman sows to the Spirit when she is reconciled to her sister in Christ. A husband and wife sow to the Spirit when they repent of their selfishness and begin to work together in true spiritual partnership. In short, sowing to the Spirit means living for Christ in every area of life. Every time we think a thought, speak a word, or perform a deed, we plant a seed. Every time we think, say, or do anything for the glory of God, we are sowing to his Spirit.

If it is true that we reap what we sow, then the more we sow, the more we will reap. I am reminded of this every spring when I walk past a nearby vacant lot. Some years ago, a man took a tub of wildflower seeds and scattered them around an empty yard in Center City Philadelphia. In springtime the lot is a riot of color. There are hundreds of red poppies, mixed with orange, yellow, and blue wildflowers.

The seed we sow to the Spirit should be scattered just as widely: "whoever sows sparingly will also reap sparingly, and whoever sows bountifully will also reap bountifully" (2 Cor. 9:6). Whoever sows to the Spirit reaps the richest harvest of all: eternal life. This does not mean, of course, that salvation comes by works. Eternal life is a gift that is based on believing, not on doing. However, believers are doers, and although no one is ever saved by works, no one is ever saved without them either. Therefore, having been saved by grace, the believer goes out and sows to please the Spirit. God, in

261

his grace, will give the reward of eternal life to everyone who sows good spiritual seed.

The Scripture teaches that the one who has the power to impart eternal life is the Holy Spirit. It is "from the Spirit" that the believer "will reap eternal life" (Gal. 6:8). Eternal life is God's gift to everyone who believes in God the Son, Jesus Christ, "for God so loved the world, that he gave his only Son, that whoever believes in him should not perish but have eternal life" (John 3:16). But the one who grants the gift of life without end is the Holy Spirit. Whereas sowing to the flesh brings nothing but death and destruction, sowing to the Spirit produces eternal life. The glorious life of the immortal resurrection body comes from God's Spirit. The same Spirit who raised Christ from the dead will also raise the Christian from the dead.

In some ways, eternal life has already begun. Those who sow to please the Spirit begin to reap his rewards already in this life. In this respect, spiritual harvesting is like picking blueberries. When a family goes out to gather berries, they gather enough to last until the next harvest. But not all the berries make it into the pies and jellies. Every now and then, one of the harvesters picks a juicy blueberry, tosses it into his mouth, and eats it right away.

In a similar way, we begin to taste eternal life as soon as we come to Christ. Everyone who is born again by God's Spirit has the life of the eternal God within. Baptist theologian Timothy George explains that eternal life "is not merely life that lasts eternally. It is rather God's very own life, the life of the Father, the Son, and the Holy Spirit, graciously bestowed upon the children of God through faith in the Redeemer. Eternal life is the present possession of all who truly trust in Christ as Savior and Lord."[4] Therefore, not all the benefits of eternal life are deferred. The Holy Spirit gives us the assurance of our faith, the joy of our salvation, and the hope of our resurrection right here and now.

The Spirit also gives us something to look forward to. We are waiting for the promised harvest of the life to come. All through this life, we sow our seeds to please the Spirit, knowing that one day we will reap a bumper crop of God's blessing. William Perkins wrote, "If men could be persuaded of this, that the time of this life is the seed time; that the last judgment is the har-

4. Timothy George, *Galatians*, New American Commentary 30 (Nashville: Broadman & Holman, 1994), 424.

vest; and that as certainly as the husbandman which sows his seed looks for increase, so we for our good works, a recompence to the full; O how fruitful should we be, how plentiful, how full of good works?"[5]

KEEP UP THE GOOD WORK!

As any farmer will say, sowing is hard work, especially when it is done by hand. Planting seed requires long hours of persistent labor. Sowing in the Spirit is hard work, too, which is why we need this exhortation: "And let us not grow weary of doing good, for in due season we will reap, if we do not give up" (Gal. 6:9). To "grow weary" means to "grow faint" or to "lose heart." Originally, the term was used to describe something that had gone slack, like an unstrung bow.

The apostle Paul knew how easy it is to slack off in the Christian life. Human beings are weak. This is why it is so hard for ministries to maintain their spiritual vitality, and why so many Christians who are active in ministry get burned out. People grow tired. They are tempted to sin. They experience opposition, sometimes from the very people they are trying to help. And they get discouraged when they do not see results. In an accelerated culture, people get used to instant gratification; it is hard to wait for things to grow. Then there is the sheer immensity of human need. As we have learned from Galatians, there are neighbors to love, sinners to restore, burdens to bear, and ministers to support. And this is only the beginning. There is always someone who needs more help. But who has the time or the energy to help everyone? Sometimes it is tempting simply to give up.

There are many things that Christians can do when they grow weary of doing good. One of them is to get some rest. Spiritual failure is often brought on by physical fatigue. Another thing to do is to stop striving to minister in our own strength and start resting in the Lord. We are called to live according to Isaiah's great promise:

He gives power to the faint,
    and to him who has no might he increases strength.

5. Perkins, *Commentary on Galatians*, 489.

> Even youths shall faint and be weary,
>> and young men shall fall exhausted;
> but they who wait for the LORD shall renew their strength;
>> they shall mount up with wings like eagles;
> they shall run and not be weary;
>> they shall walk and not faint. (Isa. 40:29–31)

While we are waiting on the Lord, we can get other Christians to pray for us, and perhaps even to help us. But whatever we do, we can't quit! And of all the reasons not to give up, we need to remember this one especially: One day there will be a harvest.

God's command to "keep on keeping on" comes with an incentive: "And let us not grow weary of doing good, for in due season we will reap, if we do not give up" (Gal. 6:9). There is no doubt about it: If you labor for Christ, you will get your reward. "Every act of Christian duty," wrote John Brown, "every sacrifice made, every privation submitted to, every suffering endured, from a regard to Christ's authority, with a view to Christ's honour, shall assuredly be recompensed."[6] If the recompense is not granted in this life, it will certainly be granted in the life to come. The Bible often speaks about eternal rewards, not to make us anxious about whether we have done enough for God, but to encourage us to do as much as we can.

Notice that the coming harvest is for those who do not give up. This is part of the biblical doctrine of perseverance. If we want to claim our reward, we must persevere to the very end, not growing weary of doing good. By the grace of God, we will persevere. The old saying is true: "Once saved, always saved." What Christians sometimes forget, however, is that once they are saved, they are always to serve. We must continue to do good, not because we are struggling to earn our salvation—which is a gift of God's grace—but because we are grateful for the salvation we have in Christ.

Sometimes it is very tempting to give up, or at least to rest on our oars for a little while. When a rower pulls his oars out of the water, his boat continues to glide upriver. But not for long. The moment that he breaks his stroke, he starts to lose speed. The current gradually slows him down, and soon he will stop altogether. Something similar happens in the spiritual life,

---

6. Brown, *Exposition of Galatians*, 344.

264

which is why the Scripture tells us not to give up when we grow weary. Christians who coast lose their spiritual momentum. We will reap a harvest only if we persevere in doing good.

The harvest will come. It will come at the proper time, a time determined not by the seasons or the weather, but by the will of God. Whether it comes during this life or when Christ comes again (cf. 1 Tim. 6:15), the harvest will come in God's own good time. In due season, those who do good will reap their reward. Jesus says, "Behold, I am coming soon, bringing my recompense with me, to repay everyone for what he has done" (Rev. 22:12).

Until the harvest comes, we must keep sowing. A good example of what it means to sow and then to wait for the reaping comes from the life of William Carey, the first modern missionary to India. From the day that he arrived on the subcontinent in 1793, Carey began to teach the Bible to anyone who would listen. This he continued to do for the next seven years without winning so much as a single convert to Christ.

Not surprisingly, Carey sometimes got discouraged. On one occasion he wrote back to his family in England: "I feel as a farmer does about his crop: sometimes I think the seed is springing, and thus I hope; a little time blasts all, and my hopes are gone like a cloud. They were only weeds which appeared; or if a little corn sprung up, it quickly dies, being either choked with weeds, or parched up by the sun of persecution. Yet I still hope in God, and will go forth in his strength."[7] Though he sometimes grew weary in doing good, Carey refused to give up. In 1800 he finally began to reap what he had sown, baptizing his first Hindu convert in the Ganges River. This was the firstfruits of a great harvest among the Indian people.

Or consider another example, this one from the colony of Virginia. It concerns the conversion of a man named Luke Short at the ripe old age of 103. Short was sitting under a hedge when he happened to remember a sermon he had once heard preached by the famous Puritan John Flavel (d. 1691). As he recalled the sermon, he asked God right then and there to forgive his sins through Jesus Christ. Short lived for three more years, and when he died,

7. William Carey, quoted in Timothy George, *Faithful Witness: The Life and Mission of William Carey* (Birmingham, AL: New Hope, 1991), 116.

this inscription was put on his tombstone: "Here lies a babe in grace, aged three years, who died according to nature, aged 106."

But here is the remarkable part of the story: The sermon Short remembered had been preached by Flavel back in England *eighty-five years before!* Nearly a century had passed between the sermon and the conversion, between the sowing and the reaping. But a man reaps what he sows, and at the proper time Flavel reaped his harvest.[8]

This is a reminder not to evaluate ministry on the basis of immediate results. Too many churches, especially in America, want to taste the fruits of their labors the day they are planted. Yet most spiritual produce takes time to grow. A long time. Often it takes years before parents, teachers, or ministers are able to see their work pay off. "Be patient, therefore, brothers," wrote the apostle James, "until the coming of the Lord. See how the farmer waits for the precious fruit of the earth, being patient about it, until it receives the early and the late rains. You also, be patient. Establish your hearts, for the coming of the Lord is at hand" (James 5:7–8).

Do Good to Everyone

While we wait patiently for the harvest, our instructions are very specific: "So then, as we have opportunity, let us do good to everyone, and especially to those who are of the household of faith" (Gal. 6:10). According to this verse, a Christian is someone who does all kinds of good to all kinds of people. Doing good means meeting people's needs by performing the six acts of charity: feeding the hungry, giving drink to the thirsty, showing hospitality to strangers, clothing the naked, caring for the sick, and visiting prisoners (Matt. 25:34–36). Doing good means tutoring the ignorant and picking up the trash. It means watching out for our neighbors and helping our community. It also means doing some spiritual good: praying for people and giving them the good news about Jesus Christ. Doing good means doing every good thing it is possible to do.

These good things are to be done both inside and outside the church. The Scripture strikes the proper balance: "let us do good to everyone, and especially to those who are of the household of faith" (Gal. 6:10). Be careful not

---

8. See John Flavel, *The Mystery of Providence* (Edinburgh: Banner of Truth, 1963), 11.

to skip past the first phrase too quickly. Christians are to do some good for all. Charity only *begins* at home; then it also goes out into the neighborhood. This is what the ancient pagans considered so unusual about the first Christians—and so attractive. They not only took care of their own needs, but also met the needs of everyone else. One of the reasons the church has such a mixed reputation in our day is that Christians do not do as much good as they ought to do.

Christians are to do good to all; nevertheless, we have a special responsibility to care for other Christians. We are all children of God by adoption. We are all members of the same household, the same spiritual family. Therefore, our brothers and sisters in Christ have a special claim on us:

> Christians, therefore, are particularly bound to do good to one another. Every poor and distressed man has a claim on me for pity, and, if I can afford it, for active exertion and pecuniary relief. But a poor Christian has a far stronger claim on my feelings, my labours, and my property. He is my brother, equally interested with myself in the blood and love of the Redeemer. I expect to spend an eternity with him in heaven. He is the representative of my unseen Saviour, and He considers everything done to his poor afflicted brother as done to himself. For a Christian to be unkind to a Christian, is not only wrong, it is monstrous.[9]

It is absolutely necessary for Christians to be good to one another. This is not a matter of being selfish; it is a matter of witness. How can we fulfill our mission to show God's love to the world without showing love to one another? Taking care of our own is part of our witness to the watching world.

The last thing to notice is that we are to do good to one another, and to everyone else, "as we have opportunity" (Gal. 6:10). This does not mean that the good is something we do only every now and then, that is, when we have the time, or if we get the chance. On the contrary, the Greek word for "opportunity" is the word for "time" or "season." Thus it conveys the urgency of the coming harvest: This is a limited opportunity, so don't miss it! There is a time to sow, as there will also be a time to reap. Soon the seedtime will be over and the day of harvest will come. Reaping is for the life to come; this

9. Brown, *Exposition of Galatians*, 348.

lifetime is for sowing. We must seize the opportunity to sow good works while we still have the time.

So what kind of seeds are you sowing? Are you sowing the seeds of destruction, or are you sowing good deeds in the Spirit? Either way, one thing is for certain: You will reap what you sow!

22

GLORY IN THE CROSS

Galatians 6:11–18

But far be it from me to boast except in the cross of our Lord Jesus
Christ, by which the world has been crucified to me, and I to
the world. For neither circumcision counts for anything, nor
uncircumcision, but a new creation. (Gal. 6:14–15)

*I*t must have been a dramatic moment—the world premiere of an epistle. The Galatian church had gathered for the public reading of a letter from none other than the apostle Paul. As the letter drew to a close, they heard these words: "See with what large letters I am writing to you with my own hand" (Gal. 6:11). Perhaps, for emphasis, the reader held up the papyrus to show everyone the large-print portion of Paul's letter.

What had probably happened was this: According to his usual custom (e.g., Rom. 16:22), Paul had dictated most of this epistle to his amanuensis, or secretary. But he finished the document in his own handwriting, personally adding his autograph in order to give his letter to the Galatians the stamp of his apostolic authority. And he wrote his signature in large letters to underscore his conclusion.

The last section of Galatians, therefore, is more than a hastily written postscript, the afterthought of an apostle. Instead, these verses constitute a summary of the entire letter. They place circumcision over against the cross,

269

showing that justification by grace alone, through faith alone, in Christ alone means boasting in the cross alone. To understand this is to understand Galatians. More than that, it is to understand the gospel.

COMPELLED TO BE CIRCUMCISED

The summary at the end of Galatians begins with a problem statement: "It is those who want to make a good showing in the flesh who would force you to be circumcised" (Gal. 6:12). This verse explains why Paul wrote to the Galatians in the first place. Some Jewish-Christian missionaries had come to do follow-up work on Paul's evangelism. These missionaries, whom we have termed the Judaizers, probably came from Jerusalem. They claimed to believe the good news about Jesus Christ. They taught about the cross and the empty tomb—the crucifixion and the resurrection of Jesus Christ.

There was one thing that these teachers wanted to add to Paul's gospel, however, and this was the Jewish rite of circumcision. In the Old Testament God had commanded his people to remove every male foreskin as a sign of belonging to his covenant (Gen. 17). The Judaizers said that circumcision was still a prerequisite for salvation. They summarized their missionary program with the following slogan: "Unless you are circumcised according to the custom of Moses, you cannot be saved" (Acts 15:1). This was a way of saying that a convert had to become a Jew in order to become a Christian. For the Judaizers, salvation meant the cross *plus* circumcision.

There is a continual temptation for the church to turn the gospel into the cross plus something else. Whether that "something else" is a deed or a duty, a sacrament or a social cause, the problem is always the "plus." For the gospel to be the gospel, the cross has to stand alone.

Since the Judaizers believed that circumcision was necessary for salvation, they naturally wanted to circumcise as many people as possible. When they came to Galatia, they pressured the Gentile Christians there to be circumcised. The problem was not so much circumcision as it was their *compelling* people to be circumcised. The Judaizers were demanding that the Galatians be circumcised in order to be saved.

Why were they doing this? The Judaizers thought they were doing God's work, but the apostle Paul, under the inspiration of the Holy Spirit, discerned their real motive: "only in order that they may not be persecuted for the cross of Christ" (Gal. 6:12). They were trying to avoid persecution.

When we think of the sufferings of the early church, we often think of all the persecution that came from the Romans. However, the first attacks came from the Jews. Think of Stephen, who was stoned by the Sanhedrin (Acts 7), or of Paul before his conversion, dragging Christians out of their homes (Acts 9:1–2). Some of the most severe persecution that Christians faced came from Jewish people.

As the church spread through Asia Minor, Jewish persecution spread with it. But there was one easy way to avoid it, and this was to become circumcised. What made devout Jews angry was people who failed to maintain the proper boundaries between Jews and Gentiles. Yet even Gentiles were welcome *if* they agreed to join God's covenant by circumcision. So what must have happened was something like this: Some Jewish-Christian missionaries followed Paul into Galatia. They found, to their horror, that Jewish Christians there were mingling with uncircumcised Gentiles. They were even eating with them! The visitors knew that if this continued much longer, there would be trouble from the authorities at the local synagogue. So they urged the Gentiles in the Galatian church to get circumcised as soon as possible. This was a clear case of overcontextualizing the gospel. Instead of simply putting the gospel into terms that the Galatians could understand and explain to their Jewish neighbors, the Judaizers were changing the terms of salvation itself.

The Judaizers said that circumcision was necessary to belong to God's covenant, but their real motivation was fear. They were afraid of what other Jews would say and do if they found out that they were worshiping with Gentiles. It would be much easier to defend their involvement with Christianity if they could say that the Gentiles in their house church kept the law of Moses. If only the Gentiles would agree to be circumcised like Jews, it would solve everything. Deep down, they were not willing to be persecuted for the cause of Christ.

Christians inevitably face this temptation because the cross has a way of inviting persecution. It arouses opposition because it says that we are sinners under God's curse. It tells us that we need someone else to die for our sins, that there is nothing we can do to save ourselves, only trust in Jesus.

271

I once had a conversation with a woman who was wrestling with the claims of Christ. She had begun to realize that surrendering to God's will for her salvation would require radical changes. "If I believed that my friends at the pool were really going to hell," she said, "then I would have to tell them about Jesus, wouldn't I? But then I wouldn't have any more friends!" Maybe not. People generally do not like being told that they are sinners who need a Savior. But this is what it means to be a Christian: it means standing up for Christ and his cross.

AN EMPTY BOAST

There was another reason the Judaizers urged the Galatians to get circumcised. Not only did they want to avoid persecution, but they also wanted to seem successful. They were hoping "to make a good showing in the flesh" (Gal. 6:12). More specifically, "they desire to have you circumcised that they may boast in your flesh" (Gal. 6:13).

This was a strange boast to make, and it shows how important circumcision had become to the Jews. Apparently, the more foreskins they collected, the more impressed people would be back home in Jerusalem. The Judaizers were not really concerned about whether or not the Galatians kept God's law; they just wanted to brag about how many converts they had made. One can almost imagine them sending a "Mission to Galatia" newsletter back to Jerusalem. "ONE HUNDRED CIRCUMCISED!" the headline might read. But they were just keeping up appearances. Their ministry was all for show.

Showing off is one of the differences between true and false religion. False religion gets caught up in externals, like attendance figures and worship rituals. Outward religion is what cult leaders strive for when they pressure members to recruit new "converts." It is what churches are after when they seek to entertain rather than to edify, or when they base salvation on what people do for God rather than on what God has done for them.

True religion is inward. Although it always works its way out, it starts within, where the Holy Spirit regenerates a sinner's heart. The problem with making something like circumcision the essence of Christianity is that it is only an outward sign. It is merely external, something done to the body, to the flesh of sinful self-reliance. True religion is not based on outward works; it is based on inward faith.

Not only was circumcision a strange subject for the Judaizers to boast about, but it was also an empty boast. It was supposed to be a sign of total commitment to God's law. The Judaizers said of the Gentiles, "It is necessary to circumcise them and to order them to keep the law of Moses" (Acts 15:5). The irony was that the Judaizers couldn't even keep the law themselves! "For even those who are circumcised do not themselves keep the law, but they desire to have you circumcised that they may boast in your flesh" (Gal. 6:13).

It was a case of hypocrisy. The legalists were lawless. They boasted about circumcision because they thought it made them more righteous, but getting circumcised also meant that they had to keep God's whole law (see Gal. 5:3). The problem with that, of course, is that no one can keep God's law perfectly: "For all who rely on works of the law are under a curse; for it is written: 'Cursed be everyone who does not abide by all things written in the Book of the Law, and do them'" (Gal. 3:10). The problem with the law is not the law; the problem with the law is sin. The law saves only those who keep it, which no one does.

What circumcision amounted to was justification by works. It was a way of saying, "I can be saved by my own efforts, by my own keeping of the law." But those who insist on saving themselves cannot measure up to their own standard, let alone measure up to God's. In the end, they have nothing to boast about: "Then what becomes of our boasting? It is excluded. By what kind of law? By a law of works? No, but by the law of faith. For we hold that one is justified by faith apart from works of the law" (Rom. 3:27–28).

No wonder the apostle Paul opposed the Judaizers at every turn! They were the very worst kind of preachers. They were unwilling to endure persecution for the cause of Christ. They sought the glory of their own success. They never practiced what they preached. Worst of all, by trusting in circumcision rather than in the cross, they denied the free grace of the gospel.

SOMETHING TO BOAST ABOUT

If the boast of the Judaizers was strange, Paul's boast sounded even stranger: "But far be it from me to boast except in the cross of our Lord Jesus Christ" (Gal. 6:14). It is difficult to capture the meaning of the Greek word for "boast" (*kauchasthai*) because there is no precise equivalent in English.

273

It means something more than bragging. "It means," writes John Stott, "to boast in, glory in, trust in, rejoice in, revel in, live for. The object of our boast or 'glory' fills our horizons, engrosses our attention, and absorbs our time and energy. In a word, our 'glory' is our obsession."[1]

Paul's obsession with the cross was strange for two reasons. First, he refused to live for any of the things that people usually live for. He did not boast about his popularity, intellect, influence, appearance, income, or job performance. Nor did he boast about his circumcision (or about anything else in his spiritual record, for that matter; see Phil. 3:3–9). Paul absolutely refused to take pride in any of his abilities or accomplishments at all, which was strange, because those are exactly the things that people usually *do* take pride in.

Second, what Paul was willing to boast about was even stranger: the cross of Christ. Christians are used to thinking about the cross as something noble, or even beautiful, but to ancient people it was nearly the ugliest thing imaginable—the ultimate humiliation. The Romans considered the cross degrading, disgusting, despicable, detestable, and disgraceful. In his commentary on these verses, F. F. Bruce observes that the

> object of Paul's present boasting was, by all ordinary standards of his day, the most ignoble of all objects—a matter of unrelieved shame, not of boasting. It is difficult, after sixteen centuries and more during which the cross has been a sacred symbol, to realize the unspeakable horror and loathing which the very mention or thought of the cross provoked in Paul's day. The word *crux* was unmentionable in polite Roman society; even when one was being condemned to death by crucifixion the sentence used an archaic formula which served as a sort of euphemism: "hang him on the unlucky tree."[2]

It is hard to think of a contemporary cultural equivalent to the cross. One that might come close is suggested by the Cotton Patch paraphrase: "God forbid that I should ever take pride in anything, except in the lynching of our Lord Jesus Christ."

What a strange thing to boast about! The cross should have been an embarrassment to the early church. What would people think when they

1. John R. W. Stott, *The Cross of Christ* (Downers Grove, IL: InterVarsity, 1986), 349.

2. F. F. Bruce, *The Epistle to the Galatians: A Commentary on the Greek Text*, New International Greek Testament Commentary (Grand Rapids: Eerdmans, 1982), 271.

discovered that the founder of Christianity had been executed like a low-life criminal? But instead of denying this, or covering it up, Christians advertised it. The very thing that most people considered too obscene to whisper in polite company, Christians were broadcasting in the streets.

Paul boasted about the cross in his letter to the Galatians. "I have been crucified with Christ" (2:19), he wrote; "Jesus Christ was publicly portrayed as crucified" (Gal. 3:1). He kept right on boasting through the rest of his epistles: "we preach Christ crucified" (1 Cor. 1:23); "I decided to know nothing among you except Jesus Christ and him crucified" (1 Cor. 2:2). He spoke of the message of the cross (1 Cor. 1:18), the offense of the cross (Gal. 5:11), the triumph of the cross (Col. 2:15), and the wonder of the cross (Phil. 2:8).

Paul was always boasting about the cross . . . and God forbid that he should ever boast about anything else. Christ crucified meant the world to him, as it should to us. The cross is not just *something* to boast about; it is the *only thing* to boast about. The cross is the only thing to boast about because it means that God loves us enough to die for us, that he saved us through the death of his own dear Son. It means that we have been redeemed, that Christ has paid the whole price for our salvation. The cross means that we have forgiveness for our sins, that Christ offered himself as an atoning sacrifice to take away our guilt. It means that we are justified, that God now accepts us as righteous in his sight. His wrath has been turned away, and now we stand innocent before him.

We can boast about Christ crucified, however, only if we renounce anything and everything we can do to save ourselves. When it comes right down to it, although there are many religions, there are only two religious options: glorying in ourselves and glorying in the cross. To glory in the cross is to stop trusting in our own merits—our church attendance, worship style, devotional habits, social involvement, theological orthodoxy, or number of converts—and to start trusting in the merits of Jesus Christ alone. The cross rejects any merely human attempt to please God. It declares that "sinners may be justified before God and by God, not because of any works of their own, but because of the atoning work of Christ; not because of anything that they have done or could do, but because of what Christ did once, when He died."[3]

3. John R. W. Stott, *The Message of Galatians: Only One Way*, The Bible Speaks Today (Downers Grove, IL: InterVarsity, 1968), 70.

The Galatians had to make a choice between the cross and circumcision. It was either one or the other, but it could not be both. Circumcision was a way of claiming a share in one's own salvation, but the cross says that Jesus paid it all: his sacrifice is the total basis for our salvation. Thus there is no way to boast about what we have done and what Christ has done at the same time. John Stott writes: "The truth is that we cannot boast in ourselves and in the cross simultaneously. If we boast in ourselves and in our ability to save ourselves, we shall never boast in the cross and in the ability of Christ crucified to save us. We have to choose. Only if we have humbled ourselves as hell-deserving sinners shall we give up boasting of ourselves, fly to the cross for salvation and spend the rest of our days glorying in the cross."[4]

The cross of Christ is the all-sufficient ground for the salvation of sinners. It claims to be sturdy enough to support the whole weight of our guilt *all by itself.* Therefore, to boast in the cross properly at all is to boast in the cross alone.

A WHOLE NEW WORLD

Boasting in the cross means more than simply believing that Jesus died for your sins; it also means living a crucified life. This is what Paul meant when he wrote, "But far be it from me to boast except in the cross of our Lord Jesus Christ, by which the world has been crucified to me, and I to the world" (Gal. 6:14).

This verse describes not one crucifixion, but three. There is only one cross, of course, but at least three times that many crucifixions. First, the cross was the place where Christ died for our sins. But when we put our faith in Jesus Christ, we are personally joined to him and to everything he has ever done for our salvation. This is the doctrine of union with Christ: Christ is in the Christian and the Christian is in Christ. Being united to Christ in this way includes being united to him in his death. We were practically crucified with Christ, so that when Christ died on the cross, we were crucified to the world, and the world was crucified to us. "In reality," therefore, "there is a triple crucifixion to be considered in this text: the crucified Christ, the crucified world, and the crucified Christian."[5]

4. Ibid., 180.
5. Timothy George, *Galatians,* New American Commentary 30 (Nashville: Broadman & Holman, 1994), 437.

The "world" refers to all the godless values and hopeless pleasures of the present age. It is unredeemed humanity dominated by sin. It is the world apart from God, the mind-set of the self seeking its own desire. But the cross strikes a deathblow to all such worldliness. As Christians we no longer think the way the world thinks, talk the way the world talks, or misbehave the way the world misbehaves. We no longer take comfort in the comforts the world has to offer. We no longer value what the world values. We no longer care what the world thinks at all because we have been crucified to the world. What means the world to us now is the cross. As far as we are concerned, they can take the whole world away from us, as long as they leave us Jesus.

Being crucified to the world is simply another way to describe what Paul was talking about back at the end of the previous chapter: "And those who belong to Christ Jesus have crucified the flesh with its passions and desires" (Gal. 5:24). Paul has already told us to crucify the flesh, to mortify it, to put it to death. Now he tells us that the world needs to join our flesh on the cross. Whether the sinful nature is called "the flesh" or "the world," the point is the same: our sin needs to be nailed to the cross and left there to die.

In both of these verses (Gal. 5:24 and 6:14), the word "crucified" occurs in the perfect tense, which is used for a past event that has a present consequence. This is precisely what the cross is: a past event with a present consequence. Our sinful nature was crucified when Christ died on the cross. The present consequence of that past event is that the world is gradually losing its hold on us. Now we are dead to the world with its temptations, but alive to God by his grace.

The cross really did change the world. It was revolutionary, in the proper sense of the word. It turned things upside down. Now we live in a whole new world, a world in which "neither circumcision counts for anything, nor uncircumcision, but a new creation" (Gal. 6:15). Once we come to the cross for salvation, circumcision becomes irrelevant, for it has nothing to do with our salvation at all.

It is surprising to hear Paul say that circumcision didn't matter. He had said it once before: "In Christ Jesus neither circumcision nor uncircumcision counts for anything" (Gal. 5:6). Nevertheless, it is surprising to hear him say it because the whole reason for his writing to the Galatians in the first place was that circumcision *did* matter. However, circumcision mattered to Paul only because it mattered to the Judaizers, who were making it a matter of salvation. In and of itself, however, circumcision means nothing. If we are in Christ, circumcision can do nothing to improve our standing before God; and if we are not in Christ, circumcision can do nothing to save us. It has nothing to do with Christianity at all!

What does count is a new creation, the inward transformation by which the Holy Spirit turns a sinner into a whole new person. "If anyone is in Christ," Paul later told the Corinthians, "he is a new creation. The old has passed away; behold, the new has come" (2 Cor. 5:17). Anyone who is born again by God's Spirit gets a whole new life. He or she becomes a brand-new creation. The outward sign and seal of this cosmic transformation is baptism, but what really counts is the transformation itself.

The theological term for this inward transformation is *regeneration*. In regeneration, the Holy Spirit makes the believer a new creature in Christ. But regeneration is only the beginning. As Timothy George says, the new creation "involves the whole process of conversion: the regenerating work of the Holy Spirit leading to repentance and faith, the daily process of mortification and vivification, continual growth in holiness leading to eventual conformity to the image of Christ. The new creation implies a new nature with a new system of desires, affections, and habits, all wrought through the supernatural ministry of the Holy Spirit in the life of the believer."[6]

As far as salvation is concerned, the only thing that matters is whether this change has taken (and is taking) place. It matters not whether a person is a circumcised Jew or an uncircumcised Gentile; what matters is whether or not a person is a regenerated Christian, a new creature in Christ. Anyone who has not yet experienced this spiritual transformation should ask God to change him (or her) from the inside out.

Everyone who is a new creation receives this blessing: "And as for all who walk by this rule, peace and mercy be upon them, and upon the Israel of God" (Gal. 6:16). This benediction grants peace and mercy—peace between Jew and Gentile and mercy from God for sinners. But notice that the blessing is conditional. Peace and mercy are only for those who "walk by this rule." A rule is a norm or a principle. In this case, what Paul means by "rule" is salvation through the cross alone. For the Judaizers, circumcision was the norm. It was the standard for determining whether people were inside or

6. Ibid., 438.

outside the family of God. But circumcision means nothing to those who are part of the new creation. The Christian's standard is the cross of Christ. The principle that determines whether one is inside or outside the family of God is faith in Christ crucified.

The phrase "upon the Israel of God" (Gal. 6:16) has significant implications for biblical theology. The blessing of peace and mercy comes from a traditional Jewish benediction. However, here Paul uses it to refer not merely to Jews, but to all true children of Abraham, whether Jews or Gentiles. It is a way of saying that the church is the new Israel. There is continuity between the old covenant and the new, between the Old Testament people of God and the New Testament church. The promises that God made to Israel are fulfilled in the true spiritual Israel, which is the church of Jesus Christ. God has one people in Christ, and what unites them is the cross. We share a common boast in the cross, and in the cross alone.

THE MARK OF A CHRISTIAN

The apostle Paul was a member of God's true Israel, and he had the battle scars to prove it. The last thing he said to the Galatians—almost as an afterthought—was this: "From now on let no one cause me trouble, for I bear on my body the marks of Jesus" (Gal. 6:17). This statement was partly a warning to Paul's old enemies, the Judaizers. They had followed him all the way from Jerusalem to interfere with his gospel of justification by grace alone, through faith alone, in Christ alone. The apostle had finally had enough, and thus he warned his opponents not to cause him any more trouble.

This statement is also a warning to every Christian, however, for it shows what kind of treatment we can expect for boasting in the cross. Sooner or later, every Christian who glories in the cross will face opposition. Some will even bear on their bodies "the marks of Jesus." The Greek word for these marks is *stigmata*. It does not mean, as some people have wrongly supposed, that Christians can receive exactly the same wounds that Christ received on the cross. For example, it is sometimes asserted that blood dripped from the hands, feet, and side of Francis of Assisi during the last years of his life. It is even said that he had nails growing out of his flesh!

Not only is this way of interpreting "the marks of Jesus" historically inaccurate, but it is also biblically incorrect (not to mention morbidly incredible). What Paul meant by *stigmata* were the various wounds that he had received for the cause of Christ. By this point in his ministry, the apostle had really taken a beating. Among other things, he had been stoned and left for dead in Lystra (see Acts 14:8–20), one of the cities of Galatia. And Paul's sufferings had left their mark on him.

If we ask why Paul was such a marked man, the answer is that people were offended by his preaching of the cross. As he had already mentioned (Gal. 5:11), he was persecuted for boasting in the cross rather than boasting in circumcision. As far as the Judaizers were concerned, the badge of true religion was the mark made by circumcision. But the apostle Paul had a different insignia, one that came from glorying in the cross, and not in himself. He was bruised and beaten for boasting in the cross. His scars were a badge of his faith in Jesus Christ.

In the Greek world, the word *stigmata* was sometimes used to refer to the branding of a slave. Such usage would be appropriate in Paul's case because his scars marked him as a servant of God. But John Calvin drew a different comparison. After describing all the "imprisonment, chains, scourging, blows, stonings and every kind of ill treatment which he [Paul] had suffered for the testimony of the Gospel," Calvin said: "For even as earthly warfare has its decorations with which generals honour the bravery of a soldier, so Christ our leader has His own marks, of which He makes good use in decorating and honouring some of His followers. These marks, however, are very different from the others; for they have the nature of the cross, and in the sight of the world they are disgraceful."[7]

The marks of Jesus may seem disgraceful to the world, but they are precious in the sight of God. They are so precious, in fact, that on occasion Paul prayed for the privilege of becoming so united to Christ that he would come to share in his sufferings: "I want to know Christ and the power of his resurrection and the fellowship of sharing in his sufferings, becoming like him in his death, and so, somehow, to attain to the resurrection from the dead" (Phil. 3:10 NIV; cf. Rom. 8:17; 2 Cor. 1:5; 4:8–10; Col. 1:24).

7. John Calvin, *The Epistles of Paul the Apostle to the Galatians, Ephesians, Philippians and Colossians,* Calvin's New Testament Commentaries, trans. T. H. L. Parker, ed. David W. and Thomas F. Torrance (Grand Rapids: Eerdmans, 1996), 119.

This should be the prayer of every Christian, but sharing in Christ's sufferings is especially important for ministers. As G. Campbell Morgan (1863–1945) once wrote: "It is the crucified man that can preach the cross. Said Thomas 'except I shall see in his hands the print of the nails . . . I will not believe.' . . . what Thomas said of Christ, the world is saying about the church. And the world is also saying to every preacher: Unless I see in your hands the print of the nails, I will not believe. It is true. It is the man . . . who has died with Christ . . . that can preach the cross of Christ."[8]

Boasting in the cross is not just for preachers, however, and therefore suffering is not just for preachers either. Every Christian who has died with Christ must live for his cross. Nowhere is the crucified life expressed more eloquently than in the words of the great hymn by Isaac Watts (1674–1748) that is based on the closing verses of Galatians 6:

When I survey the wondrous cross
    Where the young Prince of glory died,
My richest gain I count but loss,
    And pour contempt on all my pride.

Forbid it, Lord, that I should boast
    Save in the death of Christ, my God;
All the vain things that charm me most,
    I sacrifice them to his blood.

See from his head, his hands, his feet,
    Sorrow and love flow mingled down;
Did e'er such love and sorrow meet,
    Or thorns compose so rich a crown?

His dying crimson, like a robe,
    Spreads o'er his body on the tree;
Then am I dead to all the globe,
    And all the globe is dead to me.

Were the whole realm of nature mine,

8. G. Campbell Morgan, *Evangelism* (London: Henry E. Walter, 1964), 59–60.

> That were a present far too small;
> Love so amazing, so divine,
>> Demands my soul, my life, my all.

To this great statement of the gospel and call to a crucified life, we can only add the apostle's own benediction for the Galatians. It is really a prayer for God's blessing on everyone who trusts in the gospel of free grace and seeks to be justified by faith alone in Christ alone: "The grace of our Lord Jesus Christ be with your spirit, brothers. Amen" (Gal. 6:18).

INDEX OF SCRIPTURE

Index of Scripture

Index of Subjects and Names